Stand Out 3

Lesson Planner

Second Edition

Staci Johnson

Rob Jenkins

NATIONAL GEOGRAPHIC LEARNING | HEINLE CENGAGE Learning

Australia • Brazil • Japan • Korea • Mexico • Singapore • Spain • United Kingdom • United States

Stand Out 3: Lesson Planner, Second Edition
Staci Johnson and Rob Jenkins

Editorial Director: Joe Dougherty

Publisher, ESL and Dictionaries: Sherrise Roehr

Acquisitions Editor: Tom Jefferies

VP, Director of Content Development:
Anita Raducanu

Development Editor: John Hicks

Director of Product Marketing: Amy T. Mabley

Executive Marketing Manager, U.S.:
Jim McDonough

Senior Field Marketing Manager:
Donna Lee Kennedy

Product Marketing Manager: Katie Kelley

Senior Content Project Manager:
Maryellen Killeen

Content Project Manager: Dawn Marie Elwell

Senior Print Buyer: Mary Beth Hennebury

Development Editors: Kasia McNabb,
Judi Lauber

Project Manager: Tunde Dewey

Composition: Pre-Press PMG

Cover and Interior Design: Studio Montage

Cover Art: ©Lisa Henderling/Getty Images

Photo Researcher: Erika Hokanson

Illustrators: James Edwards; S.I. International

Credits appear on page 176, which constitutes a
continuation of the copyright page.

ISBN-13: 978-1-4240-1935-9

ISBN-10: 1-4240-1935-4

National Geographic Learning
20 Channel Center Street
Boston, MA 02210
USA

Cengage Learning is a leading provider of customized learning solutions with
office locations around the globe, including Singapore, the United Kingdom,
Australia, Mexico, Brazil, and Japan.

Cengage Learning products are represented in Canada by Nelson Education, Ltd.

Visit National Geographic Learning online at **elt.heinle.com**

Visit our corporate website at **www.cengage.com**

Printed in the United States of America
3 4 5 6 7 16 15 14

Elizabeth Aderman
New York City Board of Education, New York, NY

Lisa Agao
Fresno Adult School, Fresno, CA

Sharon Baker
Roseville Adult School, Roseville, CA

Lillian Barredo
Stockton School for Adults, Stockton, CA

Linda Boice
Elk Grove Adult Education, Elk Grove, CA

Chan Bostwick
Los Angeles Unified School District, Los Angeles, CA

Debra Brooks
Manhattan BEGIN Program, New York, NY

Anne Byrnes
North Hollywood-Polytechnic Community Adult School, Sun Valley, CA

Rose Cantu
John Jay High School, San Antonio, TX

Toni Chapralis
Fremont School for Adults, Sacramento, CA

Melanie Chitwood
Miami-Dade College, Miami, FL

Geri Creamer
Stockton School for Adults, Stockton, CA

Stephanie Daubar
Harry W. Brewster Technical Center, Tampa, FL

Irene Dennis
San Antonio College, San Antonio, TX

Eileen Duffell
P.S. 64, New York, NY

Nancy Dunlap
Northside Independent School District, San Antonio, TX

Gloria Eriksson
Grant Skills Center, Sacramento, CA

Marti Estrin
Santa Rosa Junior College, Santa Rosa, CA

Lawrence Fish
Shorefront YM-YWHA English Language Program, Brooklyn, NY

Victoria Florit
Miami-Dade College, Miami, FL

Sally Gearheart
Santa Rosa Junior College, Santa Rosa, CA

Rhoda Gilbert
New York City Board of Education, New York, NY

Debbie Glass
Merced Adult School, Merced, CA

Laurie Hartwick
Lawrence High School/Adult Learning Center, Lawrence, MA

Kathleen Jimenez
Miami-Dade College, Miami, FL

Nancy Jordan
John Jay High School Adult Education, San Antonio, TX

Renee Klosz
Lindsey Hopkins Technical Education Center, Miami, FL

David Lauter
Stockton School for Adults, Stockton, CA

Patricia Long
Old Marshall Adult Education Center, Sacramento, CA

Daniel Loos
Seattle Community College, Seattle, WA

Maria Miranda
Lindsey Hopkins Technical Education Center, Miami, FL

Karen Moore
Stockton School for Adults, Stockton, CA

George Myskiw
Malcolm X College, Chicago, IL

Dr. Betty Payne
Montgomery College, Rockville, MD

Heidi Perez
Lawrence Public Schools Adult Learning Center, Lawrence, MA

Marta Pitt
Lindsey Hopkins Technical Education Center, Miami, FL

Sylvia Rambach
Stockton School for Adults, Stockton, CA

Eric Rosenbaum
BEGIN Managed Programs, New York, NY

Laura Rowley
Old Marshall Adult Education Center, Sacramento, CA

Stephanie Schmitter
Mercer County Community College, Trenton, NJ

Amy Schneider
Pacoima Skills Center, Pacoima, CA

Sr. M. B. Theresa Spittle
Stockton School for Adults, Stockton, CA

Andre Sutton
Belmont Adult School, Los Angeles, CA

Jennifer Swoyer
Northside Independent School District, San Antonio, TX

Marcia Takacs
Coastline Community College, Fountain Valley, CA

Claire Valier
Palm Beach County School District, West Palm Beach, FL

Sarah Young
Arlington Education and Employment Program (REEP), Arlington, VA

Rob Jenkins

Staci Johnson

I love teaching. I love to see the expressions on my students' faces when the light goes on and their eyes show such sincere joy of learning. I knew the first time I stepped into an ESL classroom that this was where I needed to be and I have never questioned that resolution. I have worked in business, sales, and publishing, and I've found challenge in all, but nothing can compare to the satisfaction of reaching people in such a personal way.

Ever since I can remember, I've been fascinated with other cultures and languages. I love to travel and every place I go, the first thing I want to do is meet the people, learn their language, and understand their culture. Becoming an ESL teacher was a perfect way to turn what I love to do into my profession. There's nothing more incredible than the exchange of teaching and learning from one another that goes on in an ESL classroom. And there's nothing more rewarding than helping a student succeed.

We are so happy that instructors and agencies have embraced the lesson planning and project-based activities that we introduced in the first edition and are so enthusiastically teaching with **Stand Out**. It is fantastic that so many of our colleagues are as excited to be in this profession as we are. After writing over 500 lesson plans and implementing them in our own classrooms and after personal discussions with thousands of instructors all over the United States and in different parts of the world, we have found ourselves in a position to improve upon our successful model. One of the most notable things in the new edition is that we have continued to stress integrating skills in each lesson and have made this integration more apparent and obvious. To accomplish any life skill, students need to incorporate a combination of reading, writing, listening, speaking, grammar, pronunciation, and academic skills while developing vocabulary and these skills should be taught together in a lesson! We have accomplished this by extending the presentation of lessons in the book, so each lesson is more fully developed. You will also notice an extended list of ancillaries and a tighter correlation of these ancillaries to each book. The ancillaries allow you to extend practice on particular skill areas beyond the lesson in the text. We are so excited about this curriculum and know that as you implement it, you and your students will *stand out*.

Our goal is to give students challenging opportunities to be successful in their language-learning experience so they develop confidence and become independent, lifelong learners.

Rob Jenkins
Staci Johnson

ABOUT THE SERIES

The **Stand Out** series is designed to facilitate *active* learning while challenging students to build a nurturing and effective learning community.

The student books are divided into eight distinct units, mirroring competency areas most useful to newcomers. These areas are outlined in CASAS assessment programs and different state model standards for adults. Each unit in *Stand Out 3* is then divided into five lessons, a review, and a team project. Lessons are driven by performance objectives and are filled with challenging activities that progress from teacher-presented to student-centered tasks.

SUPPLEMENTAL MATERIALS

- The *Stand Out 3 Lesson Planner* is in full color with 60 complete lesson plans, taking the instructor through each stage of a lesson from warm-up and review through application.

- The *Stand Out 3 Activity Bank CD-ROM* has an abundance of customizable worksheets. Print or download and modify what you need for your particular class.

- The *Stand Out 3 Grammar Challenge* is a workbook that gives additional grammar explanation and practice in context.

- The *Reading and Writing Challenge* workbooks are designed to capture the principle ideas in the student book, and allow students to improve their vocabulary, academic, reading, and writing skills.

- The *Stand Out 3 Assessment CD-ROM with ExamView®* allows you to customize pre- and post-tests for each unit as well as a pre- and post-test for the book.

- Listening scripts are found in the back of the student book and in the Lesson Planner. CDs are available with focused listening activities described in the Lesson Planner.

STAND OUT 3 LESSON PLANNER

The *Stand Out 3 Lesson Planner* is a new and innovative approach. As many seasoned teachers know, good lesson planning can make a substantial difference in the classroom. Students continue coming to class, understanding, applying, and remembering more of what they learn. They are more confident in their learning when good lesson planning techniques are incorporated.

We have developed lesson plans that are designed to be used each day and to reduce preparation time. The planner includes:

- Standard lesson progression (Warm-up and Review, Introduction, Presentation, Practice, Evaluation, and Application)

- A creative and complete way to approach varied class lengths so that each lesson will work within a class period.

- 180 hours of classroom activities

- Time suggestions for each activity

- Pedagogical comments

- Space for teacher notes and future planning

- Identification of LCP standards in addition to SCANS and CASAS standards

USER QUESTIONS ABOUT *STAND OUT*

- **What are SCANS and how do they integrate into the book?**
  SCANS is the Secretary's Commission on Achieving Necessary Skills. SCANS was developed to encourage students to prepare for the workplace. The standards developed through SCANS have been incorporated throughout the **Stand Out** student books and components.

  Stand Out addresses SCANS a little differently than do other books. SCANS standards elicit effective teaching strategies by incorporating essential skills such as critical thinking and group work. We have incorporated SCANS standards in every lesson, not isolating these standards in the work unit. All new texts have followed our lead.

- **What about CASAS?** The federal government has mandated that states show student outcomes as a prerequisite to receiving funding. Some states have incorporated the **C**omprehensive **A**dult **S**tudent **A**ssessment **S**ystem (CASAS) testing to standardize agency reporting. Unfortunately, many of our students are unfamiliar with standardized testing and therefore struggle with it. Adult schools need to develop lesson plans to address specific concerns. **Stand Out** was developed with careful attention to CASAS skill areas in most lessons and performance objectives.

- **Are the tasks too challenging for my students?**
  Students learn by doing and learn more when challenged. **Stand Out** provides tasks that encourage critical thinking in a variety of ways. The tasks in each lesson move from teacher-directed to student-centered so the learner clearly understands what's expected and is willing to "take a risk." The lessons are expected to be challenging. In this way, students learn that when they work together as a learning community, anything becomes possible. The satisfaction of accomplishing something both as an individual and as a member of a team results in greater confidence and effective learning.

- **Do I need to understand lesson planning to teach from the student book?** If you don't understand lesson planning when you start, you will when you finish! Teaching from **Stand Out** is like a course on lesson planning, especially if you use the Lesson Planner on a daily basis.

  Stand Out does *stand out* because, when we developed this series, we first established performance objectives for each lesson. Then we designed lesson plans, followed by student book pages. The introduction to each lesson varies because different objectives demand different approaches. **Stand Out's** variety of tasks makes learning more interesting for the student.

- **What are team projects?** The final lesson of each unit is a **team project**. This is often a team simulation that incorporates the objectives of the unit and provides an additional opportunity for students to actively apply what they have learned. The project allows students to produce something that represents their progress in learning. These end-of-unit projects were created with a variety of learning styles and individual skills in mind. The team projects can be skipped or simplified, but we encourage instructors to implement them, enriching the overall student experience.

- **What do you mean by a customizable Activity Bank?** Every class, student, teacher, and approach is different. Since no one textbook can meet all these differences, the *Stand Out Activity Bank CD-ROM* allows you to customize **Stand Out** for your class. You can copy different activities and worksheets from the CD-ROM to your hard drive and then:

  - change items in supplemental vocabulary, grammar, and life skill activities;

  - personalize activities with student names and popular locations in your area;

  - extend every lesson with additional practice where you feel it is most needed.

  The Activity Bank also includes the following resources:

  - Multilevel worksheets – worksheets based on the standard worksheets described above, but at one level higher and one level lower.

  - Graphic organizer templates – templates that can be used to facilitate learning. They include graphs, charts, VENN diagrams, and so on.

  - Computer worksheets – worksheets designed to supplement each unit and progress from simple

to complex operations in word processing; and spreadsheets for labs and computer enhanced classrooms.

- Internet Worksheets – worksheets designed to supplement each unit and provide application opportunities beyond the lessons in the book.

- **Is *Stand Out* grammar-based or competency-based?** **Stand Out** is a competency-based series; however, students are exposed to basic grammar structures. We believe that grammar instruction in context is extremely important. Grammar is a necessary component for achieving most competencies; therefore it is integrated into most lessons. Students are first provided with context that incorporates the grammar, followed by an explanation and practice. At this level, we expect students to learn basic structures, but we do not expect them to acquire them. It has been our experience that students are exposed several times within their learning experience to language structures before they actually acquire them. For teachers who want to enhance grammar instruction, the *Activity Bank CD-ROM* and/or the *Grammar Challenge* workbooks provide ample opportunities.

  The six competencies that drive **Stand Out** are basic communication, consumer economics, community resources, health, occupational knowledge, and lifelong learning (government and law replace lifelong learning in Books 3 and 4).

- **Are there enough activities so I don't have to supplement?** **Stand Out** stands alone in providing 180 hours of instruction and activities, even without the additional suggestions in the Lesson Planner. The Lesson Planner also shows you how to streamline lessons to provide 90 hours of classwork and still have thorough lessons if you meet less often. When supplementing with the *Stand Out Activity Bank CD-ROM*, the *Assessment CD-ROM with ExamView®* and the *Stand Out Grammar Challenge* workbook, you gain unlimited opportunities to extend class hours and provide activities related directly to each lesson objective. Calculate how many hours your class meets in a semester and look to **Stand Out** to address the full class experience.

  Stand Out is a comprehensive approach to adult language learning, meeting needs of students and instructors completely and effectively.

CONTENTS

● Grammar points that are explicitly taught   ◊ Grammar points that are presented in context   △ Grammar points that are being recycled

	Numeracy/Academic Skills	EFF	SCANS	CASAS
Pre-Unit	• Writing a paragraph • Comparing and contrasting • Setting goals	• Taking responsibility for learning • Reflecting and evaluating • Planning • Conveying ideas in writing	Many SCAN and EFF skills are incorporated in this unit with an emphasis on: • Understanding systems • Decision making	**1:** 0.1.2; 0.1.4; 0.2.1; 0.2.2 **2:** 0.2.1; 7.2.6 **3:** 0.1.2, 0.1.6, 0.2.1, 7.1.1
Unit 1	• Pronunciation • Reading a chart • Active reading • Focused listening • Writing a paragraph • Active reading • Making inferences • Using an outline • Using a pie graph • Reviewing	Most EFF skills are incorporated into this unit with an emphasis on: • Taking responsibility for learning • Using information and communication technology • Conveying ideas in writing • Solving problems and making decisions • Planning (Technology is optional.)	Many SCAN and EFF skills are incorporated in this unit with an emphasis on: • Allocating time • Understanding systems • Applying technology to task • Responsibility • Self management • Writing • Decision making	**1:** 0.1.2, 0.2.4 **2:** 7.1.1, 7.1.2, 7.1.3, 7.2.5, 7.2.6 **3:** 7.1.1, 7.1.2, 7.1.3, 7.2.5, 7.2.6 **4:** 0.1.5, 7.4.1, 7.4.3, 7.4.5 **5:** 7.4.2 **R:** 7.2.1 **TP:** 4.8.1., 4.8.5., 4.8.6.
Unit 2	• Pronunciation: Focus • Test taking skills • Comparing and contrasting • Sequence writing • Reviewing	Most EFF skills are incorporated into this unit with an emphasis on: • Reflecting and evaluating • Learning through research • Cooperating with others • Solving problems and making decisions. (Technology is optional.)	Many SCAN skills are incorporated in this unit with an emphasis on: • Responsibility • Participating as a member of a team • Acquiring and evaluating information • Organizing and maintaining information • Decision making • Reasoning	**1:** 0.1.2, 1.3.7 **2:** 1.2.1 **3:** 1.2.1, 1.2.2 **4:** 1.3.1 **5:** 1.2.5 **R:** 7.2.1 **TP:** 4.8.1., 4.8.5., 4.8.6.

Contents

CONTENTS

• Grammar points that are explicitly taught   ◇ Grammar points that are presented in context   Grammar points that are being recycled

	Numeracy/ Academic Skills	EFF	SCANS	CASAS
Unit 3	• Pronunciation: Rising and falling intonation • Scanning • Active reading • Focused listening • Reading a bar graph • Budget arithmetic • Writing a business letter • Reviewing	Most EFF skills are incorporated into this unit with an emphasis on: • Learning through research • Reading with understanding • Conveying ideas in writing • Solving problems and making decisions (Technology is optional.)	Many SCAN skills are incorporated in this unit with an emphasis on: • Allocating money • Understanding systems • Monitoring and correcting performance • Interpreting and communicating information • Reading • Writing • Decision making	**1:** 1.4.1, 1.4.2 **2:** 1.4.2, 7.2.7 **3:** 1.4.4, 1.5.3 **4:** 1.5.1, 6.0.3, 6.0I.5, 6.1.1, 6.1.2 **5:** 1.4.7 **R:** 7.2.1 **TP:** 4.8.1, 4.8.5, 4.8.6.
Unit 4	• Pronunciation: Rising and falling intonation • Pronunciation: Phrasing • Focused listening • Making inferences • Reading charts • Reading a map • Paragraph writing • Reviewing	Most EFF skills are incorporated into this unit with an emphasis on: • Learning through research • Conveying ideas in writing • Solving problems and making decisions (Technology is optional.)	Many SCAN skills are incorporated in this unit with an emphasis on: • Understanding systems • Interpreting and communicating information • Writing • Decision making • Seeing things in the mind's eye	**1:** 0.1.2 **2:** 1.8.5, 2.5.6 **3:** 2.2.1, 2.2.5 **4:** 7.2.6 **5:** 7.2.2 **R:** 7.2.1 **TP:** 4.8.1, 4.8.5, 4.8.6
Unit 5	• Active listening • Active reading • Reviewing	Most EFF skills are incorporated into this unit with an emphasis on: • Reflecting and evaluating • Learning through research • Reading with understanding • Speaking so others can understand (Technology is optional.)	Many SCAN skills are incorporated in this unit with an emphasis on: • Understanding systems • Self management • Acquiring and evaluating information • Interpreting and communicating information	**1:** 3.1.1, 3.1.3, 3.2.1 **2:** 3.1.1 **3:** 3.4.2, 3.5.9 **4:** 3.5.1, 3.5.3, 3.5.5 3.5.9, 6.7.3 **5:** 3.5.9 **R:** 7.2.1 **TP:** 4.8.1, 4.8.5, 4.8.6.

• Grammar points that are explicitly taught   ◊ Grammar points that are presented in context   △ Grammar points that are being recycled

	Numeracy/ Academic Skills	EFF	SCANS	CASAS
Unit 6	• Paragraph writing • Reading for understanding • Focused listening • Reviewing	Most EFF skills are incorporated into this unit with an emphasis on: • Speaking so others can understand • Planning • Learning through research (Technology is optional.)	Most SCAN skills are incorporated in this unit with an emphasis on: • Self-esteem • Sociability • Acquiring and evaluating information • Speaking • Decision making	**1:** 4.1.8 **2:** 4.1.9 **3:** 4.1.3 **4:** 4.1.2 **5:** 4.1.5, 4.1.7 **R:** 7.2.1 **TP:** 4.8.1, 4.8.5, 4.8.6.
Unit 7	• Pronunciation: Rising intonation for polite requests • Pronunciation: Tone of voice • Focused listening • Reading for understanding • Reviewing	Most EFF skills are incorporated into this unit with an emphasis on: • Reflecting and evaluating • Cooperating with others (Technology is optional.)	Most SCAN skills are incorporated in this unit with an emphasis on: • Understanding systems • Participating as a member of a team • Acquiring and evaluating information	**1:** 4.1.9, 4.4.1 **2:** 4.2.1, 4.4.3 **3:** 4.2.1 **4:** 4.3.3, 4.3.4, 4.5.1 **5:** 4.4.1, 4.6.1 **R:** 7.2.1 **TP:** 4.8.1, 4.8.5, 4.8.6
Unit 8	• Focused listening • Active reading • Paragraph writing • Speech writing • Reviewing	Most EFF skills are incorporated into this unit with an emphasis on: • Speaking so others can understand • Listening actively • Reflecting and evaluating (Technology is optional.)	Most SCAN skills are incorporated in this unit with an emphasis on: • Listening • Speaking • Responsibility • Self-esteem	**1:** 5.1.6 **2:** 5.1.4, 5.1.6 **3:** 5.1.4, 5.2.1 **4:** 5.5.7, 5.5.8 **5:** 5.1.6 **R:** 7.2.1 **TP:** 4.8.1, 4.8.5, 4.8.6.

Contents

Welcome to Stand Out, Second Edition

Stand Out works.

And now it works even better!

Built from the standards necessary for adult English learners, the second edition of *Stand Out* gives students the foundation and tools they need to develop confidence and become independent, lifelong learners.

- **Grammar** Charts clearly explain grammar points, and are followed by personalized exercises.
- **Pronunciation** activities are integrated through the program.

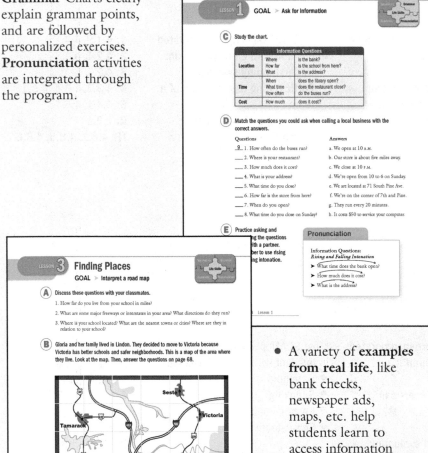

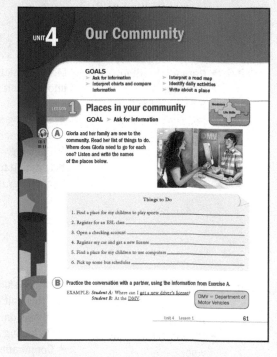

- Clearly defined **goals** provide a roadmap of learning for the student.
- Key **vocabulary** is introduced visually and orally.

- A variety of **examples from real life**, like bank checks, newspaper ads, maps, etc. help students learn to access information and resources in their community.

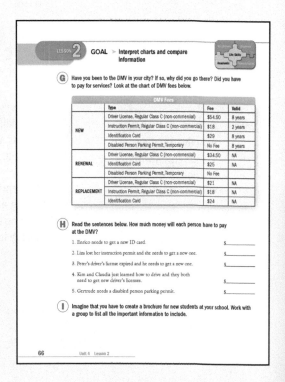

- State and federally required life skills and competencies are taught, helping students meet necessary benchmarks.

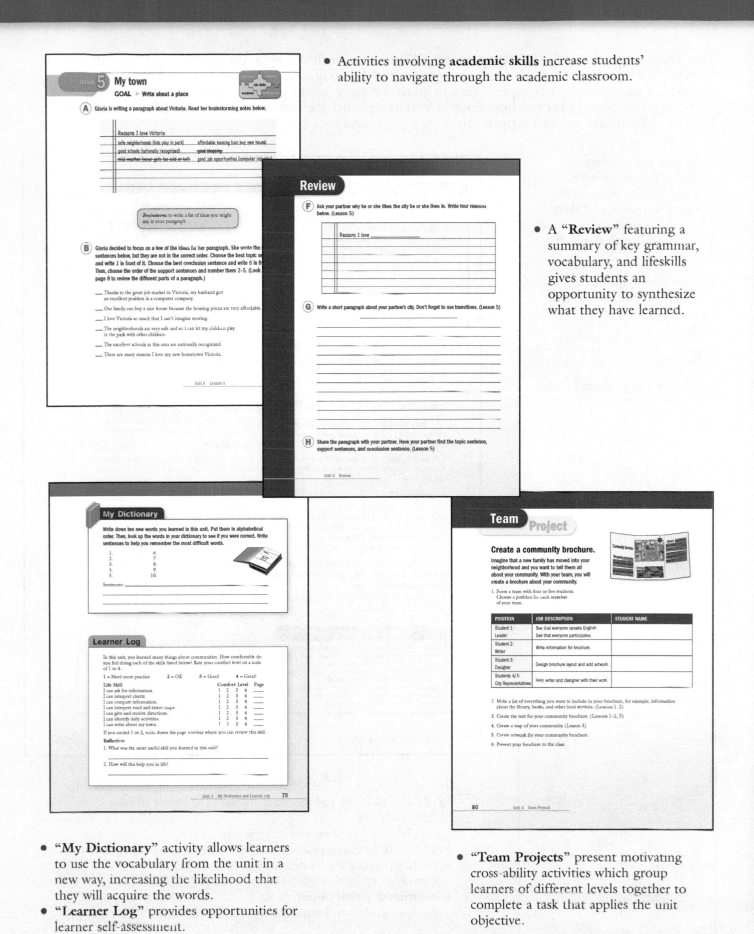

- Activities involving **academic skills** increase students' ability to navigate through the academic classroom.

- A **"Review"** featuring a summary of key grammar, vocabulary, and lifeskills gives students an opportunity to synthesize what they have learned.

- **"My Dictionary"** activity allows learners to use the vocabulary from the unit in a new way, increasing the likelihood that they will acquire the words.
- **"Learner Log"** provides opportunities for learner self-assessment.

- **"Team Projects"** present motivating cross-ability activities which group learners of different levels together to complete a task that applies the unit objective.

The ground-breaking *Stand Out* **Lesson Planners** take the guesswork out of meeting the standards while offering high-interest, meaningful language activities, and three levels of pacing for each book. A complete **lesson plan** for each lesson in the student book is provided, following the *Stand Out* methodology – **Warm-up and Review, Introduction, Presentation, Practice, Evaluation,** and **Application** (see page xviii).

- An **at-a-glance prep** section for each lesson ensures that instructors have a clear knowledge of what will be covered in the lesson. References to **unit-specific resources** are also included.

- Clear **pacing guide** icons offer three different pacing strategies.

  ■ = for 1 ½-hour classes

  ■ = for 2 ½-hour classes

  ■ = for 3-hour or more classes

- **Standards Correlations** appear directly on the page, detailing how *Stand Out* meets CASAS, SCANS, and EFF standards.

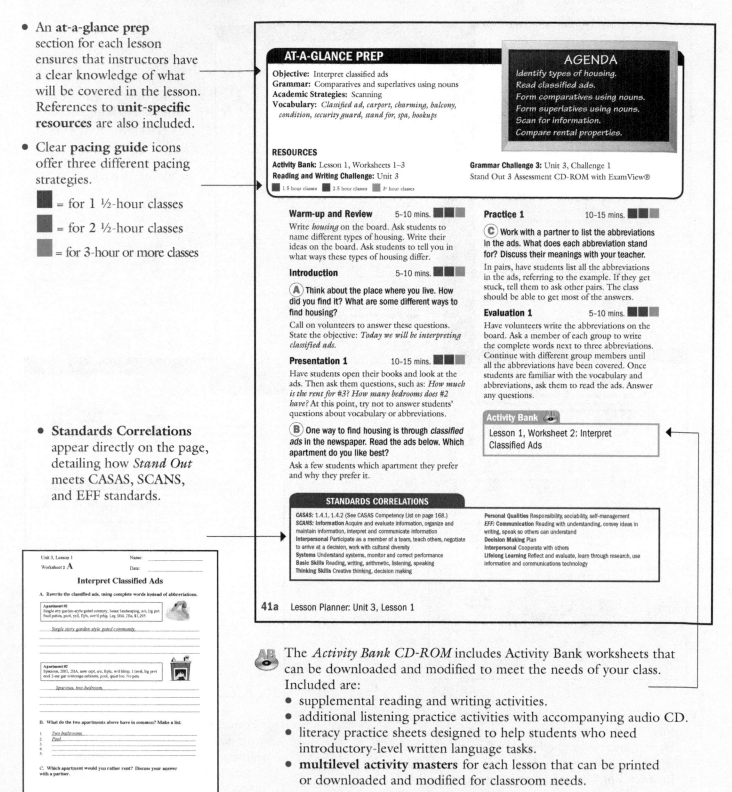

AT-A-GLANCE PREP

Objective: Interpret classified ads
Grammar: Comparatives and superlatives using nouns
Academic Strategies: Scanning
Vocabulary: *Classified ad, carport, charming, balcony, condition, security guard, stand for, spa, hookups*

RESOURCES

Activity Bank: Lesson 1, Worksheets 1–3
Reading and Writing Challenge: Unit 3

Grammar Challenge 3: Unit 3, Challenge 1
Stand Out 3 Assessment CD-ROM with ExamView®

■ 1.5 hour classes ■ 2.5 hour classes ■ 3+ hour classes

AGENDA

Identify types of housing.
Read classified ads.
Form comparatives using nouns.
Form superlatives using nouns.
Scan for information.
Compare rental properties.

Warm-up and Review   5–10 mins. ■■■
Write *housing* on the board. Ask students to name different types of housing. Write their ideas on the board. Ask students to tell you in what ways these types of housing differ.

Introduction   5–10 mins. ■■■
Ⓐ Think about the place where you live. How did you find it? What are some different ways to find housing?

Call on volunteers to answer these questions. State the objective: *Today we will be interpreting classified ads.*

Presentation 1   10–15 mins. ■■■
Have students open their books and look at the ads. Then ask them questions, such as: *How much is the rent for #3? How many bedrooms does #2 have?* At this point, try not to answer students' questions about vocabulary or abbreviations.

Ⓑ One way to find housing is through *classified ads* in the newspaper. Read the ads below. Which apartment do you like best?

Ask a few students which apartment they prefer and why they prefer it.

Practice 1   10–15 mins. ■■■
Ⓒ Work with a partner to list the abbreviations in the ads. What does each abbreviation stand for? Discuss their meanings with your teacher.

In pairs, have students list all the abbreviations in the ads, referring to the example. If they get stuck, tell them to ask other pairs. The class should be able to get most of the answers.

Evaluation 1   5–10 mins. ■■■
Have volunteers write the abbreviations on the board. Ask a member of each group to write the complete words next to three abbreviations. Continue with different group members until all the abbreviations have been covered. Once students are familiar with the vocabulary and abbreviations, ask them to read the ads. Answer any questions.

Activity Bank 🅰🅱

Lesson 1, Worksheet 2: Interpret Classified Ads

STANDARDS CORRELATIONS

CASAS: 1.4.1, 1.4.2 (See CASAS Competency List on page 168.)
SCANS: Information Acquire and evaluate information, organize and maintain information, interpret and communicate information
Interpersonal Participate as a member of a team, teach others, negotiate to arrive at a decision, work with cultural diversity
Systems Understand systems, monitor and correct performance
Basic Skills Reading, writing, arithmetic, listening, speaking
Thinking Skills Creative thinking, decision making

Personal Qualities Responsibility, sociability, self-management
EFF: Communication Reading with understanding, convey ideas in writing, speak so others can understand
Decision Making Plan
Interpersonal Cooperate with others
Lifelong Learning Reflect and evaluate, learn through research, use information and communications technology

41a   Lesson Planner: Unit 3, Lesson 1

Unit 3, Lesson 1   Name: _____
Worksheet 2 A   Date: _____

Interpret Classified Ads

A. Rewrite the classified ads, using complete words instead of abbreviations.

Apartment #1
Single stry garden-style gated comnty, beaut landscaping, a/c, lrg pvt fncd patios, pool, yrd, frp's, cov'd prkg, Lrg 3Bd, 2Ba, $1,295.

Single story garden style gated community,

Apartment #2
Spacious, 2BD, 2BA, new crpt, a/c, frplc, w/d hkup, 1 level, lrg pvt end 2-car gar w/storage cabinets, pool, quiet loc. No pets.

Spacious, two-bedroom,

B. What do the two apartments above have in common? Make a list.

1. *Two bathrooms*
2. *Pool*
3.
4.
5.

C. Which apartment would you rather rent? Discuss your answer with a partner.

Copyright © Heinle
Stand Out 3 Activity Bank

🅰🅱 The *Activity Bank CD-ROM* includes Activity Bank worksheets that can be downloaded and modified to meet the needs of your class. Included are:
- supplemental reading and writing activities.
- additional listening practice activities with accompanying audio CD.
- literacy practice sheets designed to help students who need introductory-level written language tasks.
- **multilevel activity masters** for each lesson that can be printed or downloaded and modified for classroom needs.

- **Teaching Tips** and **Culture Tips** provide ideas and strategies for teaching diverse learners in the classroom.

- **Listening Scripts** from the *Audio CD* are included next to the student book page for ease-of-use.

Presentation 2 10–15 mins. ■■■

Ask students to imagine they are moving to a new home. Tell them they need to cancel the electricity in their current home and get it turned on at their new home. Ask them how they would do this. (Call the electric company.) Ask what sort of information they would need to give to the company's representative to make this happen.

Practice 2 5–10 mins. ■■■

Tell students they will be listening to Vu call the electric company to prepare for his family's move. Direct their attention to Exercise C and tell them they will be listening for four pieces of information.

Teaching Tip

Focused listening

The purpose of teaching focused listening is to help students learn how to understand the main ideas in a conversation even when they don't understand every word.

It's important to remind students that they will not understand every word each time they do a focused listening activity. Otherwise, they may become frustrated and stop listening all together. Preparing students for the listening activity will make them much more effective listeners.

1. Explain the context of the conversation.
2. Ask students what they think they might hear.
3. Show students specifically what they are listening for.

C Vu and his family are getting ready to move. Vu calls the electric company to speak to a customer service representative. Listen to the recording and write short answers for the following information.

 Listening Script CD 1, Track 8

Recording: *Thank you for calling Texas Electric. Your call is very important to us. Please choose from the following options. For new service or to cancel your existing service, press 1. To report a problem with your service, press 2. If you have questions about your bill, press 3. For all other questions, press 4. (Vu presses 1.) Thank you. Just one moment.*

Representative: *Hello, my name is Kristen. How may I help you?*
Vu: *Um, yes. My family is moving next week. We need to cancel our current service and get service in our new home.*
Representative: *What is your current address?*
Vu: *3324 Maple Road.*
Representative: *Are you Vu Nguyen?*
Vu: *Yes.*
Representative: *When would you like the service turned off?*
Vu: *Next Wednesday, please.*
Representative: *And what is your new address?*
Vu: *5829 Bay Road.*
Representative: *And when would you like the service turned on?*
Vu: *This Monday, please.*
Representative: *OK. Your current service will be turned off sometime between 8 and 12 on Wednesday the 11th. Your new service will be on before 9 on Monday morning the 9th. Is there anything else I can do for you?*
Vu: *No, that's it.*
Representative: *Thank you for calling Texas Electric. Have a nice day.*
Vu: *You, too.*

D Listen to the recording again and answer the questions.

Prepare students for the information they are to listen for. (CD 1, Track 8)

Evaluation 2 5 mins. ■■

Go over the answers with the class.

Pronunciation

Rising and Falling Intonation

Ask students a few information questions. Ask if your voice goes up or down at the end of each question. Students should be able to recognize the rising and falling intonation. Explain that this rising and falling intonation helps the listener know that you are asking a question that requires an answer.

Go over the examples in the box in the student book, emphasizing the intonation. Have students practice by repeating after you, first as a class and then individually.

Lesson Planner: Unit 3, Lesson 3 **48a**

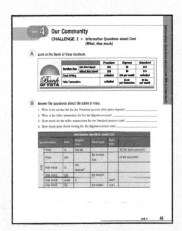

- *Grammar Challenge* workbooks include supplemental activities for students who desire even more **contextual grammar** and **vocabulary practice**.

- *Reading & Writing Challenge* workbooks provide challenging materials and exercises for students who want even **more practice in reading, vocabulary development, and writing**.

 • **Exam*View*® Test Bank** allows you to create **customizable pre- and post- tests for every unit.** The questions are correlated to CASAS and state standards and include multiple choice, true/false, numeric response, and matching types. Listening questions are included along with an audio CD.

The *Stand Out* Lesson Planner methodology ensures success!

Stand Out ensures student success through good lesson planning and instruction. Each of the five Lessons in every Unit has a lesson plan. Unlike most textbooks, the Lesson Planner was written before the student book materials. A lot of learning occurs with the student books closed so by writing the lesson plans first, we could ensure that each objective was clearly achieved. Each lesson plan follows a systematic and proven format:

W	**Warm-up and/or review**
I	**Introduction**
P	**Presentation**
P	**Practice**
E	**Evaluation**
A	**Application**

WARM-UP AND/OR REVIEW
The warm-up activities establish a context and purpose to the lesson. Exercises use previously learned content and materials that are familiar to students from previous lessons.

INTRODUCTION
In the introduction step, exercises focus the students' attention on the goals of the lesson by asking questions, showing visuals, telling a story, etc. Instructors should state the objective of the lesson and tell students what they will be doing. The objective should address what students are expected to be able to do by the end of the lesson.

PRESENTATION
The presentation activities provide students with the building blocks and skills they need to achieve the objectives set in the introduction. The exercises introduce new information to the students through visuals, realia, description, listenings, explanation, or written text. This is the time to check students' comprehension.

PRACTICE
Practice activities provide meaningful tasks for students to practice what they have just learned through different activities. These activities can be done as a class, in small groups, pairs, or individually. All of these activities are student centered and involve cooperative learning. Instructors should model each activity, monitor progress, and provide feedback.

EVALUATION
Evaluation ensures that students are successful. Instructors should evaluate students on attainment of the objective set at the start of the lesson. This can be done by oral, written, or demonstrated performance. At this point, if students need more practice, instructors can go back and do additional practice activities before moving onto the application.

APPLICATION
Application activities help students apply new knowledge to their own lives or new situations. This is one of the most important steps of the lesson plan. If students can accomplish the application task, it will build their confidence to be able to sue what they've learned out in the community. The Team Projects are an application of unit objectives that involves task-based activities with a product.

In addition to each lesson plan following the WIPPEA model, each Unit in *Stand Out* follows this same approach. The first lesson is always in Introduction to the Unit, introducing new vocabulary and the basic concepts that will be expanded upon in the unit. The following four lessons are the Presentations and Practices for the unit topic. Following the five lessons is a Review lesson, which allows students to do more practice with everything they already learned. The final lesson is an Application for everything they learned in the unit, a team project.

Text Credits

Pre-Unit
Page P10 Source: *Heinle Newbury House Dictionary of American English*, 4th edition

Unit 1
Page 7 "Educational Attainment and Earning Power for Men and Women 18 and Over" chart.
Source: U.S. Census Bureau, Current Population Survey 2006. Annual Social and Economic Supplement.

Unit 2
Page 34 "The Four Keys to Great Credit" is used by permission. Liz Pulliam Weston is a personal finance columnist for **MSN Money** (Web site source: http://money.msn.com), where this article first appeared. Her column appears every Monday and Thursday, exclusively on *MSN Money*. She also answers reader questions in the Your Money message board.

Unit 3
Page 60 "Occupant Fatalities in 2004 by Age and Restraint Use in Passenger Vehicles"
Web site source: http://www.nhtsa.dot.gov
Page 61 "Facts on alcohol-related accidents"
Web site source: http://www.cdc.gov/ncipc/factsheets/drving.htm

Unit 4
Page 82 "Theft Prevention Newsletter" Web site source: http://www.jcsd.org/burglary_prevention.htm

Unit 5
Page 97 "Percentage of persons without health insurance, by three measurements and age group, and percentage of persons with health insurance, by coverage type and age group: United States, January, 2007–June, 2007" Source: Family Core component of the 2007 National Health Interview Survey. The estimates for 2007 are based on data collected January through June. Data are based on household interviews of a sample of the civilian non-institutionalized population.
Page 98 "Percentage of persons under 65 years of age without health insurance coverage at the time of interview, by age group and sex: United States, January, 2007–June, 2007" Source: Family Core component of the 2007 National Health Interview Survey. The estimates for 2007 are based on data collected January through June. Data are based on household interviews of a sample of the civilian non-institutionalized population.

Page 99 "Percentage of persons who lacked health insurance coverage at the time of interview, for at least part of the past year, or for more than a year, by selected demographic characteristics: United States, January, 2007–June, 2007." Source: Family Core component of the 2007 National Health Interview Survey. The estimates for 2007 are based on data collected in January through June. Data are based on household interviews of a sample of the civilian non-institutionalized population.
Page 107 "Health Insurance Coverage of Adults 19–64 Living in Poverty, New York State (2005–2006)" Sources: Urban Institute and Kaiser Commission on Medicaid and the Uninsured estimates based on the Census Bureau's March 2006 and 2007 Current Population Survey (CPS: Annual Social and Economic Supplements). Web site source: http://www.statehealthfacts.org/comparebar.jsp?ind=131&cat=3

Unit 7
Page 143-146 "Conflict Resolution: Resolving Conflict Rationally and Effectively" Used with permission from ©Mind Tools Ltd, 1995–2008. All Rights Reserved.
Page 147 Progress report guidelines. Reprinted with permission from David A. McMurrey, author of *Power Tools for Technical Communication*, Boston: Heinle, 2001.

Unit 8
Page 158 U.S. Citizenship and Immigration Services, Web site source: www.uscis.gov
Page 163 "The Mothers' Club of Northville" Reprinted by permission of the City of Northville, MI.
Web site source: http://www.ci.northville.mi.us
Page 166 "Create Less Trash" and "In Your Home—Conserve Energy" Used with permission from Sustainable Environment for Quality of Life,
Web site source: www.seql.org
Page 167 "Carpooling—What is it?" Used with permission from Sustainable Environment for Quality of Life,
Web site source: www.seql.org

AT-A-GLANCE PREP

Objective: Introduce yourself and greet your friends
Grammar: Contractions
Vocabulary: *application, registration, date of birth, first name, last name, middle initial, occupation, education, goal*

RESOURCES

Activity Bank: Lesson 1, Worksheets 1–5
Grammar Challenge 3: Pre-Unit, Challenge 1

Audio: CD 1, Tracks 1–2

 1.5 hour classes   2.5 hour classes  3+ hour classes

Stand Out 3 Assessment CD-ROM with Exam*View*®

 Preassessment *(optional)*

Use the *Stand Out 3 Assessment CD-ROM with* Exam*View*® to create a pretest for Pre-Unit.

Warm-up and Review   5-10 mins.

As students enter the class, introduce yourself by shaking hands with each student and saying: *Nice to meet you.*

Introduction   5-10 mins.

Welcome students to the class and introduce yourself. Give students any practical information they need, such as what days the class meets, what time it meets, and how long it meets. State the objective: *Today we will introduce ourselves and greet our friends.*

Presentation 1   10-15 mins.

Write the word *application* on the board. Ask students what types of applications they are familiar with. Their answers may include applications for a credit card, a driver's license, or a school registration form. Talk about the meaning of the word. Explain that when you fill out an application, you are *applying* for

something. Ask students if they had to fill out an application to enroll in your English class. Ask them what information was on the application. Make a list on the board, such as name, address, telephone number, etc.

Have students turn to the school registration form in their books. Go over the application and make sure students understand all of the information they will need to fill in.

Practice 1   10-15 mins.

(A) **Fill out the school registration form with your personal information.**

Have students work alone to fill out the application.

Evaluation 1   10 mins.

Walk around the classroom. Make sure students are filling out the form correctly.

Activity Bank

Lesson 1, Worksheet 1: Adult School Registration Form

STANDARDS CORRELATIONS

CASAS: 0.1.2, 0.1.4, 0.2.1, 0.2.2 (See CASAS Competency List on pages 169–175.)
SCANS: **Information** Acquire and evaluate information, organize and maintain information, interpret and communicate information
Interpersonal Participate as a member of a team, teach others, work with cultural diversity
Basic Skills Reading, writing, listening, speaking

Thinking Skills Decision making
Personal Qualities Sociability
EFF: **Communication** Convey ideas in writing, speak so others can understand, listen actively, read with understanding
Interpersonal Cooperate with others
Lifelong Learning Learn through research

Getting to Know You

GOALS
➤ Introduce yourself and greet your friends
➤ Write about yourself
➤ Identify educational goals

LESSON 1

Nice to meet you!

GOAL ➤ Introduce yourself and greet your friends

A Fill out the school registration form with your personal information. (Answers will vary.)

☀ SANTA ANA ADULT SCHOOL
Registration Form

First Name _____ Middle Initial _____

Last Name _____

Address:
Number and Street _____

City _____ State _____ Zip _____

Phone:
Home _____ Cell _____

E-mail address _____

Date of birth (mm/dd/yy) ___ / ___ / ___

Languages Spoken _____

Occupation _____

GOAL ➤ Introduce yourself
and greet your friends

B Write questions for the information on the registration form. (Answers will vary.)

Question	Student A	Student B
What is your first name?		

C Now interview two classmates. Use the questions you wrote in Exercise B. Fill in the chart above with their answers. (Answers will vary.)

EXAMPLE: *You:* What is your first name?
Student A: My first name is Michel.
You: What's your first name?
Student B: My first name is Selma.

Contractions

What is = *What's*

What's your name?

D Introduce the two classmates you interviewed to the rest of the class.

EXAMPLE: This is Michel. His last name is Caron. He is from Haiti. This is Selma. Her last name is Bezerra. She is from Brazil.

Presentation 2   5-10 mins.

Ask students questions based on the information they provided on the form. Ask them to help you write a few questions on the board, such as: *What is your name?* Ask for two volunteers to practice asking and answering these questions.

Practice 2   15-20 mins.

B Write questions for the information on the registration form.

Have students choose from the questions on the board or write their own, based on the information on the registration form. (Shorter classes can do this exercise for homework.)

C Now interview two classmates. Use the questions you wrote in Exercise B. Fill in the chart above with their answers.

Have students walk around the classroom and interview two classmates, writing their answers down in their books. Prepare students for this exercise by modeling it with a few students in front of the class.

Teaching Tip

Modeling

In order to better prepare students for a speaking activity, it is always good to model the target language first. After explaining to students what they are supposed to do, you can model the activity in a variety of different ways.

1. Divide the class in half and have half of the class take one role while the other half takes the second role.
2. Ask a student volunteer to do the interview with you, switching roles after you have completed the activity one time.
3. Ask for two student volunteers to model the interview.

Model activities as many times as necessary so that students will feel confident in their own attempts.

Grammar Box

Contractions

Go over the grammar box with students and help them with the difference in pronunciation between *What is* and *What's*. Make sure students understand that contractions have the same meaning as the longer version of the phrase, but they are used in more informal conversation. See if students can come up with some other contractions they know.

 Refer students to *Stand Out 3 Grammar Challenge*, Pre-Unit, Challenge 1 for more practice with contractions.

Evaluation 2   10-20 mins.

Walk around the classroom and observe students as they interview one another.

D Introduce the two classmates you interviewed to the rest of the class.

Model an introduction first, and then ask a volunteer to introduce the classmates he or she interviewed. If you don't have time for each student to introduce the classmates he or she interviewed, have students introduce them to another student in the class.

Activity Bank

Lesson 1, Worksheet 2: Meet Your Classmates

Presentation 3   5-10 mins. ▪▪▫

 E **Juan and Michel take English class together. Read their conversation.**

Practice the conversation with a few students.

F **Practice the conversation above with a partner.**

Have students practice the conversation a few times with classmates who are sitting near them.

G **Listen to the greetings and responses.**

Play the recording. Encourage students to repeat each greeting and response as they hear it.

> 🎧 *Listening Script*   *CD 1, Track 1*
>
> The listening script matches the chart in Exercise G.

Practice 3   5-10 mins. ▪

 H **Now listen to the greetings and respond after each one.**

Tell students they will hear the greetings again and, this time, they must respond to them. Play the recording as many times as students want.

> 🎧 *Listening Script*   *CD 1, Track 2*
>
> *Hi!*
> *Good morning!*
> *How are you today?*
> *How's it going?*
> *How are you doing?*
> *What's up?*
> *What's new?*

Evaluation 3   5-10 mins. ▪

Walk around the classroom and listen to students as they respond to the greetings.

Application   10-20 mins. ▪▪▫

I **Greet three different classmates. Ask them a few personal information questions.**

As a class, write a conversation on the board, complete with a greeting and a few personal information questions. Have students walk around the room and have conversations with three different classmates. After they have spoken with three classmates, erase the conversation from the board. Encourage students to talk to three more classmates they haven't met yet,

creating the conversation as they go. Ask for volunteers to share what they learned about the classmates they interviewed.

Activity Bank

Lesson 1, Worksheet 3: Fill Out the Form
Lesson 1, Worksheet 4: Greetings
Lesson 1, Worksheet 5: Greeting Cards

Instructor's Notes

_____
_____
_____
_____
_____
_____
_____
_____
_____
_____
_____
_____
_____
_____
_____
_____
_____
_____

GOAL ➤ Introduce yourself
and greet your friends

E Juan and Michel take English class together. Read their conversation.

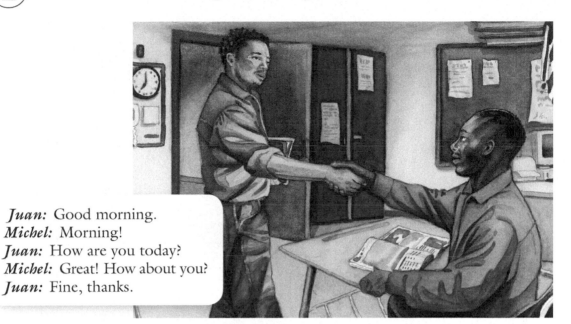

Juan: Good morning.
Michel: Morning!
Juan: How are you today?
Michel: Great! How about you?
Juan: Fine, thanks.

F Practice the conversation above with a partner.

  G Listen to the greetings and responses.

CD 1
TR 1

Greetings	Responses
Hi!	Hello!
Good morning!	Morning!
How are you today?	Fine. / Great!
How's it going?	Pretty good.
How are you doing?	OK. / Not bad.
What's up?	Nothing.
What's new?	Not much.

  H Now listen to the greetings and respond after each one.

CD 1
TR 2

  I Greet three different classmates. Ask them a few personal information questions.

Tell your story.

GOAL ➤ Write about yourself

Vocabulary | Grammar
Life Skills
Academic | Pronunciation

A Read about Akiko.

My name is Akiko Sugiyama and I'm a student at Santa Ana Adult School. I came to the United States five years ago from Japan with my husband and three children. We live in Santa Ana, California. My husband works in a computer assembly factory. I go to school and take care of our children. We are all studying English because we want to be successful in this country. Someday we hope to buy a house and send our children to college.

B Answer the questions about Akiko.

1. When did Akiko come to the United States? _Five years ago._

2. Where is she from? _She is from Japan._

3. Who did she come to the United States with? _Her husband and three children._

4. Where does she live? _She lives in Santa Ana, California._

5. What does her husband do? _Her husband works in a computer assembly factory._

6. What does she do? _She goes to school and takes care of the children._

7. Why is she studying English? _Because she wants to be successful._

8. What are her future goals? _She would like to buy a house and send her children to college._

AT-A-GLANCE PREP

Objective: Write about yourself
Grammar: Present tense
Academic Strategy: Paragraph writing
Vocabulary: *successful, paragraph, margins, indent, title, formatting, model*

RESOURCES

Activity Bank: Templates (Paragraph, Editing-Formatting)

Grammar Challenge 3: Pre-Unit, Challenge 2

■ 1.5 hour classes ■ 2.5 hour classes ■ 3+ hour classes

AGENDA

Define and read a paragraph.
Write information about yourself.
Study paragraph format.
Write a paragraph.

Warm-up and Review   5–10 mins.

Review greetings by having students greet three classmates. Extend the review by having them ask two information questions to each person they greet.

Introduction   1 min.

State the objective: *Today we will be writing about ourselves.*

Presentation 1   5–10 mins.

Write the word *paragraph* on the board. Ask students to help you define it. Explain that a paragraph is a group of sentences that are about the same topic. Ask students where they might find paragraphs. Their answers might include newspapers, books, magazines, etc.

A **Read about Akiko.**

Ask students to read the paragraph to themselves. Then ask for a volunteer to read the paragraph out loud to the class. Go over any vocabulary questions students might have.

Practice 1   10–15 mins.

B **Answer the questions about Akiko.**

Have students write the answers to the questions by themselves. When they are finished, have them discuss their answers with a partner.

Evaluation 1   3–5 mins.

Go over the answers as a class.

STANDARDS CORRELATIONS

CASAS: 0.2.1, 7.2.6 (See CASAS Competency List on pages 169–175.)
SCANS: Information Acquire and evaluate information, organize and maintain information, interpret and communicate information, use computers to process information (optional)
Interpersonal Participate as a member of a team, teach others, work with cultural diversity
Systems Understand systems, monitor and correct performance
Technology Apply technology to a task (optional)

Basic Skills Reading, writing, arithmetic, listening, speaking
Thinking Skills Creative thinking, decision making
Personal Qualities Responsibility, sociability, self-management
EFF: Communication Reading with understanding, convey ideas in writing, speak so others can understand, listen actively
Interpersonal Cooperate with others
Lifelong Learning Take responsibility for learning, reflect and evaluate, use information and communications technology (optional)

Presentation 2   10-15 mins.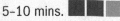

Write the following table on the board.

	Akiko	*You*
school		
native country		
family members		
job		
future goals		

As a class, fill in the column for Akiko. Then have students work with a partner and talk about how they would fill in the column for themselves.

Practice 2   15-20 mins.

C Now answer the questions about yourself.

Have students write the answers to these questions in their books. When they are finished, have them share their answers with a partner. (Shorter classes can do this exercise for homework.)

Teaching Tip

Partners

Throughout this book, students will be asked to work with a partner. In the beginning, it may be easier to have them talk to the person sitting next to them. However, as the class progresses, it is a good idea to pair them up with different students to help build a strong sense of community in the classroom. There are several ways to pair students.

1. Give students either the beginning or end of a sentence and have them find the student with the other half.
2. Have students find another student who speaks a different native language.
3. Have students work with the person in front, behind, to the right, or to the left of them.

Evaluation 2   5-10 mins.

Evaluate the students by asking the questions from Exercise C. Call on various students to answer each question.

 Refer students to *Stand Out 3 Grammar Challenge*, Pre-Unit, Challenge 2, for practice with verbs in the simple present tense.

Presentation 3   5-10 mins.

D Study the paragraph below. Notice the title, the margins, and the indented first line.

Go over Akiko's paragraph with students, pointing out all of the formatting features. As you go over each formatting aspect, have students put their fingers on the place you are referring to. For example: *Point to the title.*

Instructor's Notes

_____

_____

_____

_____

_____

_____

_____

_____

_____

_____

_____

_____

_____

_____

_____

_____

_____

_____

_____

_____

_____

C **Now answer the questions about yourself.** (Answers will vary.)

1. When did you come to this country? _____

2. Where are you from? _____

3. Who did you come to this country with? _____

4. Where do you live? _____

5. What do you do? _____

6. Why are you studying English? _____

7. What are your future goals? _____

D **Study the paragraph below. Notice the title, the margins, and the indented first line.**

title

indent

space between title and paragraph

My Story

My name is Akiko Sugiyama and I'm a student at Santa Ana

Adult School. I came to the United States five years ago from

Japan with my husband and three children. We live in Santa Ana,

California. My husband works in a computer assembly factory.

I go to school and take care of our children. We are all studying

English because we want to be successful in this country. Someday

we hope to buy a house and send our children to college.

right margin

left margin

GOAL ➤ **Write about yourself**

E Write a paragraph about yourself with the answers you wrote in Exercise C.
Use correct paragraph formatting like Akiko's paragraph in Exercise D. (Answers will vary.)

F Show your paragraph to your partner. Read your partner's paragraph and ask questions about anything you want to know more about.

Practice 3   10-15 mins.

Have students take out a lined piece of paper and copy Akiko's paragraph, using correct formatting.

Note: If you are using *Stand Out 3 Grammar Challenge* for this lesson and want to focus on the present tense, you can ask students to find all of the present tense verbs in Akiko's paragraph.

Evaluation 3   10-15 mins.

Walk around the classroom and observe students. Point out any formatting mistakes they make.

Application   15-25 mins.

E Write a paragraph about yourself with the answers you wrote in Exercise C. Use correct paragraph formatting like Akiko's paragraph in Exercise D.

Remind students to use Akiko's paragraph as a model. At this point, it's OK if they copy most of her sentences, inserting their own personal information.

Activity Bank AB

Templates Folder: Paragraph

F Show your paragraph to your partner. Read your partner's paragraph and ask questions about anything you want to know more about.

Activity Bank AB

Templates Folder: Editing—Formatting

Instructor's Notes

Objective: Identify educational goals

Grammar: Simple past

Academic Strategies: Comparing and contrasting, setting goals, writing a paragraph

Vocabulary: *community college, elementary school, graduate, high school, junior high school, kindergarten, middle school, preschool, technical school, vocational, university, achieve*

AGENDA

Learn about the U.S. educational system.

Understand educational abbreviations.

Discuss your educational system.

Set educational goals.

RESOURCES

Activity Bank: Lesson 3, Worksheets 1–2

Grammar Challenge 3: Pre-Unit, Challenge 3

■ 1.5 hour classes   ■ 2.5 hour classes   ■ 3+ hour classes

Warm-up and Review   5-10 mins.

Have students take out their paragraphs from the previous lesson and ask for a few volunteers to read their paragraphs out loud.

Introduction   5-10 mins.

Ask students a few questions about education: *Did you go to school in your native country? Did you graduate from high school in your native country?* State the objective: *Today we will identify our educational goals.*

Presentation 1   15-20 mins.

A This pyramid represents the educational system in the United States. Read the pyramid with your teacher.

Start at the bottom and work your way up the pyramid, discussing each educational step in the United States.

B What do these abbreviations stand for and mean? Have your teacher help you complete the chart.

Write the chart on the board and fill in the answers as you go over them with students.

STANDARDS CORRELATIONS

CASAS: 0.1.2, 0.1.6, 0.2.1, 7.1.1 (See CASAS Competency List on pages 169-175.)

SCANS: Information Acquire and evaluate information, organize and maintain information, interpret and communicate information
Interpersonal Participate as a member of a team, teach others, work with cultural diversity
Systems Understand systems
Basic Skills Reading, writing, listening, speaking

Thinking Skills Creative thinking, decision making
Personal Qualities Responsibility, sociability
EFF: Communication Convey ideas in writing, speak so others can understand, listen actively
Decision Making Plan
Interpersonal Cooperate with others
Lifelong Learning Take responsibility for learning, reflect and evaluate, use information and communications technology (optional)

Are you college bound?

GOAL ➤ Identify educational goals

A This pyramid represents the educational system in the United States. Read the pyramid with your teacher.

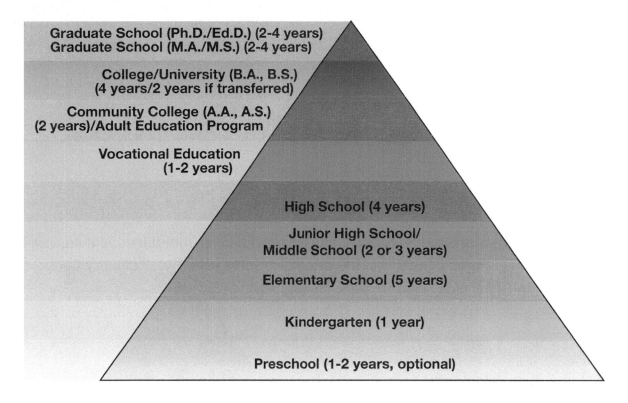

Graduate School (Ph.D./Ed.D.) (2-4 years)
Graduate School (M.A./M.S.) (2-4 years)

College/University (B.A., B.S.)
(4 years/2 years if transferred)

Community College (A.A., A.S.)
(2 years)/Adult Education Program

Vocational Education
(1-2 years)

High School (4 years)

Junior High School/
Middle School (2 or 3 years)

Elementary School (5 years)

Kindergarten (1 year)

Preschool (1-2 years, optional)

B What do these abbreviations stand for and mean? Have your teacher help you complete the chart.

Abbreviation	Stands for . . .	Meaning
A.A.	Associate of Arts	a two-year degree from a community college with an arts-related major
A.S.	Associate of Science	a two-year degree from a community college with a science-related major
M.A.	Master of Arts	a degree from a graduate school with an arts-related major
M.S.	Master of Science	a degree from a graduate school with a science-related major
Ph.D.	Doctor of Philosophy	an advanced degree from a graduate school (a doctorate): the major can be related to arts or to science
Ed.D.	Doctor of Education	a professional doctorate that prepares students for administrative or specialized positions in education

C Choose the best answer. Look back at the pyramid if you need help.

1. What is the lowest level of education in the United States?

    a. kindergarten   (b.) preschool   c. graduate school

2. How many years do students go to high school?

    a. three years   b. two years   (c.) four years

3. What is the highest degree you can get?

    a. M.A.   b. M.S.   (c.) Ph.D.

4. Where can you get a B.A. or B.S. degree?

    (a.) college   b. graduate school   c. technical college

D How is the U.S. educational system different from the educational system in your country? Use the pyramid below to show your country's educational system. Then, compare pyramids with a classmate. (Answers will vary.)

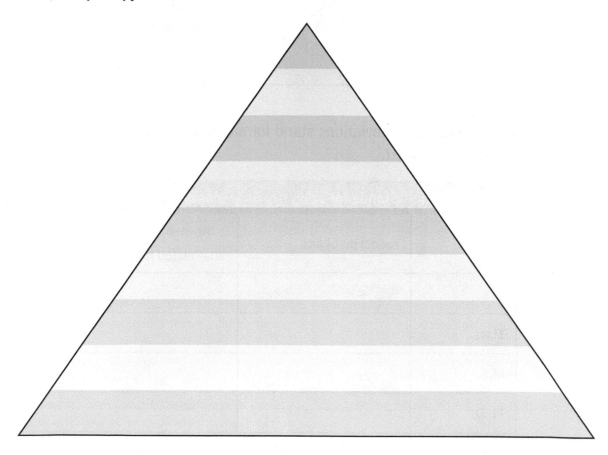

Practice 1

5-10 mins. ■■■■

C Choose the best answer. Look back at the pyramid if you need help.

Have students answer the questions by themselves.

Evaluation 1

5 mins. ■■■■

Go over the answers as a class.

Presentation 2

5-10 mins. ■■■■

Have students look back at the pyramid on page P7. Ask them questions to help them compare the U.S. educational system to the systems in their countries: *Does your country have preschool? At what age do children go to preschool? How many years of elementary school does your country have?*

Practice 2

15-20 mins. ■■■

D How is the U.S. educational system different from the educational system in your country? Use the pyramid below to show your country's educational system. Then, compare pyramids with a classmate.

Have students work by themselves to create a pyramid showing their country's educational system. If you have some students from the same country, you may want to put these students in pairs to create the pyramid together.

Evaluation 2

10-15 mins. ■■■

Ask for some volunteers to draw their pyramids on the board. As a class, discuss how these pyramids are different from the pyramid describing the U.S. educational system.

Activity Bank 🔵

Lesson 3, Worksheet 2: Compare Educational Systems

Instructor's Notes

Presentation 3   5–10 mins. ▪▪▫

Go through the educational pyramid with students, either on the board, in the book, or on an overhead. Starting at the bottom, explain your educational background. For example: *I didn't go to preschool. I started kindergarten when I was six, and I started elementary school when I was seven.*

Practice 3   5–10 mins. ▪

(E) Where are you on the educational pyramid?

Go through steps 1 and 2 with students, explaining what they are supposed to do.

Evaluation 3   5–10 mins. ▪

Walk around the classroom and help students as necessary.

Application   10–20 mins. ▪▪▫

(F) How do you plan to achieve your educational goals? Write a short paragraph.

Brainstorm ideas with students about what they will write in their paragraph. Have students work alone on their paragraphs and then share with a partner when they are finished.

📖 Refer students to *Stand Out 3 Grammar Challenge*, Pre-Unit, Challenge 3, for practice with past tense verbs.

> **Activity Bank** 💿
>
> Lesson 3, Worksheet 1: Educational History

E Where are you on the educational pyramid? (Answers will vary.)

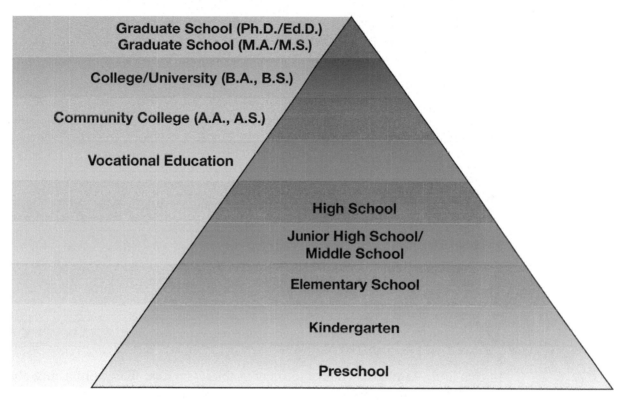

1. Put a check (✓) on the pyramid next to the educational levels you have completed (in any country).

2. Where do you want to be? Circle the educational level that you would like to achieve.

F How do you plan to achieve your educational goals? Write a short paragraph.

(Answers will vary.)

_____

_____

_____

_____

_____

My Dictionary

Find three new words you learned in this unit. Write the word and the sentence where you found the word. (Answers will vary.)

EXAMPLE: Word: future   Page: P5
Sentence: What are her <u>future</u> goals?

1. Word: _____   Page: _____

   Sentence: _____

2. Word: _____   Page: _____

   Sentence: _____

3. Word: _____   Page: _____

   Sentence: _____

Learner Log

In this unit, you had a chance to meet your classmates, share something about yourself, and think about your educational goals. How comfortable do you feel doing each of the skills listed below? Rate your comfort level on a scale of 1 to 4.

1 = Need more practice   **2** = OK   **3** = Good   **4** = Great!

Life Skill	Comfort Level				Page
I can fill out a registration form.	1	2	3	4	P1
I can introduce myself.	1	2	3	4	P3
I can greet my friends.	1	2	3	4	P3
I can ask personal information questions.	1	2	3	4	P3
I can write a paragraph.	1	2	3	4	P6
I can write my educational goals.	1	2	3	4	P9

If you circled 1 or 2, write down the page number where you can review this skill.

Reflection

1. What was the most useful skill you learned in this unit? _____

2. How will this help you in life? _____

Presentation 1 5–10 mins.

My Dictionary

Write the word *dictionary* on the board. Ask students what the purpose of a dictionary is. Tell them they are going to be creating their own mini dictionaries for each unit. Go over the directions and example with them.

Practice 1 10–15 mins.

Have students work by themselves to find three new words they learned in this unit.

Evaluation 1 10 mins.

Walk around the classroom and help students as necessary.

Presentation 2 5–10 mins.

Learner Log

Explain the Learner Log to students. Go through the instructions and discuss the rating scale. Make sure students understand what each of the numbers represents. Since this is the first time students have done this type of self-evaluation, ask them to go back in the unit and find the page numbers for each of the skills listed. Do the first two together.

Teaching Tip

Learner Logs

Learner Logs function to help students in many different ways:

1. They serve as part of the review process.
2. They help students to gain confidence and document what they have learned. Consequently, students see that they are making progress and want to move forward in learning.
3. They provide students with a tool that they can use over and over to check and recheck their understanding. In this way, students become independent learners.

Practice 2 5 mins.

Now have students circle numbers next to each of the skills, describing how they feel about doing each one.

Evaluation 2 5 mins.

Take a poll to see how students feel about doing each of the skills.

Reflection 10–20 mins.

Go over the questions, making sure students understand what they can write. Have students complete the reflection on their own.

Instructor's Notes

_____
_____
_____
_____
_____
_____
_____
_____
_____
_____
_____
_____
_____
_____
_____
_____
_____
_____
_____
_____
_____
_____
_____
_____
_____

Objective: Make a schedule
Grammar: Adverbs of frequency
Pronunciation: Focus
Academic Strategy: Reading a chart
Vocabulary: *schedule, routine,* adverbs of frequency

RESOURCES

Activity Bank: Lesson 1, Worksheets 1–2
Reading and Writing Challenge 3: Unit 1

Grammar Challenge 3: Unit 1, Challenge 1

■ 1.5 hour classes ■ 2.5 hour classes ■ 3⁺ hour classes

Stand Out 3 Assessment CD-ROM with Exam*View*®

AGENDA

Talk about schedules.
Do a dictation.
Use adverbs of frequency.
Practice focus in pronunciation.
Write your schedule.

 Preassessment *(optional)*

Use the Stand Out 3 Assessment CD-ROM with
Exam*View*ⓟ to create a pretest for Unit 1.

Warm-up and Review   5-10 mins.

Write the word *schedule* on the board. Ask
students: *What is a schedule?* They may mention
a bus or train schedule. Present the idea of a
personal schedule to them before you ask the
next questions: *What information goes on a
schedule? Who keeps schedules? Do any of you have
a schedule? What information do you keep on it?*

Introduction   1 min. ■■■

State the objective: *Today we will make
a schedule.*

Presentation 1   10-15 mins.

(A) **Look at Luisa's schedule. What are
her routines?**

After students study Luisa's schedule, ask them
specific questions about it. For example: *What
activity does Luisa do on Mondays, Wednesdays,
and Saturdays? When does she go to work?* Ask
additional questions to familiarize them with
the schedule.

Practice 1   10-15 mins.

(B) **Talk about Luisa's schedule with a partner.
Ask questions using:** *What time . . . ?,
When . . . ?,* **and** *What . . . ?*

STANDARDS CORRELATIONS

CASAS: 0.1.2, 0.2.4 (See CASAS Competency List on pages 169–175.)
SCANS: **Resources** Allocate time
Information Acquire and evaluate information, organize and maintain
information, interpret and communicate information
Interpersonal Participate as a member of a team, teach others, work
with cultural diversity
Systems Understand systems, monitor and correct performance
Basic Skills Reading, writing, listening, speaking

Thinking Skills Creative thinking, decision making, problem solving,
seeing things in the mind's eye
Personal Qualities Responsibility, sociability, self-management
EFF: **Communication** Convey ideas in writing, speak so others can
understand, listen actively
Interpersonal Cooperate with others
Lifelong Learning Reflect and evaluate, learn through research

Balancing Your Life

GOALS

➤ Make a schedule
➤ Identify goals, obstacles, and solutions
➤ Write about your goal

➤ Identify study habits
➤ Identify time-management strategies

Everyday life

GOAL ➤ Make a schedule

 Look at Luisa's schedule. What are her routines?

	Monday	Tuesday	Wednesday	Thursday	Friday	Saturday	Sunday
Morning 6-8 A.M.	Go running	Go to grocery store	Go running	Clean house	Breakfast with coworkers	Go running	
8-12 A.M./P.M.	Day off	Work 10:00	Work 10:00	Work 10:00	Work 10:00	Work 10:00	Day off
Afternoon 12-1 P.M.	Go shopping with Mary	Go to bank on lunch break				Go to library on lunch break	Have lunch with family
1-5 P.M.		Finish work 5:00	Finish work 5:00		Finish work 5:00	Finish work 5:00	
Evening 5-9 P.M.		ESL class 7-8	Computer class 6:30-7:30	Finish work 5:00	ESL class 7-8	Rent a video	

 Talk about Luisa's schedule with a partner. Ask questions using: *What time . . . ?*, *When . . . ?*, and *What . . . ?* (Answers will vary.)

EXAMPLE: *Student A:* What time does Luisa start work?
     Student B: She starts work at 10:00 A.M.

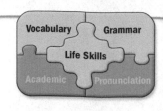

C With a partner, ask questions about Luisa's schedule. Use *How often . . . ?* Answer the questions using the frequency expressions from the box. (Answers will vary.)

once a week	twice a week	three times a week
every morning	every weekday	every other day	every Saturday

EXAMPLE: *Student A:* How often does Luisa rent a movie?
Student B: Luisa rents a movie every Saturday.

D Where do these adverbs of frequency go in a sentence? Study the charts below.

0%   50%   100%

never   rarely   sometimes   usually   always

Placement rules for frequency adverbs	Examples
before the main verb	Luisa *always / usually / often* <u>goes</u> running. She *sometimes / rarely / never* <u>makes</u> dinner.
after the main verb *be*	She <u>is</u> *usually* busy on the weekends.
sometimes / usually / often can come at the beginning or at the end of a sentence	*Usually / Sometimes* Luisa studies in the library. Luisa studies in the library *sometimes / usually*.
between the subject and verb in short answers	Yes, <u>I</u> *always* <u>do</u>. / No, <u>he</u> *usually* <u>isn't</u>.
Rarely and *never* are negative words. Do not use *not* and *never* in the same sentence.	**Correct:** He *never* goes to the movies. **Incorrect:** He ~~doesn't~~ never go to the movies.

E Write the frequency adverb in parentheses in the correct place in each sentence below. Remember, sometimes the adverb can go in more than one place.

          rarely
EXAMPLE: Roberto finishes his homework before class. (rarely)

     always
1. Jerry comes to class on time. (always)
 Sometimes   *sometimes*
2. Sue eats lunch with her husband. (sometimes)
      never
3. Our teacher sits at her desk while she is teaching. (never)
 Often *often*
4. Elia goes running in the morning before school. (often)
    usually
5. Hugo works at night. (usually)

Practice 1 *(continued)*

 With a partner, ask questions about Luisa's schedule. Use *How often . . . ?* **Answer the questions using the frequency expressions from the box.**

Have students work with a partner. Make sure they take turns asking and answering questions.

Evaluation 1   5 mins.

Observe the students while they work. When they are finished, ask them additional questions about the schedule using *How often . . . ?*

Activity Bank

Lesson 1, Worksheet 1: Schedule Information Gap

Presentation 2   15-25 mins.

Dictate the following sentences.

1. The children *always* go to school on time.
2. Do you *usually* work on Saturdays?
3. Their family is *seldom* at the park.
4. I am *generally* in good spirits.
5. *Sometimes* José studies in the library.
6. José studies in the library *often*.
7. Yes, I *always* do.
8. No, he *usually* isn't.

Ask students to underline the word in each sentence that tells how often something happens. Have volunteers write these words on the board. Explain that these words are called *adverbs of frequency*. Have students look at each pair of sentences (Sentences 1 and 2, Sentences 3 and 4, etc.) and try to find a pattern with the order of the verb and the adverb of frequency. Help them discover the rules. Then go over the chart in Exercise D.

Practice 2   10-15 mins.

Ⅾ Where do these adverbs of frequency go in a sentence? Study the charts below.

(Shorter classes can do this exercise for homework.)

Teaching Tip

Dictation

The purpose of dictation is to help students improve their listening skills.

1. Write the following steps on the board and go over them.
   Listen first. (The most important step!)
   Repeat it to yourself.
   Write.
2. To encourage students to listen carefully, tell them that you will only read the statements one time.
3. Tell students to listen to the whole sentence before they begin writing. Remind them that if they start writing before you've finished talking, they won't hear the end of what you say.
4. Dictate the sentences (one time each) at a normal pace, pausing between each one to allow students time to write.
5. Once you've finished dictating, have students check their answers with a partner or group. Encourage them to write down what they missed or fix what they think they got wrong.
6. Read the dictation one more time at normal speed. This time, don't pause.
7. Ask volunteers to write each statement on the board.
8. Ask the class to check the statements and have different volunteers come up to the board and correct what they think is wrong.
9. Continue having students check the statements until all of them are correct.

Ⅾ Write the frequency adverb in parentheses in the correct place in each sentence below. Remember, sometimes the adverb can go in more than one place.

Go over the example with students and make sure they understand the directions.

Evaluation 2   5-10 mins.

Go over the answers as a class by asking volunteers to write the completed sentences on the board.

Presentation 3   5-10 mins.

Have students turn back to page 1 in their books and look at Luisa's schedule. Ask them questions using frequency adverbs such as: *Does Luisa always run in the morning?* If they say *no* to any of the questions, ask them to use a different adverb of frequency to make the answer true. For example: *Luisa often goes running in the morning.*

Practice 3   10-15 mins. ▪

F Write sentences about Luisa, using frequency adverbs. Look back at her schedule on page 1.

Have students write four sentences in their books. (Shorter classes can do this exercise for homework.)

Activity Bank

Lesson 1, Worksheet 2: Adverbs of Frequency

Evaluation 3   5-10 mins. ▪

Ask for volunteers to write their sentences on the board. Evaluate them as a class, making sure the frequency adverbs are in the correct place.

Refer students to *Stand Out 3 Grammar Challenge*, Unit 1, Challenge 1, for more practice with adverbs of frequency.

Pronunciation

Focus

It is important for students to understand that the emphasis they put on different words may change the meaning of a sentence. Also, by putting the focus in the correct place, they will be better understood. Go over the examples in the pronunciation box with students, having them practice out loud.

G Practice reading the sentences you wrote in Exercise F. Focus on the important words.

Have students work with a partner. Walk around the classroom and listen.

Application   10-20 mins.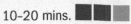

H Make a schedule of everything you do in one week. Talk about your schedule with your partner.

After students create a schedule, have them talk about it with a partner using present tense verbs and adverbs of frequency. If time allows, students can write sentences about their schedules.

Instructor's Notes

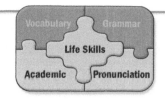

F Write sentences about Luisa, using frequency adverbs. Look back at her schedule on page 1. (Answers will vary.)

EXAMPLE: <u>Luisa usually finishes work at 5:00.</u>

1. _____

2. _____

3. _____

4. _____

G Practice reading the sentences you wrote in Exercise F. Focus on the important words.

H Make a schedule of everything you do in one week. Talk about your schedule with your partner. (Answers will vary.)

EXAMPLE: I NEVER cook on my day off because I'm a cook in a restaurant!

Pronunciation

Focus: In a phrase or sentence, certain words get the most stress or *focus.* In the sentences below, the words with the most focus are in CAPITAL letters.

Luisa OFTEN goes RUNNING.
She is NEVER HOME on the weekends.
SOMETIMES I go to the MOVIES.
He RARELY studies in the MORNING.

	Monday	Tuesday	Wednesday	Thursday	Friday	Saturday	Sunday
Morning							
Afternoon							
Evening							

The future

GOAL ➤ Identify goals, obstacles, and solutions

Zhou is worried about the future.
What is he thinking about?

A Read about Zhou.

Zhou's life is going to change very soon. His wife, Huixen, is going to have twins in July.
His parents are going to come from China to live in the United States. He's happy, but his
apartment will to be too small for everyone. He needs a better job, but his boss won't promote
him because he doesn't have a college degree.

Zhou has three goals. When his parents come to the United States, he will buy a house
large enough for two families. His father will work and help pay for the house. His mother
will help take care of the children. Then, Zhou plans to go to night school and get his
bachelor's degree. When he graduates, he will apply for a new position at work. He will
work hard to achieve his goals.

B A *goal* is something you would like to achieve in the future. What are Zhou's three goals?

Contractions
will not = *won't*
His boss *won't* promote him.

1. He will buy a house.

2. He plans to go to night school and get his bachelor's degree.

3. He will apply for a new position at work.

C An *obstacle* is a problem, or something that gets in the way of your goal. Zhou has two obstacles. What are they?

1. His apartment is too small for everyone.

2. His boss won't promote him because he doesn't have a college degree.

AT-A-GLANCE PREP

Objective: Identify goals, obstacles, and solutions
Grammar: *When in the future*
Academic Strategies: Active reading, focused listening
Vocabulary: *goals, obstacle, solution, personal, occupational*

RESOURCES

Activity Bank: Lesson 2, Worksheets 1–3
Reading and Writing Challenge 3: Unit 1

Grammar Challenge 3: Unit 1, Challenge 2
Audio: CD 1, Track 3

■ 1.5 hour classes ■ 2.5 hour classes ■ 3⁺ hour classes

AGENDA
Discuss goals, obstacles,
and solutions.
Use when in the future.
Create a goal chart.
Write about your goals.

Warm-up and Review   5-10 mins. ■■■

Write the word *goal* on the board. Ask students to help you define it. Write down anything they say that could be considered a definition of the word. Keep in mind that you are trying to solicit definitions, not examples.

Introduction   5-10 mins. ■■■

Have students open their books and look at the picture of Zhou. Ask them what he is thinking about. State the objective: *Today we will be identifying goals, obstacles, and solutions.*

Presentation 1   10-15 mins. ■■■

 Read about Zhou.

Have students silently read the story. When they are finished, read the story out loud so they can hear the correct intonation. Ask basic comprehension questions, such as: *Why won't his boss promote him?* Then ask students if they have any vocabulary questions.

Practice 1   10-15 mins. ■■■

B A *goal* is something you would like to achieve in the future. What are Zhou's three goals?

Go over the definition of *goal* and find the first goal together. Have students complete the other two goals by themselves.

C An *obstacle* is a problem, something that gets in the way of your goal. Zhou has two obstacles. What are they?

Go over the definition of *obstacle* and find the first obstacle together. Have students find the second obstacle by themselves.

Presentation 1 (continued)

D Review vocabulary.

Have students complete the items by themselves.

Evaluation 1   5-10 mins.

Go over the answers as a class. Make sure students understand all the definitions. Go back to Zhou's story and ask students what Zhou's solutions are.

Presentation 2   5-10 mins.

Tell students they will listen to two different speakers talk about their goals. Write the words *goal*, *obstacle*, and *solutions* on the board. Tell students that they will listen for these items.

Teaching Tip

Focused listening

The purpose of focused listening is to learn how to pick out important information.

1. Tell students that they don't need to understand every word to grasp the speaker's meaning.
2. Present the context.
3. Make sure students understand what they are listening for.
4. Start with a few examples and allow students to gain confidence.
5. After students complete the task, ask them to summarize what they heard.

Practice 2   15-20 mins.

E Listen to Tuba and Lam. Identify their goals, obstacles, and solutions and write them in the spaces below.

Play the recording. Ask students to identify each person's goal, obstacle, and solutions. Have them fill in the answers in their books.

 Listening Script   CD 1, Track 3

My name is Tuba Kambriz. I came here from Afghanistan five years ago. My husband had to come here for business so my whole family moved here. Right now, we don't have enough money to pay the bills so my goal is to get a job to help my husband with money. But I have an obstacle—time. It will be difficult to work because I have to take care of the children and the house. One solution is to work part time while my children are in school. Another solution is to have my mother help out around the house and help take care of the children. If we all work together, we will achieve our goal.

I'm Lam and I came to the United States from Vietnam many years ago. I was a political prisoner during the Vietnam War and now I'm happy to be safe in America with my family. The most important people in my life are my grandchildren. My goal is to send my grandchildren to college. But there is an obstacle. We don't have enough money to send them to college. I want them to have the education I never did so I think it's very important for them to go to school. My wife thought of one solution. She suggested they apply for scholarships. This is a good idea because both girls are very smart. The girls came up with another solution. They said they could work part time while going to school. We have been saving every penny we can to help them. I hope everything works out in the end.

Evaluation 2   5-10 mins.

Go over the answers as a class. See if students can suggest any more solutions.

Presentation 3   15-20 mins.

Have student close their books and take out a sheet of paper. Dictate the following sentences.

1. When Zhou's parents come from China, his house will be too small for everyone.
2. Zhou will buy a two-family house when his parents move to the United States.
3. When he graduates, he will apply for a new position at work.

After students write the sentences, write them on the board and have students check their work. Have volunteers underline the verbs in the *when* clause with <u>one</u> line and in the other clause with <u>two</u> lines. Help them find the pattern of tenses.

F Look at how we can talk about Zhou's goals.

Go over the examples and explanations.

D **Review vocabulary.**

1. What is a goal? _A goal is something you would like to achieve in the future._

2. What is an obstacle? _An obstacle is a problem, something that gets in the way of your goal._

3. What is a solution? **A solution is an idea of how to solve a problem.**

4. Zhou's apartment is too small. What is his solution?

   His solution is to buy a house.

5. Zhou needs a better job. What is his solution?

   His solution is to go to night school and get his bachelor's degree. When he graduates, he will apply for a new position.

CD 1
TR 3

E **Listen to Tuba and Lam. Identify their goals, obstacles, and solutions and write them in the spaces below.**

1. **Goal:** Tuba wants to _get a job to help her husband_ .

   Obstacle: Her obstacle is _time_ .

   Solutions: _____

   A. Maybe she can _work part time while her children are in school_ .

   B. Maybe her mother can _help around the house and help take care of the children_ .

2. **Goal:** Lam wants to _send his grandchildren to college_ .

   Obstacle: His obstacle is _that he doesn't have enough money to send them to college_ .

   Solutions: _____

   A. Maybe his grandchildren can _apply for scholarships_ .

   B. Maybe his grandchildren can _work part time while going to school_ .

F **Look at how we can talk about Zhou's goals.**

When Zhou *graduates*, he *will* apply for a new position at work.
This sentence means:
First, he will graduate. *Then*, he will apply for a new position at work.

When his parents *come* to the United States, he *will* buy a house.
This sentence means:
First, his parents will come to the United States. *Then*, he will buy a house.

GOAL ➤ Identify goals, obstacles, and solutions

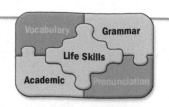

Future Time Clauses with *When*			
When	**Present tense**	**Will**	**Base verb**
When Zhou	graduates,	he will	apply for a new position at work.*
When his parents	come to the United States	he will	buy a house.
*Note: The order of the clauses does not matter. You can also say, *Zhou will apply for a new position at work when he graduates.*			

G Complete the sentences below with your own ideas.

EXAMPLE: When his parents come to the United States, <u>Zhou's house</u>

<u>will be too small</u>.

1. When <u>Zhou's parents come to the United States</u>, they will buy a bigger house.

2. When Zhou's mother comes to stay, <u>she will help take care of the children</u>.

3. When <u>Zhou gets his bachelor's degree</u>, his boss will promote him.

4. When Zhou gets a better job, <u>he will have achieved his goals</u>.

H Look back at Zhou's goals. He has a *personal* goal (buy a new home), an *educational* goal (graduate from college), and an *occupational* goal (get a new position at work). What are your goals? Write them in the chart below. (Answers will vary.)

Personal	Educational	Occupational
<u>run a 5k race</u>	<u>take an English course</u>	<u>get a raise at work</u>
1. _____	1. _____	1. _____
2. _____	2. _____	2. _____
3. _____	3. _____	3. _____

I In groups, discuss your goals for the future. Then, write sentences about yourself.

EXAMPLE: <u>When I graduate, I will get a new job.</u> (Answers will vary.)

J Active Task. Write or type your goals on a piece of paper. Hang it up in a special place where you can read your goals each day. (Answers will vary.)

Presentation 3 (continued)

Go over the grammar chart with students. Answer questions as needed.

Practice 3   10-15 mins.

G Complete the sentences below with your own ideas.

Go over the example with students and have them complete the exercises on their own.

Activity Bank

Lesson 2, Worksheet 1: *When* in the Future

Evaluation 3   10-15 mins.

Ask for volunteers to write their completed sentences on the board. Go over the answers as a class. Encourage other students to share what they wrote.

GC Refer students to *Stand Out 3 Grammar Challenge*, Unit 1, Challenge 2 for more practice with *when* in the future.

Application   10-20 mins. ■■■

H Look back at Zhou's goals. He has a *personal* goal (buy a new home), an *educational* goal (graduate from college), and an *occupational* goal (get a new position at work). What are your goals? Write them in the chart below.

Make sure students understand the different types of goals before you have them complete the chart. As a class, come up with a few examples for each type. Walk around the classroom and help students with vocabulary as they are writing down their goals.

Activity Bank

Lesson 2, Worksheet 2: My Goals

I In groups, discuss your goals for the future. Then, write sentences about yourself.

Put students in small groups and have them spend 5–10 minutes discussing their future goals. Encourage them to use *when*. After students have finished talking, have them write sentences about their goals.

J Active Task. Write or type your goals on a piece of paper. Hang it up in a special place where you can read your goals each day.

Discuss with students how writing their goals down and posting them where they will see them each day will help them stay focused and make sure they are working toward their goals.

Activity Bank

Lesson 2, Worksheet 3: My Own Store

Instructor's Notes

_____

_____

_____

_____

_____

_____

_____

_____

_____

_____

_____

_____

_____

_____

_____

_____

_____

Objective: Write about your goal
Academic Strategy: Writing a paragraph
Vocabulary: *topic, support, conclusion*

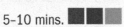

AGENDA

Discuss goals, obstacles, and solutions.

Identify topic, support, and conclusion sentences in a paragraph.

Write about your goal.

RESOURCES

Activity Bank: Lesson 3, Worksheet 1
Reading and Writing Challenge 3: Unit 1

Grammar Challenge 3: Unit 1, Challenge 3

■ 1.5 hour classes ■ 2.5 hour classes ▨ 3⁺ hour classes

Warm-up and Review 5-10 mins. ■■▨

Ask students to give you examples of goals. Write everything they say on the board, but put their ideas in three separate clusters without giving the clusters a name: *personal, educational,* and *occupational*. Once you have quite a few goals on the board, ask students to read over each cluster separately and try to identify the types of goals it contains.

Introduction 5-10 mins. ■■▨

A Read the paragraph and review the meanings of the words in italics.

State the objective: *In this lesson, we will write about one of our goals.*

Presentation 1 10-15 mins. ■■▨

Ask for a volunteer to share his or her goals with the class. Write the list on the board. Now ask the class to come up with some possible obstacles to reaching these goals. Then have

them come up with a few solutions for each obstacle. Repeat this presentation until you think all of the students are comfortable with the terms *goal, obstacle,* and *solution*.

Practice 1 10-15 mins. ■■▨

B Choose one of the goals you wrote in the chart on page 6. Think of one obstacle to reaching your goal and two possible solutions. Write the information below.

Have students complete this exercise by themselves.

Evaluation 1 5-10 mins. ■■▨

C Share your ideas with a partner. Can your partner suggest other possible solutions?

After students complete this exercise, ask for volunteers to share their goals, obstacle, solutions, and any additional solutions their partners came up with.

Goals, obstacles, and solutions

GOAL ➤ **Write about your goal**

Vocabulary   Grammar
Life Skills
Academic   Pronunciation

A Read the paragraph and review the meanings of the words in italics.

In the previous lesson, you wrote your *goals*. Goals are things you want to *achieve*. Sometimes we can have *problems* achieving our goals. These problems are called *obstacles*. When we figure out how to *solve* these problems, we have *solutions*.

B Choose one of the goals you wrote in the chart on page 6. Think of one obstacle to reaching your goal and two possible solutions. Write the information below.

(Answers will vary.)

Goal: _____

Obstacle: _____

Solutions:

1. _____

_____

2. _____

_____

C Share your ideas with a partner. Can your partner suggest other possible solutions?

Solutions from my partner: (Answers will vary.)

_____

_____

_____

_____

GOAL ➤ **Write about your goal**

D What is a paragraph? Discuss the following terms with your teacher.

➤ A *paragraph* is a group of sentences about the same topic.

➤ A *topic sentence* is usually the first sentence in a paragraph and it introduces the topic or *main idea*.

➤ *Support sentences* are the sentences that follow the topic sentence. They give *details* about the topic.

➤ A *conclusion sentence* is the final sentence of the paragraph. It gives a *summary* of the paragraph.

E In Lesson 2, you heard Tuba talk about her goal. Now, read about her goal. Study the paragraph with your teacher.

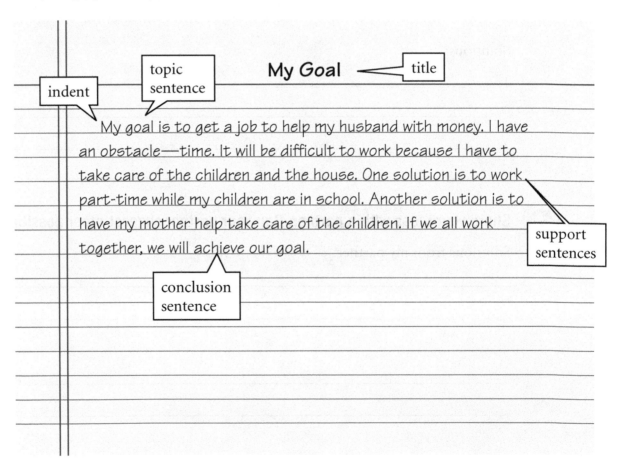

Presentation 2   5–10 mins.

Write the word *paragraph* on the board. Ask if students can remember what a paragraph is. Write their ideas on the board.

 What is a paragraph? Discuss the following terms with your teacher.

Go over the parts of a paragraph with students.

E **In Lesson 2, you heard Tuba talk about her goal. Now, read about her goal. Study the paragraph with your teacher.**

As a class, read the paragraph. Then discuss the different parts of the paragraph.

Practice 2   5–10 mins.

Have students close their books. Quiz them on the different parts of a paragraph by reading sentences from Tuba's paragraph out loud and asking the students which type of sentence it is—topic, support, or conclusion.

Activity Bank

Lesson 3, Worksheet 1: Paragraph Practice

Evaluation 2   5–10 mins.

Listen and make sure students are calling out the correct sentence type.

Presentation 3   5–10 mins.

Ask students to choose one of the sentence types and write an example sentence on a sheet of paper. You may have to get them started by giving them an example. Have them keep their sentences secret. Collect the papers and read each one out loud. The class must guess if it is a topic sentence, a support sentence, or a conclusion sentence.

Instructor's Notes

_____

_____

_____

_____

_____

_____

_____

_____

_____

_____

_____

_____

_____

_____

_____

_____

_____

Practice 3   5-10 mins. ■

F Answer the questions about Tuba's paragraph. Then, write ideas for your own paragraph about the goal you chose on page 7.

Evaluation 3   10-20 mins. ■

As a class, go over the answers about Tuba's paragraph. Then ask for volunteers to read some of their ideas out loud. If you have time, you may want to ask volunteers to write their sentences on the board so you can go over them as a class.

Application   20-30 mins. ■■■

G Write a paragraph about your goal using correct paragraph formatting. Make sure your first sentence is a topic sentence. Follow your topic sentence with support sentences. Write a conclusion sentence at the end of your paragraph.

Teaching Tip

Error correction

There is often the temptation to overcorrect our students. Students will make errors, but too much correcting without explanation can intimidate students so much so that they are afraid to produce the target language. We suggest that you correct students on the concept you are teaching or have taught. In this case, focus on the sentence types more than the grammar. If you want to focus on some grammar errors, limit it to the ones you have already taught in this course.

Refer students to *Stand Out 3 Grammar Challenge*, Unit 1, Challenge 3 for more practice with *be* + infinitive.

GOAL ➤ **Write about your goal**

F Answer the questions about Tuba's paragraph. Then, write ideas for your own paragraph about the goal you chose on page 7.

1. What is Tuba's topic sentence?

   My goal is to get a job to help my

   husband with money.

2. Tuba's support sentences are about her obstacle and her two possible solutions. What are her support sentences?

   It will be difficult to work because I have to take care of the children and the house.

   One solution is to work part time while my children are in school.

   Another solution is to have my mother help take care of the children.

3. What is Tuba's conclusion sentence?

   If I plan carefully and ask for help,

   I will achieve my goal.

1. Write your topic sentence.

   (Answers will vary.)

   _____

2. Write your three support sentences.

   A. (Answers will vary.)

   B. _____

   C. _____

3. Write your conclusion sentence.

   (Answers will vary.)

   _____

G Write a paragraph about your goal using correct paragraph formatting. Make sure your first sentence is a topic sentence. Follow your topic sentence with support sentences. Write a conclusion sentence at the end of your paragraph.

(Answers will vary.)

_____

_____

_____

_____

_____

_____

GOAL ➤ **Identify study habits**

 Write answers to the following questions. Then, compare your answers with a partner.

(Answers will vary.)

1. Where do you like to study? _____

2. When do you usually study? _____

3. How long do you study? _____

4. Do you listen to music when you study? Why or why not? _____

_____

 Look at the first picture. What is Luisa doing? Do you think she is learning anything? Why or why not? Look at the second picture. What is Michel doing? Is he learning anything? Discuss your ideas with a partner.

Luisa is sitting on the floor trying to do her homework. I don't think she's learning anything because the TV is on, and she is disorganized.

Michel is working at his desk. Yes, he is learning because he is organized, and he is studying.

  Listen to the reading about study habits. Listen for good and bad study habits.

CD 1
TR 4

Objective: Identify study habits
Academic Strategies: Active reading, inference
Vocabulary: *study habits, distractions, beneficial, harmful, improve, concentrate, go over*

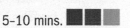

AGENDA

Discuss good and bad study habits.
Listen and read about study habits.
Use new vocabulary.
Describe your study habits.

RESOURCES

Activity Bank: Unit 1, Lesson 4, Worksheet 1
Reading and Writing Challenge 3: Unit 1

Grammar Challenge 3: Unit 1, Challenge 4
Audio: CD 1, Track 4

 1.5 hour classes   2.5 hour classes   3ᐟ hour classes

---

Warm-up and Review   5-10 mins. ■■■

Ask the class to give you the three main parts of a paragraph (topic sentence, support sentences, and conclusion sentence). Tell them that a good paragraph, like a good story, has a beginning, middle, and end.

(A) Write answers to the following questions. Then, compare your answers with a partner.

Review the questions as a class before students begin the exercise. Ask students to discuss the questions with a partner. Ask pairs to share their answers with the class.

Introduction   5-10 mins. ■■■

Ask students to list good and bad study habits. Write the list on the board. You may have to get them started with a few examples. State the objective: *Today we will identify study habits.*

Presentation 1   5-10 mins. ■■■

(B) Look at the first picture. What is Luisa doing? Do you think she is learning anything? Why or why not? Look at the second picture. What is Michel doing? Is he learning anything? Discuss your ideas with a partner.

When students have finished discussing their ideas in pairs, discuss the questions as a class.

Practice 1   5-10 mins. ■■■

(C) Listen to the reading about study habits. Listen for good and bad study habits.

Ask students to put their pencils down and listen for good and bad study habits, nothing else. You may want to play the recording more than once.

 Listening Script   CD 1, Track 4

The listening script matches the reading in Exercise D on page 11.

Evaluation 1   5-10 mins. ■■■

Draw two columns on the board and label them *good* and *bad*. Ask students to report what they heard on the recording and write the study habits in the correct columns.

STANDARDS CORRELATIONS

CASAS: 0.1.5, 7.4.1, 7.4.3, 7.4.5 (See CASAS Competency List on pages 169-175.)
SCANS: Information Acquire and evaluate information, organize and maintain information, interpret and communicate information
Interpersonal Participate as a member of a team, teach others, serve clients and customers, exercise leadership, negotiate to arrive at a decision, work with cultural diversity
Systems Understand systems, monitor and correct performance, improve and design systems
Technology Select technology, apply technology to a task, maintain and troubleshoot technology

Basic Skills Reading, writing, arithmetic, listening, speaking
Thinking Skills Creative thinking, decision making, problem solving, seeing things in the mind's eye
Personal Qualities Responsibility, sociability, self-management
EFF: Communication Read with understanding
Decision Making Plan
Interpersonal Cooperate with others
Lifelong Learning Take responsibility for learning, reflect and evaluate, learn through research, use information and communications technology (optional)

Presentation 2

10–15 mins.

D Read the paragraphs about study habits below.

Teaching Tip

Active reading

The purpose of active reading is to help students engage their reading-comprehension skills so they can tackle any reading with confidence. Explain that they may not understand the passage on the first reading. Help them realize that to understand a reading, they may need to read it more than once, maybe even three of four times.

Pre-reading: Teach students that anticipating the content of a reading and recalling information they already know about the topic will help make the reading easier to understand.

First reading: Focus on the main ideas by asking students to find the topic sentence in each paragraph, or to summarize the main point of each paragraph.

Second reading: Show students how to scan the reading quickly to find details that support the main ideas or that answer the post-reading questions.

Guessing from context: Encourage students to guess the meaning of new words from context by analyzing the words surrounding the vocabulary item. They should not let unknown words slow down their reading and should use a dictionary only after they are familiar with the context.

When students are finished, ask them some basic comprehension questions about the passage to see if they understand the general ideas.

Practice 2

10–15 mins. ■■

(Shorter classes can do these exercises for homework.)

Have students complete the two exercises by themselves.

E According to the reading, what are some bad study habits? Write them below and add one more idea.

F According to the reading, what are some good study habits? Write them below and add one more idea.

Evaluation 2

5–10 mins.

Go over the answers as a class. Encourage volunteers to share their ideas with the class.

Activity Bank

Lesson 4, Worksheet 1: Parts of Speech

Instructor's Notes

_____
_____
_____
_____
_____
_____
_____
_____
_____
_____
_____
_____
_____
_____
_____
_____

GOAL ➤ **Identify study habits**

D Read the paragraphs about study habits below.

> Good study habits can be very *beneficial* to you and your education. On the other hand, bad study habits can be *harmful* to your educational goals. First, let's talk about bad study habits.
>
> Many people have very busy schedules and it is difficult for them to find time to study. One bad study habit is not studying before class. Another bad study habit is studying with *distractions* around, such as television, people talking, or loud music. A third bad study habit is copying a friend's homework. These are just a few bad study habits, but you can easily change them into good study habits.
>
> There are many ways that you can improve your study habits. First, set a time every day to study and try to study at the same time every day. Do not make appointments at this time. This is your special study time. Second, find a good place to study, a place that is quiet and comfortable so you can *concentrate*. Finally, do your homework on your own. Afterwards, you can find a friend to help you *go over* your work and check your answers.

E According to the reading, what are some bad study habits? Write them below and add one more idea.

EXAMPLE: <u>not studying before class</u>

studying with distractions around

copying a friend's homework

(Additional answers will vary.)

F According to the reading, what are some good study habits? Write them below and add one more idea.

EXAMPLE: <u>studying at the same time every day</u>

finding a good place to study

doing your homework on your own

(Additional answers will vary.)

LESSON **4**   **GOAL** ➤ **Identify study habits**

G Match each vocabulary word or phrase with its correct definition.

1. __b__ improve   a. bad for you

2. __d__ beneficial   b. get better

3. __a__ harmful   c. review or check again

4. __f__ distractions   d. good for you

5. __e__ concentrate   e. think hard about something

6. __c__ go over   f. things that disturb your study

H Fill in the blanks with a word or phrase from Exercise G.

1. My English will _____improve_____ if I practice every day.

2. Please be quiet. I can't _____concentrate_____ on my homework.

3. Studying with a friend can be _____beneficial_____ because you can help each other.

4. When you finish taking a test, _____go over_____ your answers again.

5. It's hard to study when there are _____distractions_____. Turn off the TV!

6. Bad study habits can be _____harmful_____ to your educational goals.

I Choose three words or phrases from Exercise G and write sentences about your study habits on a piece of paper. Share your sentences with a partner. (Answers will vary.)

J Think about your study habits. Fill in the chart below. (Answers will vary.)

Good study habits	Bad study habits
EXAMPLE: I study every day.	EXAMPLE: I watch the news and do my homework at the same time.
1.	1.
2.	2.
3.	3.

K Share your answers with a partner. Which study habits are the same? Which study habits are different? (Answers will vary.)

Presentation 3   5–10 mins. ■■■

Discuss the vocabulary from the reading. Help students with pronunciation and definitions.

(G) Match each vocabulary word or phrase with its correct definition.

Have students complete as much of the exercise as they can before providing help.

Practice 3   5–10 mins. ■

(H) Fill in the blanks with a word or phrase from Exercise G.

Evaluation 3   3 mins. ■

Go over the answers as a class.

Application   10–20 mins. ■■■

(I) Choose three words or phrases from Exercise G and write sentences about your study habits on a piece of paper. Share your sentences with a partner.

(J) Think about your study habits. Fill in the chart below.

(K) Share your answers with a partner. Which study habits are the same? Which study habits are different?

Refer students to *Stand Out 3 Grammar Challenge*, Unit 1, Challenge 4 for more practice with *be* + gerund.

AT-A-GLANCE PREP

Objective: Identify time-management strategies
Math: Read and create a pie chart
Academic Strategies: Using an outline, focused listening
Vocabulary: *balance, accomplish, task, time slot, benefits*

AGENDA

Read about a problem.
Listen to a lecture on time management.
Complete an outline.
Create a pie chart.
Discuss your time-management strategies.

RESOURCES

Activity Bank: Unit 1, Lesson 5, Worksheets 1–2
Reading and Writing Challenge 3: Unit 1

Grammar Challenge 3: Unit 1, Challenge 5
Audio: CD 1, Track 5

■ 1.5 hour classes ■ 2.5 hour classes ■ 3+ hour classes

Warm-up and Review   5-10 mins.

Go over the study-habit chart from Lesson 4. Have students read their list of good habits. Ask how many people followed each habit the day before. Provide or elicit suggestions on how to make these habits a part of their daily routine.

Introduction   5-10 mins.

Write *time management* on the board and ask students what it means. If they have trouble providing a definition, ask for examples that help clarify the term. State the objective: *Today we will identify time-management strategies.*

Presentation 1   10-15 mins.

Have students look at Lara's pie chart. Ask questions about how Lara spends her time. Ask them if they think she balances her time well. If not, where are her problem areas?

(A) Read about Lara's problem.

Ask for a volunteer to read this paragraph out loud. Ask students: *What is Lara's problem? What does she want to do? How do you think she could solve her problem?*

Practice 1   10-15 mins.

(B) Answer the questions about Lara.

Have students work with a partner.

Evaluation 1   3 mins.

Go over the answers as a class.

Presentation 2   15-20 mins.

(C) Listen to the lecture about time management. Listen for the main ideas.

Tell students to put their pencils down and listen for main ideas. After they listen, ask students what they heard. Write their ideas on the board.

 Listening Script   CD 1, Track 5

The listening script matches the script for Exercise E on page 14.

STANDARDS CORRELATIONS

CASAS: 7.4.2 (See CASAS Competency List on pages 169–175.)
SCANS: Resources Allocate time
Information Acquire and evaluate information, organize and maintain information, interpret and communicate information
Interpersonal Participate as a member of a team, negotiate to arrive at a decision, work with cultural diversity
Systems Understand systems, monitor and correct performance
Basic Skills Reading, writing, arithmetic, listening, speaking
Thinking Skills Creative thinking, decision making, problem solving, seeing things in the mind's eye

Personal Qualities Responsibility, sociability, self-management
EFF: Communication Convey ideas in writing, speak so others can understand, listen actively
Decision Making Plan, use math to solve problems and communicate
Interpersonal Cooperate with others, resolve conflict and negotiate
Lifelong Learning Take responsibility for learning, reflect and evaluate

---

LESSON 5 **Time management**

GOAL ➤ **Identify time-management strategies**

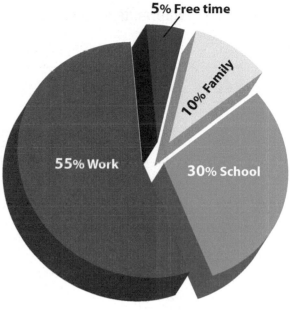

5% Free time

10% Family

55% Work

30% School

Lara's Day

 A **Read about Lara's problem.**

Lara doesn't get to spend enough time with her family. The pie chart shows how Lara spends her time. As you can see, she rarely has any free time to relax. Lara wants to find a way to balance her time. So, she has decided to attend a lecture at school to learn better time-management strategies.

B **Answer the questions about Lara.**

1. What is Lara's goal?

   Lara's goal is to find a way to balance her time.

2. What is her obstacle?

   Her obstacle is that she rarely has any free time to relax.

3. What is her solution?

   Her solution is to attend a lecture to learn better time-management skills.

 C **Listen to the lecture about time management. Listen for the main ideas.**

CD 1
TR 5

D When you listen to a lecture, you can use an outline to help record important information. Look at the outline below and discuss it with your teacher.

I. Why is time management important?
  A. You stay organized.

  B. You accomplish everything that needs to get done.

  C. You _make time for family, friends, and things that matter most._____.

II. How do you keep a schedule?
  A. Write down everything you need to do in a week.

  B. Put each task in a time slot.

  C. _Follow your schedule._____.

  D. Check off things that have been completed.

III. How can you add more time to your day?
  A. You can wake up earlier.

  B. You can ask _your family or friends to help you._____.

  C. You can try doing ____two.____ tasks at once.

IV. What are other important things to consider about time management?
  A. Remember the important people in your life.

  B. _Remember your values._____.

  C. You are the boss of your schedule.

V. What are the benefits of managing your time?
  A. You will have more time.

  B. You will feel less _stressed._____.

  C. You will have time to _see the people who matter most._____.

  D. You will feel better about yourself.

 E Listen to the lecture on time management again and complete the outline above.

CD 1
TR 5

Presentation 2 (continued)

D When you listen to a lecture, you can use an outline to help record important information. Look at the outline below and discuss it with your teacher.

Ask students if they have ever seen or used an outline before. Explain to them the purpose of the different levels of an outline. Go over the sentences already filled in the outline. Then prepare students for the focused listening activity.

Note: This listening and outline exercise may be difficult for students so do as much pre-listening discussion as possible to prepare them.

Practice 2   15–20 mins.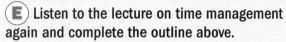

E Listen to the lecture on time management again and complete the outline above.

Have students close their books. Play the recording. The first time you play it, ask students just to listen. The second time, have them open their books and ask them to fill in the blanks in the outline as they listen. Play the recording as many times as you think necessary. Then ask students to share their sentences with a partner. After most students have completely filled in the outline, play the recording once again.

🎧 **Listening Script**   CD 1, Track 5

Time management is important for several reasons. First of all, it helps you stay organized. Second of all, you can make sure you are accomplishing everything that needs to get done. And thirdly, you can make time for family and friends and things that matter most. One of the best ways to manage your time is to keep a schedule. First, write down everything you need to do in a week. This includes work, school, children, and other tasks. Then put each of these into a time slot. Of course, you have to follow your schedule. And most important, check things off once they have been completed. There are some easy ways to add more time to your day. One, wake up a few minutes earlier. Even ten or fifteen minutes will give you some extra time to study or do things around the house. Two, have your family or friends help you with things you need to get done. For example, having your children help you with the housework will help you finish twice as fast. Three, try doing two tasks at once. Instead of just eating lunch, eat lunch and review your verb tenses. We call this killing two birds with one stone! There are some other important things to consider about time management. First of all, remember the important people in your life. Did you put time in your schedule to visit them, write them a letter, or even call them? Also remember your values. If you value exercise, you must schedule time to exercise. And finally, you are the boss of your schedule. Don't let your schedule control you. Managing your time will give you several benefits in life. You will find that you have more free time. In addition, you will feel less stressed because you are more organized. Also, you will have time to see the people in your life who matter most. And lastly, you will feel better about yourself.

Evaluation 2   10–20 mins.

Using a transparency of the outline, go over it in detail. Have students come up one by one to fill in the blanks or call on different volunteers to help you fill them in. On completion, play the recording one last time.

Presentation 3

10-15 mins.

Draw a pie chart on the board and show the class how you would fill it in to show your schedule. Then have the class look back at Lara's pie chart on page 13 and compare it to yours. Ask them questions, such as: *Who works more—me or Lara? Who has more free time?*

Brainstorm a list of different ways to spend time that students could put in a pie chart (work, school, exercise, entertainment, hobbies, volunteer, etc.).

(F) A pie chart is a circle, like a pie, and is divided up into segments that equal 100%. From the pie chart on the right, fill in the percentages below and add them up. Do they equal 100%?

The purpose of a pie chart is to represent information (percentages) in an easy-to-understand way. Do the exercise as a class, making sure students understand the purpose of a pie chart and that the pie pieces must equal 100%.

Practice 3

5-10 mins.

(G) Fill in the pie chart on the right to show how you spend your time. Make sure your graph equals 100%.

Have students fill in the pie chart. Remind them to look at the one you have just drawn on the board as well as Lara's if they need some ideas.

Evaluation 3

5-10 mins.

Ask for a few volunteers to come to the board and draw their pie charts. Compare the different charts.

Application

10-20 mins.

(H) Answer the following questions about your own time-management strategies.

Have students answer these questions on their own. When they have finished, have them get in small groups and share what they have written.

 Refer students to *Stand Out 3 Grammar Challenge*, Unit 1, Challenge 5 for more practice with imperatives.

Activity Bank

Lesson 5, Worksheet 1: Time-Management Outline
Lesson 5, Worksheet 2: Time-Management Techniques

Refer students to *Stand Out 3 Grammar Challenge*, Unit 1, Extension Challenges 1–2 for more practice with adverbial clauses and time clauses.

Instructor's Notes

_____
_____
_____
_____
_____
_____
_____
_____
_____
_____
_____
_____
_____
_____
_____
_____
_____
_____
_____

GOAL ➤ **Identify time-management strategies**

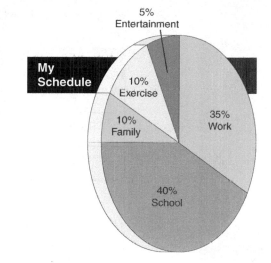

F A pie chart is a circle, like a pie, and is divided up into segments that equal 100%. From the pie chart on the right, fill in the percentages below and add them up. Do they equal 100%?

Work: _____35___ %
School: _____40___ %
Family: _____10___ %
Exercise: _____10___ %
Entertainment: _____5___ %
_____
TOTAL _____100___ %

G Fill in the pie chart on the right to show how you spend your time. Make sure your graph equals 100%! (Answers will vary.)

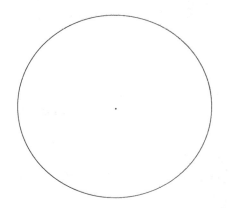

H Answer the following questions about your own time-management strategies.

(Answers will vary.)

1. What problems do you have with time?

EXAMPLE: _I work ten hours a day and I don't have time to study._

_____

_____

2. How could you add more time to your day? (Think about what you learned from the lecture.)

_____

_____

3. What are some time-management skills you learned today that you would like to use

in your life? _____

_____

Review

A Exchange books with a partner. Have your partner complete the schedule below about himself or herself. (Lesson 1) (Answers will vary.)

	Monday	Tuesday	Wednesday	Thursday	Friday	Saturday	Sunday
Morning							
Afternoon							
Evening							

B Write sentences about your partner's schedule using the frequency adverbs. (Lesson 1) (Answers will vary.)

1. (always) _____

2. (usually) _____

3. (often) _____

4. (sometimes) _____

5. (rarely) _____

6. (never) _____

C Now share your sentences with your partner and see if he or she agrees.

EXAMPLE: *Student A:* You always work in the evenings.
　　　　　　Student B: That's true.

D Complete the sentences with the correct verb form. (Lesson 2)

1. When Jason _____gets_____ (get) a better job, he _____will buy_____ (buy) a new house.

2. Lilia _____will join_____ (join) her sister at college when she _____finishes_____ (finish) her ESL class.

3. We _____will run_____ (run) a marathon when we _____complete_____ (complete) our training program.

4. When Maria _____gets_____ (get) her bachelor's degree, she

　_____will ask_____ (ask) her boss for a raise.

Objectives: All unit objectives

Grammar: All unit grammar

Academic Strategies: Reviewing previously learned material

Vocabulary: All unit vocabulary

RESOURCES

Activity Bank: Unit 1, Lessons 1–5

Reading and Writing Challenge 3: Unit 1

Grammar Challenge 3: Unit 1, Challenges 1–5

 1.5 hour classes  2.5 hour classes  3+ hour classes

Stand Out 3 Assessment CD-ROM with ExamView®

AGENDA
Discuss unit objectives.
Complete the review.
Do My Dictionary.
Evaluate and reflect on progress.

Warm-up and Review   5-10 mins.

In groups, have students list five ways to more effectively manage their time. Ask them to try to come up with ways different from those mentioned in the time-management recording in Lesson 5.

Introduction   5-10 mins.

Ask students as a class to try to recall (in general) all the goals of this unit without looking at their books. Then remind them which goals they omitted, if any. Write all the unit goals on the board: make a schedule; identify goals, obstacles, and solutions; write about your goals; identify study habits; and identify time-management strategies. Show students the first page of the unit and mention the five objectives. State the objective for the review: *Today we will be reviewing everything you have learned in this unit.*

Presentation 1   10-15 mins.

This presentation will cover the first three pages of the review. Quickly go to the first page of each lesson. Discuss the objective of each. Ask simple questions to remind students of what they have learned.

Note: Since there is little presentation in the review, you can assign the review exercises for homework and go over them in class the following day.

Practice 1   20-25 mins.

Note: There are two ways to do the review: (1) Do the exercises one at a time and, as students complete each one, go over the answers. (2) Briefly go through the instructions of each exercise, allow students to complete all of the exercises at once, and then go over the answers.

(A) Exchange books with a partner. Have your partner complete the schedule below about himself or herself. (Lesson 1)

(B) Write sentences about your partner's schedule using the frequency adverbs. (Lesson 1)

(C) Now share your sentences with your partner and see if he or she agrees.

(D) Complete the sentences with the correct verb form. (Lesson 2)

STANDARDS CORRELATIONS

CASAS: 7.2.1 (See CASAS Competency List on pages 169–175.)
SCANS: **Resources** Allocate time
Information Acquire and evaluate information
Interpersonal Participate as a member of a team, teach others, negotiate to arrive at a decision, work with cultural diversity
Systems Monitor and correct performance
Basic Skills Reading, writing, arithmetic, listening, speaking
Thinking Skills Creative thinking, decision making, problem solving, seeing things in the mind's eye

Personal Qualities Responsibility, sociability, self-management
EFF: **Communication** Convey ideas in writing, speak so others can understand, listen actively
Decision Making Solve problems and make decisions, plan
Interpersonal Cooperate with others, guide others
Lifelong Learning Take responsibility for learning, reflect and evaluate, learn through research

Practice 1 *(continued)*   25–30 mins.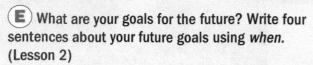

E What are your goals for the future? Write four sentences about your future goals using *when*. (Lesson 2)

F Think of one obstacle and one solution for each goal you wrote in Exercise E. Complete the chart. (Lessons 2 and 3)

G Match each word or phrase to its correct meaning. Draw a line. (Lesson 3)

Teaching Tip

Recycling/Review

The review process and the project that follows are part of the recycling/review process. Students at this level often need to be reintroduced to concepts to solidify what they have learned. Many concepts are learned and forgotten while learning other new concepts. This is because students learn but are not necessarily ready to acquire language concepts.

Therefore, it becomes very important to review and to show students how to review on their own. It is also important to recycle the new concepts in different contexts.

E What are your goals for the future? Write four sentences about your future goals using *when*. (**Lesson 2**) (Answers will vary.)

EXAMPLE: <u>When I finish this course, I will take the GED exam.</u>

1. _____

2. _____

3. _____

4. _____

F Think of one obstacle and one solution for each goal you wrote in Exercise E. Complete the chart. (**Lessons 2 and 3**) (Answers will vary.)

	Goal	Obstacle	Solution
1.			
2.			
3.			
4.			

G Match each word or phrase to its correct meaning. Draw a line. (**Lesson 3**)

1. paragraph   a. introduces your topic, or main idea

2. topic sentence   b. give details about your topic

3. support sentences   c. gives a summary of everything you wrote

4. conclusion sentence   d. a group of sentences about the same topic

Review

 H Read the following sentences that make up a paragraph. Label each as a *topic* sentence (T), a *support* sentence (S), or a *conclusion* sentence (C). Remember, there can only be one topic sentence and one conclusion sentence. (Lesson 3)

1. I will buy books to study with and I will study very hard. _S_

2. Within the next two years, I hope to have my license. _C_

3. When I'm ready, I will register for the test. _S_

4. My goal for the future is to get my real estate license. _T_

5. When I am close to taking the test, I will ask my friend, who is a realtor, to help me. _S_

 I On a piece of paper, rewrite the sentences above in the correct order, using correct paragraph formatting. (Lesson 3)

My goal for the future is to get my real estate license. I will buy some books to study with, and I will have to study very hard. When I'm ready, I will register for the test. When I am close to taking the test, I will ask my friend who is a realtor to help me. Within the next two years, I hope to have my license.

 J Write two good study habits. (Lesson 4) (Answers will vary.)

1. Studying at the same time every day.

2. Finding a good place to study.

K Write two good time-management strategies. (Lesson 5) (Answers will vary.)

1. Keep a schedule.

2. Remember the important people in your life/your values.

L Write the correct word from the box for each definition. (Lessons 2–4)

beneficial	concentrate	distractions	go over
goal	harmful	improve	obstacle

1. bad for you — harmful
2. when you get better at something — improve
3. good for you — beneficial
4. think hard about something — concentrate
5. something you want to achieve — goal
6. a problem — obstacle
7. review something or check it again — go over
8. things that bother you when you are studying — distractions

Practice 1 *(continued)*   25–30 mins. ■■■■

H Read the following sentences that make up a paragraph. Label each as a *topic* sentence (T), a *support* sentence (S), or a *conclusion* sentence (C). Remember, there can only be one topic sentence and one conclusion sentence. (Lesson 3)

I On a piece of paper, rewrite the sentence above in the correct order, using correct paragraph formatting. (Lesson 3)

J Write two good study habits. (Lesson 4)

K Write two good time-management strategies. (Lesson 5)

L Write the correct word from the box for each definition. (Lessons 2–4)

Evaluation 1   25–30 mins. ■■■■

Go around the classroom and check on students' progress. Help individuals when needed. If you see consistent errors among several students, interrupt the class and give a mini lesson or review to help students feel comfortable with the concept.

Presentation 2   5–10 mins.

My Dictionary

Ask students to brainstorm new vocabulary items they learned in this unit. Have them do this without looking in their books.

Practice 2   15–20 mins.

(Shorter classes can do this exercise for homework.)

Choose three words from this unit. Write the new words and a definition for each one in your vocabulary notebook. Draw pictures to help you remember the new words.

Go over the three examples with students. Then pick one of the words from the book and do one together as a class. Then have students do three words on their own.

Evaluation 2   15–20 mins.

Walk around the classroom and help students.

Presentation 3   5–10 mins.

Learner Log

Write the word *log* on the board. Ask students if they know what this word means. Explain to them that it is a journal, notebook, or place where you keep track of information. In this case, they will be keeping track of what they have learned. Tell them that they will be doing a learner log at the end of each unit.

In this unit, you learned many things about balancing your life. How comfortable do you feel doing each of the skills listed below? Rate your comfort level on a scale of 1 to 4.

Go over the instructions with students and make sure they understand what to do. You may want to do the first one or two with the class to make sure they understand.

Practice 3   5–10 mins. ▪

Have students complete the Learner Log.

Evaluation 3   5–10 mins. ▪

Walk around the classroom and help students.

Application   5–10 mins. ▪

Go over the two reflection questions with students and have them complete the answers by themselves.

TB Assessment

Use the Stand Out Assessment CD-ROM with Exam*View*® to create a post-test for Unit 1.

My Dictionary

Choose three words from this unit. Write the new words and a definition for each one in your vocabulary notebook. Draw pictures to help you remember the new words.

EXAMPLES:

Goal - something I want to achieve

GOAL

Obstacle - something that stops you from getting to your goal

Solution - a way to overcome the problem

Learner Log

In this unit, you learned many things about balancing your life. How comfortable do you feel doing each of the skills listed below? Rate your comfort level on a scale of 1 to 4.

1 = Need more practice   **2** = OK   **3** = Good   **4** = Great!

Life Skill	Comfort Level				Page
I can make a schedule.	1	2	3	4	1
I can identify my future goals, obstacles, and solutions.	1	2	3	4	4
I can write about my goals.	1	2	3	4	7
I know how to improve study habits.	1	2	3	4	10
I can use good time-managment strategies.	1	2	3	4	13
I can listen to a lecture and use an outline.	1	2	3	4	14

If you circled 1 or 2, write down the page number where you can review this skill.

Reflection

1. What was the most useful skill you learned in this unit? _____

2. How will this help you in life? _____

Team Project

Make a schedule.

With a team, you will design a weekly schedule that includes your class and study time. You will identify good study habits and time-management strategies that you will use during this class.

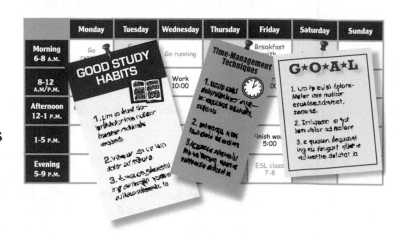

1. Form a team with four or five students. Choose a position for each member of your team.

POSITION	JOB DESCRIPTION	STUDENT NAME
Student 1: Leader	See that everyone speaks English and participates.	
Student 2: Secretary	Take notes on study habits and time-management strategies.	
Student 3: Designer	Design a weekly schedule.	
Students 4/5: Assistants	Help the secretary and the designer with their work.	

2. Design a weekly schedule. On your schedule, write in the days and times you have English class. (Lesson 1)

3. Decide on a goal that is related to learning English. Think of one obstacle to your goal. Think of two solutions. (Lessons 2–3)

4. Make a list of good study habits and a list of time-management strategies you'd like to use. (Lessons 4–5)

5. Make a poster with all of the information from above: weekly schedule, goal, obstacle, solutions, good study habits, and time-management strategies.

6. Present your poster to the class.

Make a schedule.

Each team will design a collage that includes a weekly schedule with class and study time, a list of good study habits, and a list of time-management strategies they will use.

The team project is the final application for the unit. It gives students a chance to show that they have mastered all of the Unit 1 goals.

Note: Shorter classes can extend this project over two class meetings.

Stage 1   5 mins.
Form a team with four or five students. Choose a position for each member of your team.

Have students decide who will lead each step as described on the student page. Provide well-defined directions on the board for how teams should proceed. Explain that all the students do every step as a team. Teams shouldn't go to the next stage until the previous one is complete.

Stage 2   15–20 mins.
Design a weekly schedule. On your schedule, write in the days and times you have English class. (Lesson 1)

Have students fill in the schedule with their English class time and possible study times throughout the week. (Due to students' varying schedules, this should yield some good discussion and negotiation about when they are all free to study.)

Optional Computer Activity: As a class, or as the instructor, you may want to design a blank schedule on the computer that everyone can use.

Stage 3   10–15 mins.
Decide on a goal that is related to learning English. Think of one obstacle to your goal. Make a list of two solutions. (Lessons 2–3)

Encourage students to make their goal English-related, such as talking more with native English speakers or reading the newspaper every day.

Stage 4   10–15 mins.
Make a list of good study habits and time-management strategies you'd like to use. (Lessons 4–5)

As a class, decide how many items should go on each list.

Stage 5   15 mins.
Make a poster with all the information from above: weekly schedule, goal, obstacle, solutions, good study habits, and time-management strategies.

Stage 6   15–20 mins.
Present your poster to the class.

Help teams prepare for their presentations. Suggest that each member choose a different part of the poster to present.

STANDARDS CORRELATIONS

CASAS: 4.8.1, 4.8.5, 4.8.6 (See CASAS Competency List on pages 169–175.)
SCANS: **Resources** Allocate time
Information Acquire and evaluate information, organize and maintain information, interpret and communicate information, use computers to process information
Systems Understand systems, improve and designs systems
Technology Select technology, apply technology to exercise

Basic Skills Writing
Thinking Skills Creative thinking, decision making, problem solving, seeing things in the mind's eye, reasoning
Personal Qualities Responsibility, self-esteem, self-management, integrity/honesty
EFF: **Decision Making** Solve problems and make decisions, plan
Lifelong Learning Take responsibility for learning, reflect and evaluate, use information and communication technologies (optional)

AT-A-GLANCE PREP

Objective: Identify places to purchase goods and services
Grammar: *get* + past participle (causative)
Vocabulary: *consumer, goods, services, laundromat, gas station, pharmacy, hotel, jewelry store, bank, post office, department store, grocery store, car wash, tailor's, office supply store, drugstore, dry cleaners, hardware store*

AGENDA
Identify goods and services.
Use the form "to get something done."
Use past participles.
Ask about your neighborhood.

RESOURCES

Activity Bank: Lesson 1, Worksheets 1–2
Reading and Writing Challenge: Unit 2

Grammar Challenge 3: Unit 2, Challenge 1

■ 1.5 hour classes   ■ 2.5 hour classes   ■ 3+ hour classes

 Preassessment *(optional)*

Use the Stand Out 3 Assessment CD-ROM with *ExamView*® to create a pretest for Unit 2.

Warm-up and Review   5–10 mins.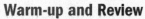

Write the word *shopping* on the board. Ask students to make a list on a sheet of paper of all the different kinds of stores they shop in during a typical week. Then ask them to list places they go for services during the week, such as the bank or the post office.

Introduction   5–10 mins.

Write the words *goods* and *services* on the board. Ask students which of their lists names places to purchase goods and which list names places to purchase services. Ask them to give you examples from each list. State the objective: *Today we will identify places to purchase goods and services.*

Presentation 1   10–15 mins.

(A) **What kind of stores or businesses are these? What goods or services can you purchase here?**

Use this activity to present the differences between goods and services.

(B) **Look at the places below. Which of them sell goods? Which of them provide services?**

Do this exercise as a class. Ask two students to write the class's answers on the board, one student listing places that sell goods, the other student listing places that sell services.

STANDARDS CORRELATIONS

CASAS: 0.1.2, 1.3.7 (See CASAS Competency List on pages 169–175.)
SCANS: **Information** Acquire and evaluate information, organize and maintain information, interpret and communicate information
Interpersonal Participate as a member of a team, teach others, exercise leadership, negotiate to arrive at a decision, work with cultural diversity
Basic Skills Reading, writing, listening, speaking

Thinking Skills Creative thinking, decision making
Personal Qualities Responsibility, sociability, self-management
EFF: **Communication** Speak so others can understand, listen actively
Decision Making Solve problems and make decisions
Interpersonal Cooperate with others, guide others

Consumer Smarts

GOALS

 Identify places to purchase goods and services

 Interpret advertisements

 Compare products

 Identify and compare purchasing methods

 Make a smart purchase

LESSON 1

Shopping for goods and services

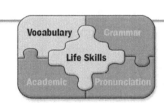

GOAL ➤ Identify places to purchase goods and services

A What kind of stores or businesses are these? What goods or services can you purchase here?

A pharmacy: You can buy medicine here.

A post office: You can buy stamps here; you can send mail here.

B Look at the places below. Which of them sell goods? Which of them provide services?

laundromat	gas station	pharmacy	hotel
jewelry store	bank	post office	department store
grocery store	car wash	tailor's	office supply store
drugstore	dry cleaners	hardware store	hair salon

Goods: jewelry store, grocery store, drugstore, gas station, pharmacy, post office, tailor's, hardware store, department store, office supply store, hair salon
Services: laundromat, jewelry store, gas station, bank, car wash, dry cleaners, post office, tailor's, hotel, hair salon

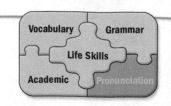

GOAL ➤ **Identify places to purchase goods and services**

C Fill in the chart using the places from Exercise B. Then, add two places of your own to each list.

Sells goods	Provides services	Both
grocery store drugstore pharmacy hardware store department store office supply store department store	laundromat bank car wash dry cleaners hotel	post office jewelry store gas station tailor's hair salon

D Where can you purchase each of the following items? Write the places. Some items may have more than one answer.

Item	Place
1. medicine	pharmacy
2. a table	furniture store
3. a notebook	office supply store
4. a bracelet	jewelry store
5. boots	shoe store
6. a refrigerator	appliance store
7. bread	grocery store
8. motor oil	gas station
9. a shirt	department store
10. stamps	post office

E We use the expression *to get something done* when we talk about services we receive. Study the chart with your teacher.

to get something done				
Subject	***get***	**Object**	**Past participle**	**Example sentence**
I	get	my hair	cut	I get my hair cut every month. (present)
she	got	her clothes	cleaned	She got her clothes cleaned yesterday. (past)
For a list of past participles, see p. 163 in the back of this book.				

Practice 1   10–15 mins.

 Fill in the chart using the places from Exercise B. Then, add two places of your own to each list.

Go over the examples in the chart so students understand what they are supposed to do. Have students complete this exercise by themselves.

Evaluation 1   5 min.

Go over the answers as a class.

Presentation 2   5–10 mins. ■■■

Ask students where you can find certain items. For example: *Where can I find a couch?* (At the furniture store.) *Where can I get a cashier's check?* (At the bank.) Write a few more similar questions on the board. Talk about the differences between asking about goods and asking about services. Have volunteers ask the same kind of questions to you.

Practice 2   10–15 mins. ■■

 Where can you purchase each of the following items? Write the places. Some items may have more than one answer.

Have students complete this exercise with a partner by asking questions like the ones they practiced in Presentation 2. (Shorter classes can do this exercise for homework.)

Evaluation 2   10–15 mins. ■■

Walk around the classroom and listen to students as they complete the exercise. When everyone has finished, ask for volunteers to ask and answer the questions.

Activity Bank

Lesson 1, Worksheet 2: Store Guessing Game Cards

On the Activity Bank CD-ROM, there are cards for students to play a guessing game.

Half of the students in the class will receive a card with the name of a kind of store on it. The other students, who haven't received a card, must each find a student who has a card and guess what store is on the student's card by asking questions. For example: *Can I buy things there? Can I buy books there?* The students holding the cards may only answer yes or no. Once a student guesses correctly, he or she takes the card and finds a classmate who doesn't have a card at the moment. Demonstrate the procedure with a few volunteers before the class tries the activity.

Have students play this game until everyone has had a chance to ask questions and try to guess the name of the store at least three times.

Presentation 3   5–10 mins. ■■■

 We use the expression *to get something done* when we talk about services we receive. Study the chart with your teacher.

Go over the chart with students. Show them the chart on p. 163 in the back of their books for a list of past participles.

Instructor's Notes

Practice 3 15–20 mins. ■

(F) Where can you receive the following services? Write the places on the lines. Some items may have more than one answer.

(G) Answer the following questions with complete sentences.

Go over the example with students.

 Refer students to *Stand Out 3 Grammar Challenge*, Unit 2, Challenge 1 for more practice with *get* + past participle.

Evaluation 3 5–10 mins. ■

As students complete each exercise, go over the answers as a class. For Exercise G, ask volunteers to write their sentences on the board.

Application 10–20 mins. ■■■

(H) Imagine you are new to the neighborhood. Ask your partner questions about businesses in the area.

Ask students to make a list of ten things they are looking for in the neighborhood, either goods or services. Then have them walk around the room with their lists and ask ten other students one question each. For example: *Where can I buy CDs?* Have them write down the answers they get next to the items on their list. When the students have finished, have them share their answers with the class.

(I) **Active Task.** Go to a mall and look at the directory. What different stores and businesses does it have? Make a list to share with your class.

Ask students if they can visit a mall within the next week to complete this activity. As a class, agree on a day when they will bring their lists back to class. If you have Internet access in your classroom, show students how to find the mall directory of a local mall on the Internet.

Instructor's Notes

GOAL ➤ **Identify places to purchase goods and services**

 Where can you receive the following services? Write the places on the lines. Some items may have more than one answer.

EXAMPLE: get your clothes cleaned __dry cleaners__

1. get your hair cut __hair salon, barbershop__

2. get your checks cashed __bank__

3. get your pants hemmed __tailor's__

4. get your car washed __car wash__

5. get your car fixed __gas station__

6. get your clothes washed __laundromat, dry cleaners__

G Answer the following questions with complete sentences.

EXAMPLE: Where do you get your clothes cleaned?

> **I get my clothes cleaned at the dry cleaners.**

1. Where do you do get your hair cut?

I get my hair cut at the barbershop/hair salon.

2. Where did you get your prescription filled?

I got my prescription filled at the pharmacy/drugstore.

3. Where do you get your packages mailed?

I get my packages mailed at the post office.

4. Where did you get your keys made?

I got my keys made at the hardware store.

5. Where did you get your gas tank filled up?

I got my gas tank filled up at the gas station.

6. Where do you get your clothes washed?

I get my clothes washed at the laundromat/dry cleaners.

H Imagine you are new to the neighborhood. Ask your partner questions about businesses in the area.

EXAMPLE: *Student A:* Where can I get my car washed?
Student B: at the car wash on Maple Street

 Active Task. Go to a mall and look at the directory. What different stores and businesses does it have? Make a list to share with your class. (Answers will vary.)

LESSON 2 Advertisements

GOAL ➤ Interpret advertisements

A Write answers to the following questions. Then, discuss your answers with your classmates.

1. What are advertisements? _Advertisements are messages that tell about a product or service. They try to persuade you to buy the product or service._

2. Where can you find them? _You can find them on TV, in magazines and newspapers, on billboards, and on the Internet._

3. What information can you find in advertisements? Make a list. _____

   price, brand name, use, where to buy the item, etc.

B Read the advertisements from the newspaper.

1. **BOB'S AUTO SERVICE**
- Save on oil change
- Most cars now **only $16.95**
- Includes up to five quarts of oil, new oil filter, and labor
- Not valid with any other offer
- Offer expires 8/5/2009

2. 16 x 7 garage doors
McKINNON'S Garage Door Sale
Includes: delivery and installation of new door, 3-year warranty
Call now for your free in home estimate
1-800-555-3936
only $599.00
licensed and insured
exp. 2-21-2009

3. **★ STEREO ★ ★ FACTORY ★ ★ OUTLET ★**
30-70% off original prices
Headphones   Speakers
starting at $9.95   starting at $79.95 a pair
$5 DISCOUNT WITH THIS AD

4. **All mountain bikes on sale!**
Wheel World Bike Sale
SAVE 25%
All bikes come with 1-year warranty
Bikes reg. priced $150 now $112.50

C Read the ads again and find words with these meanings.

1. discount ___on sale___
2. guarantee ___warranty___
3. work ___labor___
4. to come to an end ___expires___
5. no charge ___free___
6. approximate cost ___estimate___
7. to set up for use ___installation___
8. normal ___regular___

Objective: Interpret advertisements

Academic Strategy: Test-taking skills

Vocabulary: *advertisement, ad, discount, sale price, offer, expire, cut, sale, regular, save, percent off, delivery, installation, licensed, insured, guarantee, warranty*

RESOURCES

Activity Bank: Lesson 2, Worksheets 1–3

Reading and Writing Challenge: Unit 2

Grammar Challenge 3: Unit 2, Challenge 2

■ 1.5 hour classes   ■ 2.5 hour classes   ■ 3+ hour classes

AGENDA

Talk about advertisements (ads).

Read ads.

Interpret ads.

Write an ad.

Warm-up and Review   5–10 mins.

Review the Lesson 1 by asking students where you might go to find a particular item or service. At first, allow students to call out answers. Then call on individual students to make sure everyone is included in the activity.

Introduction   5–10 mins.

Discuss the following questions with your class: *What are advertisements? Where can you find them? What information can you find in advertisements?* Write student answers to this last question on the board. State the objective: *Today we will be interpreting advertisements.*

Presentation 1   10–15 mins.

(A) Write answers to the following questions. Then, discuss your answers with your classmates.

Have students look at the questions in their books and fill in the answers based on what you have just discussed.

(B) Read the advertisements from the newspaper.

Give students a few minutes to look over the ads. Then begin asking them questions, such as: *How much is the oil change? What is the regular price of mountain bikes? How much is the price of stereo speakers reduced?* Continue quizzing them until you feel they grasp how to find the information to answer your questions correctly. Make sure they understand all of the vocabulary in the ads.

(C) Read the ads again and find words with these meanings.

Go over the vocabulary items as a class and have students write the meanings in their books.

STANDARDS CORRELATIONS

CASAS: 1.2.1 (See CASAS Competency List on pages 169–175.)

SCANS: **Resources** Allocate human resources

Information Acquire and evaluate information, organize and maintain information, interpret and communicate information

Interpersonal Participate as a member of a team, teach others, serve clients and customers, exercise leadership, negotiate to arrive at a decision, work with cultural diversity

Systems Understand systems, monitor and correct performance, improve and design systems

Technology Apply technology to a task, maintain and troubleshoot technology

Basic Skills Reading, writing, arithmetic, listening, speaking

Thinking Skills Creative thinking, decision making, problem solving, seeing things in the mind's eye

Personal Qualities Responsibility, sociability, self management

EFF: **Communication** Read with understanding, speak so others can understand, listen actively, observe critically

Decision Making Solve problems and make decisions, plan

Interpersonal Cooperate with others, guide others, resolve conflict and negotiate

Lifelong Learning Reflect and evaluate, learn through research, use information and communications technology (optional)

Practice 1

10-15 mins.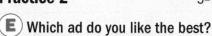

D Read the ads again and bubble in the circle next to the correct answer.

Have students check answers with a partner.

Evaluation 1

5 mins.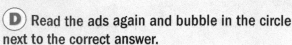

Go over the correct answers as a class.

Activity Bank

Lesson 2, Worksheet 2: Ad Practice

Presentation 2

10-15 mins.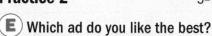

Have students look back at the ads and, as a class, discuss each one. *What makes the ad interesting or not? Would you consider buying this product? Why or why not?* Discuss the concept of marketing with students. Talk about how companies create ads to try to get you to buy their products. Talk about television advertising as well.

Practice 2

5-15 mins.

E Which ad do you like the best?

Have students answer these questions by themselves and encourage them to write several reasons why they chose the ad they did. (Shorter classes can do this exercise for homework.)

Evaluation 2

10-20 mins.

Have students raise their hands to indicate which ad they liked best. Designate each corner in the room for one of the ads and have students go to the corner of the ad they chose. Once in the corner, have students discuss the reason they wrote for their preference. Then ask each group to report its top three reasons to the class.

D   Read the ads again and bubble in the circle next to the correct answer.

1. What does the oil change NOT include?

   ○ oil   ○ oil filter   ● windshield-wiper fluid

2. When does the offer expire for the oil change?

   ○ May 8, 2009   ○ August 8, 2009   ● August 5, 2009

3. When does the garage door offer end?

   ● February 21, 2009   ○ December 2, 2009   ○ February 2, 2009

4. What does the garage door purchase NOT include?

   ○ new door installation   ● removal of old door   ○ three-year warranty

5. How do you get an in-home estimate for a new garage door?

   ● call   ○ go to the company   ○ write a letter

6. What is for sale at the stereo factory outlet?

   ○ stereo speakers   ○ headphones   ● stereo speakers and headphones

7. What is the discount at the outlet?

   ○ $9.95   ● 30-70 percent   ○ $79.95

8. What is the regular price of the bikes?

   ● $150.00   ○ $112.99   ○ $250.00

9. How much are the bikes discounted?

   ○ $25   ● 25%   ○ $37.00

10. Which item(s) come with a warranty?

   ○ garage doors   ○ bicycles   ● garage doors and bicycles

E   Which ad do you like the best? (Answers will vary.)

_____

Why?_____

_____

F Read the two ads and complete the table below.

Cleaning Services		
Company	Happy Helpers Cleaning Service	Kate's Cleaners
Phone Number	714-555-7382	562-555-0191
Product or Service	house cleaning	house cleaning
Price	$10 per room; $15 per bathroom	$45 per hour
Discounts	$20 off with ad	20% off first two services
Other Information	same-day service	They bring their own cleaning supplies.

Which cleaning service would you choose? (Answers will vary.)

Why?

G In groups, choose a product or service and create an advertisement for it. Include the name of your company, the name of your product, a small picture or illustration, and details of prices and discounts.

H **Active Task.** Find some newspaper advertisements and bring them to class. What special offers can you find?

Presentation 3   5–10 mins. ■■■

Direct students' attention to the two ads on page 26. Ask them what these ads are for. Ask students if they have ever seen any ads like this in the newspaper.

Practice 3   5–10 mins. ■

F Read the two ads and complete the table below.

Evaluation 3   10–15 mins. ■

Go over students' answers to Exercise F as a class. Then encourage students to share their answers.

Application   10–20 mins. ■■■

G In groups, choose a product or service and create an advertisement for it. Include the name of your company, the name of your product, a small picture or illustration, and details of prices and discounts.

Put students in groups and make sure they understand their task. Tell students that when they finish, they will present their ad to the class.

H Active Task. Find some newspaper advertisements and bring them to class. What special offers can you find?

Activity Bank

Lesson 1, Worksheet 1: Sample Ad Card / Matching Ad Cards

Lesson 1, Worksheet 3: Radio Ads

Refer students to *Stand Out 3 Grammar Challenge*, Unit 2, Challenge 2 for an explanation of and practice with superlative adjectives.

Objective: Compare products
Grammar: Comparative and superlative adjectives
Academic Strategies: Compare and contrast
Vocabulary: *speed, CPU, monitor, screen, disk drive, memory, CD-ROM drive*, comparative and superlative adjectives, irregular adjectives

AGENDA

Identify the parts of a computer.
Use comparative adjectives.
Use superlative adjectives.

RESOURCES

Activity Bank: Lesson 3, Worksheets 1–2
Reading and Writing Challenge: Unit 2

Grammar Challenge 3: Unit 2, Challenges 2–3

■ 1.5 hour classes   ■ 2.5 hour classes   ■ 3⁺ hour classes

Warm-up and Review   5 mins.

Go over the ads from Lesson 2 and ask students basic questions about their content to refresh their memories.

Introduction   5-10 mins.

Introduce the concept of comparison by asking students if they look at more than one ad before purchasing something. Ask them why or why not. Ask them why they might want to look at more than one ad. Write their reasons on the board. State the objective: *Today we will be comparing products.*

Presentation 1   15-20 mins. ■■■

A Think about the different parts of a computer. What do you use them for? Use the words from the box to label the picture.

Go over the computer vocabulary as a class. If you have computers in the classroom, use one to point out the parts of a computer.

B What should you look for when you buy a computer?

Mention other factors besides speed, monitor, memory, price and hard-drive size. These might include type and compatibility (PC or Mac), built-in features (CD/DVD drives, wireless Internet, video cards), warranties, and technical support.

C Study the information about five different computers. Use the adjectives above to talk about them.

Ask students to give you sentences about the computers. Write their sentences on the board. Introduce comparative adjectives by asking students questions, such as: *Which computer is cheaper, the JCN or the Vintel?* When they answer, write a comparative statement on the board, such as: *The Vintel is cheaper than the JCN.* Do a few examples and use the examples to explain comparative and superlative adjectives.

STANDARDS CORRELATIONS

CASAS: 1.2.1, 1.2.2 (See CASAS Competency List on pages 169–175.)
SCANS: Information Acquire and evaluate information, organize and maintain information, interpret and communicate information
Interpersonal Participate as a member of a team, work with cultural diversity
Basic Skills Reading, writing, arithmetic, listening, speaking
Thinking Skills Creative thinking, decision making

Personal Qualities Responsibility, sociability, self-management
EFF: Communication Convey ideas in writing, speak so others can understand, listen actively, observe critically
Decision Making Solve problems and make decisions
Interpersonal Guide others, cooperate with others
Lifelong Learning Reflect and evaluate, learn through research, use information and communications technology (optional)

Making Comparisons

GOAL ➤ Compare products

 Think about the different parts of a computer. What do you use them for?
Use the words from the box to label the picture.

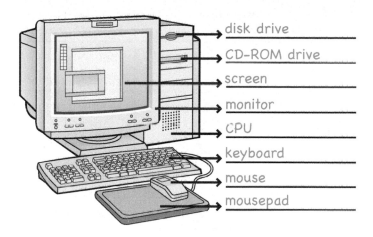

disk drive

CD–ROM drive

screen

monitor

CPU

keyboard

mouse

mousepad

monitor	CD-ROM drive
mouse	keyboard
screen	CPU
mousepad	disk drive

 What should you look for when you buy a computer?

Speed: Is the computer *fast* or *slow*?
Monitor: Is the screen *large* or *small*?
Memory: How *much* memory does the computer have?
Price: Is the computer *expensive* or *cheap*?
Hard Drive: Is the hard drive *big* or *small*?

> GHz = gigahertz
>
> 1,000 MHz = 1 GHz
>
> MB = megabytes
>
> GB = gigabytes
>
> 1,000 MB = 1 GB
>
> 15" = 15 inches

C Study the information about five different computers. Use the adjectives
above to talk about them.

EXAMPLE: The JCN computer has a large monitor.

	JCN	Doshiba	Vintel	Shepland	Kontaq
Price	$1,371	$1,549	$794	$1,168	$419
Speed	3.1 GHz	3.2 GHz	2.66 GHz	3.0 GHz	2.4 GHz
Monitor Size	20"	20"	22"	17"	17"
Memory	2 GB	3 GB	512 MB	1 GB	256 MB
Hard Drive	160 GB	250 GB	80 GB	160 GB	80 GB

GOAL ➤ **Compare products**

D Study the chart with your classmates and teacher.

Comparatives				
	Adjective	**Comparative**	**Rule**	**Example sentence**
Short adjectives	cheap	cheaper	Add *-er* to the end of the adjective.	Your computer was *cheaper* than my computer.
Long adjectives	expensive	more expensive	Add *more* before the adjective.	The new computer was *more expensive* than the old one.
Irregular adjectives	good bad	better worse	These adjectives are irregular.	The computer at school is *better* than this one.
Remember to use *than* after a comparative adjective followed by a noun.				

E Use the rules above to make comparative adjectives.

Spelling
hot ⟶ **hotter**
easy ⟶ **easier**
large ⟶ **larger**
pretty⟶ **prettier**

1. slow _____slower_____ 5. heavy _____heavier_____

2. small _____smaller_____ 6. fast _____faster_____

3. wide _____wider_____ 7. beautiful _____more beautiful_____

4. big _____bigger_____ 8. interesting _____more interesting_____

F Make comparative sentences about the computers on page 27.

EXAMPLE: The Kontaq / slow / the Vintel _The Kontaq is slower than the Vintel._

1. The JCN monitor / wide / the Shepland monitor

   The JCN monitor is wider than the Shepland monitor.

2. The Doshiba / fast / the Vintel

   The Doshiba is faster than the Vintel.

3. The JCN's hard drive / big / the Kontaq

   The JCN's hard drive is bigger than the Kontaq's hard drive.

G Talk to your partner. Which computer from page 27 would you buy? Using comparatives, give three reasons for your choice.

Presentation 1 (continued)

 Study the chart with your classmates and teacher.

Spelling

Comparatives

Remind students of the following rules:

1. One-syllable words, consonant-vowel-consonant: double the final letter
2. Words that end in -y: change the -y to -i
3. Words that end in -e: drop the -e

Practice 1   10–15 mins. ■■■

  Use the rules above to make comparative adjectives.

Go over the example with students and have them complete the exercise by themselves.

 Make comparative sentences about the computers on page 27.

Go over the example with students and have them complete the exercise by themselves.

Evaluation 1   5 mins. ■■■

Go over answers as a class by asking volunteers to write the answers on the board.

Presentation 2   10–15 mins. ■■■

Have students take out a piece of paper and write down what is most important to them when choosing a computer. Provide help and examples as necessary. For example, if they like to play video games, monitor size and speed might be important. If they like to work with pictures and video, hard-drive space and speed might be important. Also, money is probably an important factor. Ask for a few volunteers to share what is most important to them.

Practice 2   5–10 mins. ■■

Have students turn back to page 27 and decide which computer they would buy.

 Talk to your partner. Which computer from page 27 would you buy? Using comparatives, give three reasons for your choice.

 Refer students to *Stand Out 3 Grammar Challenge*, Unit 2, Challenges 2–3 for more practice with comparative and superlative adjectives. There are also two extension challenges in Unit 2, which teach students about comparatives and superlatives with nouns and comparative and superlative questions.

Evaluation 2   5–10 mins. ■■

Walk around the classroom and listen to students as they discuss the computers.

Instructor's Notes

_____

_____

_____

_____

_____

_____

_____

_____

_____

_____

_____

_____

_____

_____

_____

_____

_____

_____

_____

_____

_____

_____

_____

_____

_____

Presentation 3   5–10 mins.

Have students look back at the table on page 27. Ask them a few superlative questions, such as *Which computer is the cheapest? Which computer is the most expensive?*

H Study the chart with your teacher.

Spelling

Superlatives

Remind students of the following rules:

1. One-syllable words, consonant-vowel-consonant: double the final letter
2. Words that end in *-y*: change the *-y* to *-i*
3. Words that end in *-e*: drop the *-e*

Practice 3   5–10 mins.

I Use the rules above to make superlative adjectives.

Go over the example with students and have them complete the exercise by themselves.

J Make superlative sentences about the computers on page 27.

Go over the example with students and have them complete the exercise by themselves.

Evaluation 3   5 mins.

Go over answers as a class by asking volunteers to write the answers on the board.

Pronunciation

Focus

Remind students about pronunciation focus. They practiced focus in Unit 1. Explain to them that in comparative and superlative statements, the adjective is the word that will get the focus.

The Doshiba computer is the FASTEST.

The Kontaq is SLOWER than the Vintel.

Application   15–25 mins.

K Write six questions about the computers on page 27, using comparatives and superlatives. Walk around the room and ask your classmates to answer your questions.

Go over the examples with students and, as a class, write a few more questions. Then have students write questions on their own, not using any of the ones from the board. Walk around the classroom and help students with their questions. When students have finished, have them walk around the room and practice asking their questions.

Activity Bank

Lesson 3, Worksheet 1: Comparative and Superlative Adjectives

Lesson 3, Worksheet 2: Comparative Sentence Lists

Instructor's Notes

_____

_____

_____

_____

_____

_____

_____

_____

_____

_____

_____

_____

_____

_____

_____

_____

_____

_____

H Study the chart with your teacher.

Superlatives				
	Adjective	**Superlative**	**Rule**	**Example sentence**
Short adjectives	cheap	the cheapest	Add *-est* to the end of the adjective.	Your computer is *the cheapest*.
Long adjectives	expensive	the most expensive	Add *most* before the adjective.	He bought *the most* expensive computer in the store.
Irregular adjectives	good bad	best worst	These adjectives are irregular.	The computers at school are *the best*.
Always use *the* before a superlative.				

I Use the rules above to make superlative adjectives.

1. slow	the slowest	5. heavy	the heaviest	**Spelling**
2. small	the smallest	6. fast	the fastest	hot → the hottest
3. wide	the widest	7. beautiful	the most beautiful	easy → the easiest
4. big	the biggest	8. interesting	the most interesting	large → the largest
				pretty → the prettiest

J Make superlative sentences about the computers on page 27. (Answers will vary.)

EXAMPLE: wide   The Vintel computer has the widest screen.

1. expensive   _____

2. cheap   _____

3. slow   _____

4. large memory   _____

5. small memory   _____

K Write six questions about the computers on page 27, using comparatives and superlatives. Walk around the room and ask your classmates to answer your questions.

(Answers will vary.)

EXAMPLE: Which computer has the biggest monitor?
Which computer is faster, the JCN or the Doshiba?

LESSON 4 Cash or charge?

GOAL ➤ Identify and compare purchasing methods

 A Terron uses four different ways to make purchases. What are they?

He uses cash, check, credit card, and debit card.

B Write the correct word next to its description. You will use some of the items two times.

> cash   personal check   credit card   debit card

1. This is a written request to your bank asking them to pay money out of your account.
   ___personal check___

2. This allows you to borrow money to make purchases. ___credit card___

3. Coins and bills are this. ___cash___

4. This allows a store to take money directly from your account to pay for purchases. ___debit card___

5. This allows you to buy now and pay later. ___credit card___

6. You can get cash out of the ATM with this. ___debit card___

Objective: Identify and compare purchasing methods
Grammar: Modals: *have to* and *must*
Academic Strategies: Compare and contrast
Vocabulary: *cash, check, credit card, debit card, advantages, disadvantages, must, have to*

AGENDA

Identify purchasing methods.
Discuss advantages and disadvantages of purchasing methods.
Use have to and must appropriately.

RESOURCES

Activity Bank: Lesson 4, Worksheets 1–2
Reading and Writing Challenge: Unit 2

Grammar Challenge 3: Unit 2, Challenge 4
Audio: CD 1, Track 6

■ 1.5 hour classes   ■ 2.5 hour classes   ■ 3⁺ hour classes

Warm-up and Review   10–15 mins. ■■■

Write the words *tall, short, thin,* and *happy* on the board. Ask students to help you come up with more adjectives that can describe people. Review comparative and superlative adjectives by having students write statements comparing two people they know. Ask volunteers to write their sentences on the board.

Introduction   5–10 mins. ■■■

(A) Terron uses four different ways to make purchases. What are they?

For this exercise, you are only interested in the following purchasing methods: *cash, check, credit card,* and *debit card*. Write these methods on the board. State the objective: *Today we will compare purchasing methods.*

Presentation 1   10–15 mins. ■■■

(B) Write the correct word next to its description. You will use some of the items two times.

Do this activity as a class.

Write *advantages* and *disadvantages* on the board. Ask students if they know the meaning of either word. Go over the definitions and give them a few examples.

Practice 1   10–15 mins.

C In groups, talk about the advantages and disadvantages of each purchasing method. Complete the chart below.

Evaluation 1   10–15 mins.

Write the chart on the board and ask a representative from each group to come up and fill in some of their group's ideas.

D Talk to a partner about the purchasing method you prefer and why.

You may want to do this as a corners activity, designating each of the four corners in your room as *cash*, *check*, *credit card*, and *debit card*. Students can then discuss their preferred method with the other students in their corner.

Presentation 2   5–10 mins.

Write the words *must* and *have to* on the board. See if students can help you define the meaning of the two items by giving you example sentences. The structure isn't as important as the meaning at this point.

Practice 2   15–20 mins.

E Listen to Terron and his wife, Leilani, talk about purchasing methods. Make a list of the things they *have to* or *must* do.

Go over the directions with students and tell them they will be listening for *must* and *have to* and the phrases that follow them.

1. Play the recording with student books closed. Tell students just to listen.
2. Have them open their books and see if they can remember anything to write in the table.
3. Play the recording again and have them write what they hear.
4. Have them share their answers with a partner and fill in what they missed.
5. Play the recording one final time.

 Listening Script   CD 1, Track 6

Leilani: *Terron, you must go to the ATM tomorrow because we are out of cash.*
Terron: *What do you need cash for?*
Leilani: *I have to get groceries and I need to pick up the dry cleaning.*
Terron: *We really have to get a credit card. That way, we don't have to keep pulling cash out of the ATM.*
Leilani: *Yes, but if we get a credit card, we must pay it off every month. I don't want monthly debt hanging over our heads.*
Terron: *I agree. I have to go into the bank tomorrow anyway to cash my check so I'll get a credit card application for us to fill out then.*

Evaluation 2   5–10 mins.

Make two columns on the board, one titled *have to* and the other labeled *must*. Ask volunteers to come up and write what they heard in the correct columns.

Activity Bank

Lesson 4, Worksheet 1: Purchasing Methods

GOAL ➤ Identify and compare purchasing methods

C In groups, talk about the advantages and disadvantages of each purchasing method. Complete the chart below. (Answers will vary.)

EXAMPLE: *Student A:* Cash is good because it is quick and easy.
Student B: Yes, but if you lose cash, you cannot replace it.

	Cash	Debit card	Personal check	Credit card
Advantages	quick and easy			
Disadvantages	can't replace			

D Talk to a partner about the purchasing method you prefer and why.

CD 1
TR 6

E Listen to Terron and his wife, Leilani, talk about purchasing methods. Make a list of the things they *have to* do and *must* do.

Have to	Must
get groceries get a credit card go to the bank tomorrow	go to the ATM tomorrow pick up the dry cleaning pay off the credit card every month

GOAL ➤ Identify and compare
purchasing methods

F We use *must* and *have to* when something is necessary. *Must* is a little stronger than *have to*. Study the chart below with your teacher.

Must vs. Have to			
Subject	**Modal**	**Base verb**	
We	have to	save	money for vacation.
I	must	pay off	my credit card every month.

G Complete each statement with *must* or *have to* and a verb from the box.

> check   keep   put   make   pay

EXAMPLE: You ___**must pay**___ your bills if you want a good credit history.

1. You ___have to___ ___put___ your cash in a safe place.

2. You ___must___ ___keep___ track of the personal checks you write.

3. You ___must___ ___pay___ the minimum amount on your credit card every month.

4. You ___have to___ ___make___ sure you have enough money in the bank when you write a personal check.

5. You ___must___ ___check___ your balance before you get cash out of an ATM machine.

H Choose one purchasing method and write a paragraph on why you think it is better than all the rest. Use comparative and superlative adjectives.

___(Answers will vary.)_____

_____

_____

_____

_____

Presentation 3 10–15 mins.

F We use *must* and *have to* when something is necessary. *Must* is a little stronger than *have to.* Study the chart below with your teacher.

Practice 3 5–10 mins.

G Complete each statement with *must* or *have to* and a verb from the box.

Evaluation 3 3 mins.

Go over the answers as a class, making sure students used the base form of the verb after the modal.

Activity Bank

Lesson 4, Worksheet 2: *Must* and *Have to*

GC Refer students to *Stand Out 3 Grammar Challenge*, Unit 2, Challenge 4 for more practice with *must* and *have to.*

Application 10–20 mins.

H Choose one purchasing method and write a paragraph on why you think it is better than all the rest. Use comparative and superlative adjectives.

Instructor's Notes

Objective: Make a smart purchase
Grammar: Transition words
Academic Strategy: Sequence writing
Vocabulary: *comparison shopping, save, smart consumer, sequencing, transitions*

RESOURCES

Activity Bank: Lesson 5, Worksheets 1–2
Reading and Writing Challenge: Unit 2

 1.5 hour classes  2.5 hour classes 3⁺ hour classes

AGENDA

*Read about making a smart purchase.
Order steps.
Use sequencing transitions.
Write a paragraph with transitions.
Identify steps to making a smart purchase.*

Warm-up and Review   5-10 mins.

Write *cash, check, credit,* and *debit* on the board. Assign each one to a corner of the room. Ask students to choose their least favorite purchasing method and go to that corner. Have them work with the students in that corner to make a list of reasons why they don't like to use this purchasing method.

Introduction   5-10 mins.

Write *smart purchase* on the board. Ask students what they think this means. Ask them what they would do if they were going to make a smart purchase. Write their ideas on the board. State the objective: *In this lesson, we will learn about making smart purchases.*

Presentation 1   10-15 mins. ■■

(A) Read about making smart purchases.

Read the paragraph out loud to students. Then ask them to read it silently to themselves. Ask them some comprehension questions about the paragraph, such as: *What is a smart purchase? How do you comparison shop? What do smart consumers do?* Then ask if they have any questions about vocabulary.

Practice 1   10-15 mins.

(B) Put the steps in order from 1 to 5 according to the paragraph above.

Go over the directions and have students find the first step in the paragraph. Then have them number the rest of the steps by themselves.

(C) Rewrite the steps in Exercise B after the words below.

Evaluation 1   3 mins. ■■

Go over the answers as a class, making sure all of the students have the steps in the correct order.

STANDARDS CORRELATIONS

CASAS: 1.2.5 (See CASAS Competency List on pages 169–175.)
SCANS: Information Acquire and evaluate information, organize and maintain information, interpret and communicate information
Interpersonal Participate as a member of a team, teach others, exercise leadership, negotiate to arrive at a decision, work with cultural diversity
Basic Skills Reading, writing, listening, speaking
Thinking Skills Creative thinking, decision making, problem solving, seeing things in the mind's eye

Personal Qualities Responsibility, sociability, self-management
EFF: Communication Convey ideas in writing, speak so others can understand, listen actively, observe critically
Decision Making Solve problems and make decisions, plan
Interpersonal Cooperate with others
Lifelong Learning Reflect and evaluate, use information and communications technology (optional)

Think before you buy

GOAL ➤ **Make a smart purchase**

A Read about making smart purchases.

Making a Smart Purchase

You make a smart purchase when you think and plan before you buy something. First of all, you make a decision to buy something. This is the easy part. The second step is comparison shopping. You comparison shop by reading advertisements, going to different stores, and talking to friends and family. Third, you choose which product you are going to buy. Do you have enough money to buy this product? If you don't, the next step is to start saving. This may take a while depending on how much you need to save. Once you have enough money, you are ready to make your purchase. If you follow these steps to make a purchase, you will be a smart consumer. And smart consumers make smart purchases!

What is Leilani doing?
What is her problem?

B Put the steps in order from 1 to 5 according to the paragraph above.

_5_ make the purchase

_2_ read advertisements

_1_ decide to buy something

_3_ choose the best deal

_4_ save money

C Rewrite the steps in Exercise B after the words below.

First,   decide to buy something.

Second, read advertisements.

Next,   choose the best deal.

Then,   save money.

Finally, make the purchase.

D *Sequencing transitions* are used to describe stages of a process. Study the examples in the box.

First,	First of all,	Second,	Second of all,	Third,
Fourth,	Next,	Then,	Lastly,	Finally,

E **Put the steps in the correct order.**

_4_ You decide to buy it.

_2_ You find out the price.

_1_ You see something in a store you want to buy.

_6_ You decide to charge it.

_3_ You think about if you have enough money to pay for it or not.

_7_ You pay for it.

_5_ You think about if you want to pay cash or put it on your credit card.

You

We use *you* to talk about people in general.

F **Add sequencing transitions to the steps above to write a paragraph about making a purchase.** (Answers may vary.)

First, you see something in a store you want to buy. Second, you find out the price.

Next, you think about if you have enough money to pay for it or not. Then, you decide

to buy it. Next, you think about if you want to pay cash or put it on your credit card.

Then, you decide to charge it. Finally, you pay for it.

Presentation 2   5–10 mins. ■■■

D *Sequencing transitions* are used to describe stages of a process. Study the examples in the box.

Explain that *next* and *then* can come before or after any transition, but they must come after the first step.

Practice 2   15–20 mins. ■■

(Shorter classes can do these exercises for homework.)

E Put the steps in the correct order.

Have students work with a partner to put the steps in the correct order.

F Add sequencing transitions to the steps above to write a paragraph about making a purchase.

Refer students to *Stand Out 3 Grammar Challenge*, Unit 2, Challenge 5 for more practice with transition words.

Evaluation 2   10–20 mins. ■■

Go over the answers to Exercise E as a class and see if everyone agrees on the order of the steps.

Presentation 3

5-10 mins. ■■■

Remind students what they learned about computers in Lesson 3. Ask them if they can remember the price of the computer they liked best. Then ask them if they could go out and buy that computer today. Why or why not? Ask them what they think the best purchasing method would be.

Practice 3

10-15 mins. ■

 Imagine you are going to buy a computer. In groups, come up with a list of steps to make a smart purchase.

Evaluation 3

10-15 mins. ■

Ask volunteers to write their groups' steps on the board.

Application

10-20 mins. ■■■

(H) Write a paragraph about buying your computer. Use sequencing transitions.

Activity Bank

Lesson 5, Worksheet 1: One Consumer's Story

Lesson 5, Worksheet 2: Sequence Writing

Refer students to *Stand Out 3 Grammar Challenge*, Unit 2, Extension Challenges 1–2 for more practice with comparatives and superlatives.

Instructor's Notes

GOAL ➤ **Make a smart purchase**

G Imagine you are going to buy a computer. In groups, come up with a list of steps to make a smart purchase.

(Answers may vary.)

Steps to Buying Our Computer

1. Decide to buy a computer.

2. Decide what type of computer to buy.

3. Look for the best price.

4. Think about if you have enough money to buy the computer.

5. Save money to pay for the computer.

6. Think about if you want to pay cash or put it on your credit card.

7. Decide to charge the computer.

8. Pay for it.

H Write a paragraph about buying your computer. Use sequencing transitions. (Answers may vary.)

First, decide to buy a computer. Second, decide what type of computer you want to buy. Third, look for the best price. Next, think about if you have enough money to buy the computer. Then, save money to pay for the computer. Next, think about if you want to pay cash or put it on your credit card. Then, decide to charge the computer. Finally, pay for it.

Review

A Where can you purchase the following goods or services? Write the places below. (Lesson 1)

Goods/Services	Place	Goods/Services	Place
1. shampoo	drugstore	6. a washing machine	department store
2. soccer ball	department store	7. fruit	grocery store
3. hammer	hardware store	8. a tune-up	gas station
4. stamps	post office	9. clothes cleaned	dry cleaners
5. prescription refill	pharmacy	10. shoes	shoe store

B Write the present tense form of *get* and the past participle of the verb in parentheses. (Lesson 1)

1. He ___gets___ his car ___washed___ at the local car wash. (wash)

2. She ___gets___ her hair ___cut___ at the hair salon. (cut)

3. He ___gets___ his car ___cleaned___ at the automotive shop. (clean)

4. They ___get___ their clothes ___cleaned___ at the dry cleaners. (clean)

5. I ___get___ my checks ___cashed___ at the bank. (cash)

C Read the ads and answer the questions below. (Lesson 2)

Xonda Pilot with all the bells and whistles

Hill's Xonda

$36,999

Includes free gas for a year!

Xonda of Albilene

Fully loaded Xonda Pilot

Come test drive your new car!
0% financing

$37,999 (includes tax, title, and license)

1. Are these ads advertising the same thing? ___yes___ If so, what? ___car___

2. What is the price of the car at Hill's? ___$36,999___ At Albilene? ___$37,999___

3. Which car is cheaper? Hill's Xonda is cheaper.

4. What is good about the offer from Hill's? Free gas for a year.

5. What is good about the offer from Albilene? 0% financing; tax, title, and license included.

6. Which dealership would you buy from? (Answers will vary.)

Why?_____

AT-A-GLANCE PREP

Objective: All unit objectives
Grammar: All unit grammar
Academic Strategy: Reviewing
Vocabulary: All unit vocabulary

RESOURCES

Activity Bank: Unit 2, Lessons 1–5
Reading and Writing Challenge: Unit 2

Grammar Challenge 3: Unit 2, Challenges 1–5

■ 1.5 hour classes ■ 2.5 hour classes ■ 3⁺ hour classes

AGENDA

Discuss unit objectives.
Complete the review.
Do My Dictionary.
Evaluate and reflect on progress.

Warm-up and Review   5-10 mins.

In groups, have students come up with a list of ways to make a smart purchase.

Introduction   5-10 mins. ■■■

Ask students to try to recall (in general) all the goals of this unit without looking at their books. Then remind them which goals they omitted, if any. (Unit goals: Identify places to purchase goods and services, interpret advertisements, compare products, identify and compare purchasing methods, and make a smart purchase) Write all the goals from Unit 2 on the board. Show students the first page of the unit and mention the five objectives. State the objective: *Today we will be reviewing everything you have learned in this unit.*

Presentation 1   10-15 mins. ■■■

This presentation will cover the first three pages of the review. Quickly go to the first page of each lesson. Discuss the objective of each. Ask simple questions to remind students of what they have learned.

Note: Since there is little presentation in the review, you can assign the review exercises for homework and go over them in class the following day.

Practice 1   20-25 mins. ■■■

Note: There are two ways to do the review: (1) Go through the exercises one at a time and, as students complete each one, go over the answers. (2) Briefly go through the instructions of each exercise, allow students to complete all of the exercises at once, and then go over the answers.

(A) Where can you purchase the following goods or services? Write the places below. (Lesson 1)

(B) Write the present tense form of *get* and the past participle of the verb in parentheses. (Lesson 1)

(C) Read the ads and answer the questions below. (Lesson 2)

Evaluation 1   20-25 mins.

Go around the classroom and check on students' progress. Help individuals when needed. If you see consistent errors among several students, interrupt the class and give a mini lesson or review to help students feel comfortable with the concept.

STANDARDS CORRELATIONS

CASAS: 7.2.1 (See CASAS Competency List on pages 169–175.)
SCANS: **Resources** Allocate time
Information Acquire and evaluate information
Interpersonal Participate as a member of a team, teach others, negotiate to arrive at a decision, work with cultural diversity
Systems Monitor and correct performance
Basic Skills Reading, writing, arithmetic, listening, speaking
Thinking Skills Creative thinking, decision making, problem solving, seeing things in the mind's eye

Personal Qualities Responsibility, sociability, self-management
EFF: **Communication** Convey ideas in writing, speak so others can understand
Decision Making Solve problems and make decisions, plan
Interpersonal Cooperate with others, guide others, resolve conflict and negotiate, advocate and influence
Lifelong Learning Take responsibility for learning, reflect and evaluate, use information and communications technology (optional)

Practice 1 *(continued)*   25-30 mins.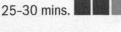

D Complete the following statements with a comparative or a superlative adjective. (Lesson 3)

E Imagine that you are going to buy a new car—your dream car. Write sentences comparing your old car to your new car. (Lesson 3)

F What is the best restaurant in your neighborhood? Write sentences comparing this restaurant to all the other restaurants in the neighborhood. (Lesson 3)

Evaluation 1 *(continued)*   25-30 mins.

Go around the classroom and check students' progress. Help individuals when needed. If you see consistent errors among several students, interrupt the class and give a mini lesson or review to help students feel comfortable with the concept.

Teaching Tip

Recycling/Review

The review process and the project that follows are part of the recycling/review process. Students at this level often need to be reintroduced to concepts to solidify what they have learned. Many concepts are learned and forgotten while learning other new concepts. This is because students learn but are not necessarily ready to acquire language concepts.

Therefore, it becomes very important to review and to show students how to review on their own. It is also important to recycle the new concepts in different contexts.

Instructor's Notes

(D) Complete the following statements with a comparative or a superlative adjective. (Lesson 3)

1. My new watch was _____cheaper than_____ my old watch. (cheap)

2. This computer is _____the fastest_____ one in the store. (fast)

3. That mirror is _____taller than_____ the one we have now. (tall)

4. This box is much _____heavier than_____ that one. What's in it? (heavy)

5. _____The most beautiful_____ paintings in the world are painted by that artist. (beautiful)

6. Do you think that the book is _____more interesting than_____ the movie? (interesting)

7. Let's go to a different store. This is _____the busiest_____ one. (busy)

8. My neighbor's house is _____bigger than_____ our house. (big)

9. Do you think this car is _____better than_____ the one you have? (good)

(E) Imagine that you are going to buy a new car—your dream car. Write sentences comparing your old car to your new car. (Lesson 3) (Answers will vary.)

EXAMPLE: _My new car is faster than my old car._

_____

_____

_____

_____

_____

(F) What is the best restaurant in your neighborhood? Write sentences comparing this restaurant to all the other restaurants in the neighborhood. (Lesson 3) (Answers will vary.)

EXAMPLE: _China Palace has the friendliest service in the neighborhood._

_____

_____

_____

_____

_____

Review

G Write a sentence about each of the following purchasing methods.
Use *must* or *have to*. **(Lesson 4)** (Answers will vary.)

EXAMPLE: cashier's check: _You must be careful not to lose a cashier's check._

1. cash: _____

2. personal check: _____

3. debit card: _____

4. credit card: _____

H Imagine that your friend is going to buy a new television. What steps would you tell him or her to take? Write them below. **(Lesson 5)** (Answers will vary.)

1. _Decide what kind of television to buy._

2. _Read advertisements about the television or visit different stores._

3. _Choose the best deal on the television._

4. _Save money for the television._

5. _Buy the television._

I Write a paragraph using the steps you wrote above. Use sequencing transitions.
(Lesson 5) (Answers will vary.)

First, decide what kind of television to buy. Second, read advertisements about the television or visit different stores. Next, choose the best deal on the television. Then, save money for the television. Finally, buy the television.

Practice 1 *(continued)*   25-30 mins. ■■■□

G Write a sentence about each of the following purchasing methods. Use *must* or *have to*. (Lesson 4)

H Imagine that your friend is going to buy a new television. What steps would you tell him or her to take? Write them below. (Lesson 5)

I Write a paragraph using the steps you wrote above. Use sequencing transitions. (Lesson 5)

Evaluation 1 *(continued)*   25-30 mins. ■■□

Go around the classroom and check students' progress. Help individuals when needed. If you see consistent errors among several students, interrupt the class and give a mini lesson or review to help students feel comfortable with the concept.

Instructor's Notes

_____

_____

_____

_____

_____

_____

_____

_____

_____

_____

_____

_____

_____

_____

_____

_____

_____

_____

_____

_____

_____

_____

_____

_____

_____

_____

_____

_____

_____

_____

Presentation 2 — 5-10 mins.

My Dictionary

Ask students to brainstorm new vocabulary they learned in this unit. Have them do this without looking in their books. Write their ideas on the board.

Practice 2 — 15-20 mins.

(Shorter classes can do these exercises for homework.)

Make flash cards to improve your vocabulary.

Go over the example flash card with students. Then pick one of the words from the board and do one together as a class. Then have students make three more flash cards for three different words on their own.

Evaluation 2 — 15-20 mins.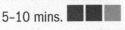

Walk around the classroom and help students.

Presentation 3 — 5-10 mins.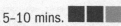

Learner Log

Write the word *log* on the board. Ask students if they know what this word means. Explain to them that it is a journal, notebook, or place where you keep track of information. In this case, they will be keeping track of what they have learned. Tell them that they will do a learner log at the end of each unit.

In this unit, you learned many things about consumer smarts. How comfortable do you feel doing each of the skills listed below? Rate your comfort level on a scale of 1 to 4.

Go over the instructions with students and make sure they understand what to do. You may want to do the first one or two items with the class to make sure students understand.

Practice 3 — 5-10 mins.

Have students complete the Learner Log.

Teaching Tip

Learner Logs

Learner Logs function to help students in many different ways.

1. They serve as part of the review process.
2. They help students to gain confidence and document what they have learned. Consequently, students see that they are making progress and want to move forward in learning.
3. They provide students with a tool that they can use over and over to check and recheck their understanding. In this way, students become independent learners.

Evaluation 3 — 5-10 mins.

Walk around the classroom and help students.

Application — 5-10 mins.

Go over the two reflection questions with students and have them complete the answers by themselves.

TB Assessment

Use the Stand Out 3 Assessment CD-ROM with Exam*View*® to create a post-test for Unit 2.

My Dictionary

Make flash cards to improve your vocabulary.

1. Choose four words from this unit.
2. Write each word on a 3-by-5 index card or on a piece of paper.
3. On the back of the card or paper, write a definition, or a sentence with the word missing, and draw a picture.
4. Study the words while you are traveling to school or work, or read them during breakfast. (Remember your time-management skills!) You can also ask a friend or family member to help you review.
5. Do this for each unit, and add other new words that you learn in or out of class. If you study a little each day, you will improve your vocabulary very quickly. By the end of this class, you will have a whole stack of flash cards!

to purchase

_____ the shirt.

Learner Log

In this unit, you learned many things about consumer smarts. How comfortable do you feel doing each of the skills listed below? Rate your comfort level on a scale of 1 to 4.

1 = Need more practice   **2** = OK   **3** = Good   **4** = Great!

Life Skill	Comfort Level				Page
I can identify places to purchase goods and services.	1	2	3	4	21
I can interpret advertisements.	1	2	3	4	24
I can compare products.	1	2	3	4	27
I can identify and compare purchasing methods.	1	2	3	4	30
I know how to make a smart purchase.	1	2	3	4	33

If you circled 1 or 2, write down the page number where you can review this skill.

Reflection

1. What was the most useful skill you learned in this unit? _____

2. How will this help you in life? _____

Team Project

Create two advertisements and a purchase plan.

1. Form a team with four or five students. Choose positions for each member of your team.

POSITION	JOB DESCRIPTION	STUDENT NAME
Student 1: Leader	See that everyone speaks English. See that everyone participates.	
Student 2: Secretary	Write the advertisement. Take notes for the family.	
Student 3: Designer	Design advertisement layout.	
Students 4/5: Spokespeople	Plan presentations.	

Part 1—Advertising Team: Create Advertisements

1. Create two different advertisements for the same product or service. (Lesson 2)

2. Present your ads to the class and then post them in the classroom.

Part 2—Family: Create a Purchase Plan

1. Walk around the room and choose a product or service to buy from all the ads created by all the teams on the wall.

2. Compare two of the ads, writing four comparative statements about why one is better than the other. (Lessons 2–3)

3. Choose one product or service to buy and write a purchase plan—the steps needed to make a smart purchase. (Lessons 4–5)

4. Present your comparisons and purchase plan to the class.

Create two advertisements and a purchase plan.

Each team will create advertisements for a product or service. Then each team will choose one of the products or services to buy by comparing the available products. Afterwards, teams will write up a purchase plan for the one they have decided to buy.

The team project is the final application for the unit. It gives students a chance to show that they have mastered all of the Unit 2 objectives.

Note: Shorter classes can extend this project over two class meetings.

Stage 1   5 mins.

Form a team with four or five students. Choose positions for each member of your team.

Have students decide who will lead each step as described on the student page. Provide well-defined directions on the board for how teams should proceed. Explain that all the students do every step as a team. Teams shouldn't go to the next stage until the previous one is complete.

Part 1—Advertising Team: Create Advertisements

Stage 1   15-20 mins.

Create two different advertisements for the same product or service. (Lesson 2)

Have teams decide on a product or service to market and create two competing ads for the product or service.

Optional Computer Activity: Students may want to use the computer to design their ads.

Stage 2   10-15 mins.

Present your ads to the class and then post them in the classroom.

Part 2—Family: Create a Purchase Plan

Stage 1   10-15 mins.

Walk around the room and choose a product or service to buy from all the ads created by all the teams on the wall.

The advertisements should all be posted around the room so students can clearly see them in order to make their decision.

Stage 2   15-20 mins.

Compare two of the ads, writing four comparative statements about why one is better than the other. (Lessons 2–3)

Stage 3   15-20 mins.

Choose one product or service to buy and write a purchase plan—the steps needed to make a smart purchase. (Lessons 4–5)

Stage 4   15-20 mins.

Present your comparisons and purchase plan to the class.

Help teams prepare for their presentations. Suggest that each member choose a different part of the poster to present.

STANDARDS CORRELATIONS

CASAS: 4.8.1, 4.8.5, 4.8.6 (See CASAS Competency List on pages 169–175.)
SCANS: Resources Allocate time
Information Acquire and evaluate information, organize and maintain information, interpret and communicate information, use computers to process information
Systems Understand systems, improve and design systems
Technology Select technology, apply technology to exercise
Basic Skills Writing
Thinking Skills Creative thinking, decision making, problem solving, seeing things in the mind's eye, reasoning

Personal Qualities Responsibility, self-esteem, self-management, integrity/honesty
EFF: Communication Convey ideas in writing, speak so others can understand
Decision Making Solve problems and make decisions, plan
Interpersonal Guide others, resolve conflict and negotiate, advocate and influence, cooperate with others
Lifelong Learning Take responsibility for learning, reflect and evaluate, use information and communication technologies (optional)

AT-A-GLANCE PREP

Objective: Interpret classified ads
Grammar: Comparatives and superlatives using nouns
Academic Strategy: Scanning
Vocabulary: *classified ad, carport, charming, balcony, condition, security guard, stand for, spa, hookup*

AGENDA

Identify types of housing.
Read classified ads.
Form comparatives using nouns.
Form superlatives using nouns.
Scan for information.
Compare rental properties.

RESOURCES

Activity Bank: Lesson 1, Worksheets 1–3
Reading and Writing Challenge: Unit 3

Grammar Challenge 3: Unit 3, Challenge 1

 1.5 hour classes   2.5 hour classes   ■ 3⁺ hour classes

Stand Out 3 Assessment CD-ROM with Exam *View*®

Warm-up and Review   5–10 mins.

Write *housing* on the board. Ask students to name different types of housing. Write their ideas on the board. Ask students to tell you in what ways these types of housing differ.

Introduction   5–10 mins.

A Think about the place where you live. How did you find it? What are some different ways to find housing?

Call on volunteers to answer these questions. State the objective: *Today we will be interpreting classified ads.*

Presentation 1   10–15 mins. ■■■

Have students open their books and look at the ads. Then ask them questions, such as: *How much is the rent for #3? How many bedrooms does #2 have?* At this point, try not to answer students' questions about vocabulary or abbreviations.

B One way to find housing is through *classified ads* in the newspaper. Read the ads below. Which apartment do you like best?

Ask a few students which apartment they prefer and why they prefer it.

Practice 1   10–15 mins.

C Work with a partner to list the abbreviations in the ads. What does each abbreviation stand for? Discuss their meanings with your teacher.

In pairs, have students list all the abbreviations in the ads, referring to the example. If they get stuck, tell them to ask other pairs. The class should be able to get most of the answers.

Evaluation 1   5–10 mins. ■■■

Have volunteers write the abbreviations on the board. Ask a member of each group to write the complete words next to three abbreviations. Continue with different group members until all the abbreviations have been covered. Once students are familiar with the vocabulary and abbreviations, ask them to read the ads. Answer any questions.

Activity Bank

Lesson 1, Worksheet 2: Interpret Classified Ads

STANDARDS CORRELATIONS

CASAS: 1.4.1, 1.4.2 (See CASAS Competency List on pages 169–175.)
SCANS: **Information** Acquire and evaluate information, organize and maintain information, interpret and communicate information
Interpersonal Participate as a member of a team, teach others, negotiate to arrive at a decision, work with cultural diversity
Systems Understand systems, monitor and correct performance
Basic Skills Reading, writing, arithmetic, listening, speaking
Thinking Skills Creative thinking, decision making

Personal Qualities Responsibility, sociability, self-management
EFF: **Communication** Reading with understanding, convey ideas in writing, speak so others can understand
Decision Making Plan
Interpersonal Cooperate with others
Lifelong Learning Reflect and evaluate, learn through research, use information and communications technology

Housing

GOALS

➤ **Interpret classified ads**
➤ **Make decisions about housing**

➤ **Arrange and cancel utilities**
➤ **Make a budget**
➤ **Write a letter to a landlord**

LESSON **1**

House hunting

GOAL ➤ Interpret classified ads

Vocabulary · Grammar · Life Skills · Academic · Pronunciation

A Think about the place where you live. How did you find it? What are some different ways to find housing?

B One way to find housing is through *classified ads* in the newspaper. Read the ads below. Which apartment do you like best?

FOR RENT

1.
Lge apartment,
2 floors, 3 bedrooms,
2 bath, gar, **pool,**
$1,500

2.
SUNNY
1 BR, 1 bath w/ huge l/r,
1 car gar, W/D, high ceilings,
security guard,
$895/mo.

3.
Charming 1BR condo,
1 bath, carport, large
balc, great condition,
carpeting, walk to ctr,
$800/mo.

4.
4 bdrm spacious condo,
pool, gar, laundry, nr school,
no pets, **$2,500/mo.**

5.
1st fl sunny studio,
yard, stove & frig, Cat OK,
first, last, & sec. dep,
$550 per month

6.
Clean 2 bedroom, 1 bath
apt in gated community
A/C, new appl, nr fwys
Gas, water, trash paid
avail 8/1, $1,195

C Work with a partner to list the abbreviations in the ads. What does each abbreviation stand for? Discuss their meanings with your teacher.

Abbreviation	Word	Meaning
lge	large	very big

bath: bathroom (a room where you wash and use the toilet); gar: garage (building that you park cars in); BR: bedroom (a room to sleep in); w/: with; l/r: living room (a room where you can sit, read, watch TV, visit with friends, etc.); W/D: washer/dryer (includes a washing machine and a dryer); mo.: month; balc: balcony (an elevated place outside where you can stand); ctr: center (middle); bdrm: bedroom (a room to sleep in); nr: near (close to); 1st fl: first floor (the floor that is above the basement, usually at ground level); frig: refrigerator (includes a refrigerator); sec dep: security deposit (extra money you pay besides rent. You get it back if you don't damage the house or apartment.); apt: apartment (a type of rented housing); A/C: air conditioning (includes a cooling system); fwys: freeways (highways); avail: available (ready to live in)

D Discuss the following questions about the ads on page 41 with your partner.

1. Which one-bedroom apartment has higher rent? #2
2. Which apartment has more rooms—#1 or #5? #1
3. Which apartment has more bathrooms—#1 or #6? #1

E Here are more ways to make comparisons. Study the charts below.

Comparatives Using Nouns	
Our new apartment has *more bedrooms* than our old one. Our old apartment had *fewer bedrooms* than our new one.	Use *more* or *fewer* to compare count nouns.
Rachel's apartment gets *more light* than Pablo's apartment. Pablo's apartment gets *less light* than Rachel's apartment.	Use *more* or *less* to compare noncount nouns.

Superlatives Using Nouns	
Rachel's apartment has *the most bedrooms*. Phuong's apartment has *the fewest bedrooms*.	Use *the most* or *the fewest* for count nouns.
Rachel's apartment has *the most light*. Phuong's apartment has *the least light*.	Use *the most* or *the least* for non-count nouns.

F Complete the sentences with the correct word: *more* or *most*.

1. Kim's house has _____more_____ bedrooms than Jen's house.

2. The Worshams' apartment gets the _____most_____ light.

3. That condo has _____more_____ appliances than this one.

4. Her house has the _____most_____ rooms.

G Complete the sentences with the correct word: *fewer, less, fewest,* or *least*.

1. John's house has _____fewer_____ bathrooms than Brad's place.

2. The small condo has _____less_____ light than the big one.

3. The small condo has the _____least_____ space.

Presentation 2   5-10 mins. ▪▪▫

Ask students questions about the ads on page 41. Use comparative and superlative forms: *Which rental is the biggest? Which rental is the cheapest? Which rental is more expensive—#3 or #7?* Review comparative and superlative forms with students. Then ask them more questions, such as: *Which rental has the most bedrooms?* and *Which apartment has cheaper rent—#2 or #4?* Write the answers on the board in complete sentences. Use these sample sentences to explain the rules for using comparatives and superlatives with nouns.

D Discuss the following questions about the ads on page 41 with your partner.

E Here are more ways to make comparisons. Study the charts below.

Present the charts.

Teaching Tip

Presenting grammar

One way to present grammar that will allow students to figure out the rules for themselves is through dictation.

1. Have students close their books.
2. Dictate the sentence examples from the grammar chart. (See page 2, Teaching Tip: Dictation.)
3. Once you have all the corrected sentences written on the board, ask students to help you formulate the grammar rules.

Practice 2   10-15 mins. ▪▪

(Shorter classes can do the following two exercises for homework.)

F Complete the sentences with the correct word: *more* or *most*.

G Complete the sentences with the correct word: *fewer, less, fewest,* or *least*.

Evaluation 2   10-15 mins. ▪▪

Go over the answers as a class, asking volunteers to read the completed sentences out loud.

Refer students to *Stand Out 3 Grammar Challenge*, Unit 3, Challenge 1 for more practice with *more/fewer/less* and *most/fewest/least*.

Activity Bank

Lesson 1, Worksheet 3: Compare Homes

Instructor's Notes

Presentation 3 5-10 mins

Draw a large four-circle Venn diagram on the board.

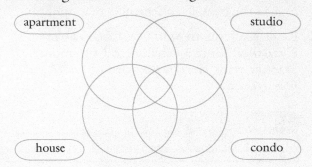

Ask students to help you come up with the similarities and differences between each of these housing types and fill in the diagram.

Teaching Tip

Graphic organizers

Graphic organizers, such as Venn diagrams, allow students to think critically. However, four-circle diagrams are rather complicated. Therefore, it is imperative that you create the diagram on the board so students can see how to complete it.

Practice 3   15-20 mins. ⬛

H **Work with a partner. Scan the ads above and ask and answer the questions below. Try to answer in complete sentences.**

Explain to students how to scan. Tell them they don't need to read every word in the ad to find the answer to the questions; they just need to look for the key words from the questions in the ads. For example, in the first item, the key words are *bedrooms*, *house*, and *condo*. Ask students to help you come up with the key words in the rest of the questions before they begin working with their partners.

Evaluation 3   5-10 mins. ⬛

Go over the answers as a class by calling on pairs to read the questions and answers.

Application   10-20 mins. ⬛⬛⬛

I **Write sentences comparing the places for rent.**

J **Active Task.** Search for classified ads for housing on the Internet. What abbreviations can you find? Tell the class. (Key words: housing ads *your city*)

Activity Bank

Lesson 1, Worksheet 1: Classified Ad Cards

On the Activity Bank CD-ROM, there is an additional worksheet where students will compare properties.

The worksheet contains classified-ad cards, each of which advertises a different rental property. Pass out a card to each student. Then have students compare the rental on their card with the one on a partner's card. Demonstrate by giving one student a card and asking: *How many bedrooms does your apartment have?* After receiving an answer, respond with a comparative sentence, such as: *My apartment is smaller than your apartment.* Encourage the same student to ask you a question and then make a comparative sentence in response to your answer. You may want to demonstrate the exchange with a few more students.

Note: Students have not yet learned information questions in this book. Since the objective of this activity is to make comparisons using comparative adjectives, the content of the questions is more important than the form.

GOAL ➤ **Interpret classified ads**

Vocabulary | Grammar
Life Skills
Academic | Pronunciation

FOR RENT

a.

Lge *apartment,*
1st floor, 2 bed, 1.5 bath,
gar, community spa,
sec dep $500, $975/month

c.

**BEAUTIFUL 3BR CONDO FOR RENT,
3 BATH, CARPORT FOR 2 CARS, LRG
PATIO, WOODS FLOORS, NR SHOPS,
SEC DEP $600, RENT $1,100/MO.**

Lge 5 BR, 2 bath *house,*
2 car gar, W/D hookups,
high ceilings, quiet nbhd.
sec dep $2,000, $2,000/mo. rent

Top fl bright studio,
balcony, new appl. Cat
OK, first, last, & sec. dep,
$550, $950 per month

b.

d.

H Work with a partner. *Scan* the ads above and ask and answer the questions below. Try to answer in complete sentences.

1. Which place has more bathrooms, the house or the condo?
   The condo has more bathrooms.
2. Which place has the most bedrooms?
   The house has the most bedrooms.
3. Which place has the highest rent?
   The house has the highest rent.
4. Which place has more bedrooms, the condo or the apartment?
   The condo has more bedrooms.
5. Which place has the lowest security deposit?
   The apartment has the lowest security deposit.

Scan: to quickly look for the answers in a text without reading everything

I Write sentences comparing the places for rent. (Answers will vary.)

EXAMPLES: The studio has fewer rooms than the house.

The house has the most bedrooms.

1. _____
2. _____
3. _____
4. _____
5. _____
6. _____

J **Active Task.** Search for classified ads for housing on the Internet. What abbreviations can you find? Tell the class. (Key words: housing ads *your city*)

Time to move

GOAL ➤ **Make decisions about housing**

Vocabulary — Grammar
Life Skills
Academic — Pronunciation

A **Read about the Nguyen family.**

The Nguyen family lives in Cedarville, Texas. Vu Nguyen came from Vietnam twenty years ago and met his wife, Maryanne, in Texas. The Nguyens have four children—two sons and two daughters. They are currently living in a two-bedroom apartment, which is too small for all six of them. They would like to stay in Cedarville, but they need a bigger place. Vu recently got a raise at work, so the Nguyen family wants to move.

CD 1
TR 7

B **Listen to the Nguyen family talk about their housing preferences. Check the boxes next to the things they would like to have in their new apartment.**

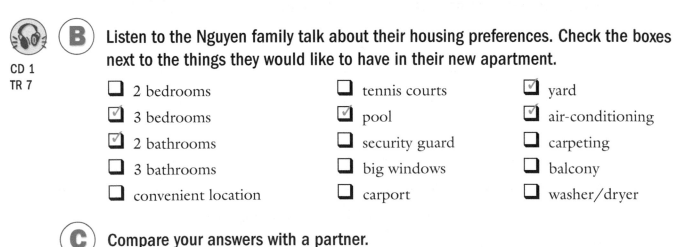

☐ 2 bedrooms	☐ tennis courts	☑ yard
☑ 3 bedrooms	☑ pool	☑ air-conditioning
☑ 2 bathrooms	☐ security guard	☐ carpeting
☐ 3 bathrooms	☐ big windows	☐ balcony
☐ convenient location	☐ carport	☐ washer/dryer

C **Compare your answers with a partner.**

AT-A-GLANCE PREP

Objective: Make decisions about housing
Grammar: Yes/No questions and answers
Pronunciation: Rising intonation
Academic Strategies: Active reading, focused listening
Vocabulary: *preferences, yard, pool, air-conditioning, garage, heating, tennis courts, carpeting*

RESOURCES

Activity Bank: Lesson 2, Worksheet 1
Reading and Writing Challenge: Unit 3

Grammar Challenge 3: Unit 3, Challenge 2
Audio: CD 1, Track 7

 1.5 hour classes   ■ 2.5 hour classes   ■ 3+ hour classes

AGENDA

Write an ad.
Identify housing preferences.
Ask yes/no questions.
Use rising intonation.
Talk about your housing preferences.

Warm-up and Review   10-15 mins.

Review Lesson 1 by having students write a classified ad for the place they live using the target abbreviations. Then have them share their ads with a partner.

Introduction   5-10 mins. ■■■

Ask students how many bedrooms they have in the place where they live. Ask them if they have a pool or tennis courts. Ask them about air-conditioning. Allow them to call out their answers. After a few questions, write *Housing Preferences* on the board. Explain this term. State the objective: *Today we will be making decisions about housing.*

Presentation 1   10-15 mins. ■■□

(A) Read about the Nguyen family.

Have students open their books and ask them some questions about the picture: *Where do you think this family is from? How many people are in the family? Where do you think they live?* Ask students to follow along as you read the paragraph out loud. When you have finished, ask some comprehension questions. Then have them read the paragraph one more time, silently.

Practice 1   10-15 mins.

(B) Listen to the Nguyen family talk about their housing preferences. Check the boxes next to the things they would like to have in their new apartment.

🎧 Listening Script   CD 1, Track 7

Maryanne: *I think it's time to move. This apartment is too small.*
Vu: *I'm making more money now. I think we can afford a bigger place.*
Truyen: *All right! Now I can have my own room.*
Maryanne: *Not so fast. We are not that rich, but it is hard with all four of you sharing one room. We need one bedroom for the girls and one for the boys.*
Vu: *Yes. A three-bedroom would be perfect.*
Truyen: *I want two bathrooms. Nga and Truc take hours to do their hair!*
Maryanne: *We don't have air-conditioning. I want air-conditioning in the new place.*
Vu: *Air-conditioning would be really nice. It gets so hot in the summer.*
Truyen: *Can we get a pool, too?*
Vu: *Well, we don't really need a pool. (Pause) Well, let's try to find a place that has one.*
Truyen: *Don't forget we need a yard for the dog. We don't have one now.*
Maryanne: *Of course, we want a nice space for Fluffy.*
Vu: *Let's get the paper and start looking for a place today!*

Evaluation 1   5 mins.

(C) Compare your answers with a partner.

Go over the answers to Exercise B as a class. Explain any other preferences on the list that students might not understand.

STANDARDS CORRELATIONS

CASAS: 1.4.2, 7.2.7 (See CASAS Competency List on pages 169–175.)
SCANS: Information Acquire and evaluate information, organize and maintain information, interpret and communicate information
Interpersonal Participate as a member of a team, teach others, work with cultural diversity
Basic Skills Reading, writing, listening, speaking
Thinking Skills Decision making

Personal Qualities Sociability
EFF: Communication Reading with understanding, speak so others can understand, listen actively
Decision Making Solve problems and made decisions, plan
Interpersonal Cooperate with others
Lifelong Learning Reflect and evaluate

Presentation 2   10-15 mins. ■■■

D Study the chart with your classmates and teacher.

Present *yes/no* questions and answers with *do/does* and *don't/doesn't*.

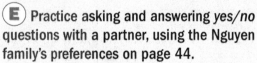

Pronunciation

Rising intonation

Ask students some *yes/no* questions) and ask them if your voice goes up or down at the end of each one. Students should be able to recognize the *rising intonation* in your voice. Explain that this rising intonation helps the listener know that you are asking a *yes/no* question that requires an answer.

Read the examples in the box in the student book, emphasizing rising intonation as you do so. Have students repeat after you as a class and then call on individuals to demonstrate rising intonation as they read the questions by themselves.

Practice 2   5-15 mins. ■■

E Practice asking and answering *yes/no* questions with a partner, using the Nguyen family's preferences on page 44.

Go over the example with students. Encourage them to practice rising intonation.

Teaching Tip

Modeling

Before students practice a question/answer exchange in pairs, it is a good idea to model it in a few different ways until they understand what to do.

1. Read the example.
2. Ask only the question in the example and have the whole class respond.
3. Have the class ask you the question and you respond
4. Divide the class in half. Have one half ask the question and the other half respond.
5. Ask a volunteer to practice with you.
6. Ask two volunteers to demonstrate for the class.

F Write five *yes/no* questions you could ask the Nguyens.

G With a partner, practice asking your questions with rising intonation.

Evaluation 2   10-20 mins. ■■

Ask volunteers to write their questions on the board and go over them as a class. Ask for volunteers to read their questions out loud using rising intonation.

Refer students to *Stand Out 3 Grammar Challenge*, Unit 3, Challenge 2 for more explanation and practice with *yes/no* questions.

GOAL ➤ **Make decisions about housing**

D Study the chart with your classmates and teacher.

Yes/No Questions and Answers with Do				
Questions				Short answers
Do	Subject	Base verb	Example question	
do	I, you, we, they	have	Do they have a yard?	Yes, they do. / No, they don't.
does	he, she, it	want	Does she want air-conditioning?	Yes, she does. / No, she doesn't.

E Practice asking and answering *yes/no* questions with a partner, using the Nguyen family's preferences on page 44.

EXAMPLE: *Student A:* Do they want five bedrooms?
Student B: No, they don't.

Pronunciation

Yes/No Questions:
Rising Intonation

➤ Do they have a yard?

➤ Do you want five bedrooms?

➤ Does it have a balcony?

F Write five *yes/no* questions you could ask the Nguyens. (Answers will vary.)

EXAMPLE: Do you want a bathtub?

1. _____

2. _____

3. _____

4. _____

5. _____

G With a partner, practice asking your questions with rising intonation.

H Imagine you are going to buy or rent a new home. What kind of home do you want? Write the number of bedrooms and bathrooms you prefer. Then, check your preferences below. Add other preferences that are not on the list. (Answers will vary.)

Yes	No		Yes	No	
		_____ bedrooms	❑	❑	convenient location
		_____ bathrooms	❑	❑	garage
❑	❑	yard	❑	❑	carport
❑	❑	balcony	❑	❑	refrigerator
❑	❑	pool	❑	❑	_____
❑	❑	washer/dryer	❑	❑	_____
❑	❑	air-conditioning	❑	❑	_____

I Write five *yes/no* questions you can ask your partner about his or her housing preferences. Don't write the answers yet. (Answers will vary.)

EXAMPLE: <u>Do you want a balcony?</u> _____

1. _____

Answer: _____

2. _____

Answer: _____

3. _____

Answer: _____

4. _____

Answer: _____

5. _____

Answer: _____

J Practice asking your questions with a partner. Use good rising intonation! Fill in the answers in Exercise I.

EXAMPLE: *Student A:* Do you want a balcony?
                Student B: Yes, I do.

Presentation 3

5–10 mins. ■■□

Ask students what things they would include in a list of housing preferences if they were looking for a new place to live. List their ideas on the board.

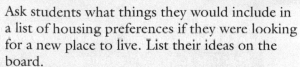 **Imagine you are going to buy or rent a new home. What kind of home do you want? Write the number of bedrooms and bathrooms you prefer. Then, check your preferences below. Add other preferences that are not on the list.**

Have students complete the checklist based on their personal preferences. When they have finished, call on individual students and ask them questions about what they prefer, such as: *(Angela), how many bedrooms do you want? (Jared), do you want a garage?*

Practice 3

5–10 mins. ■

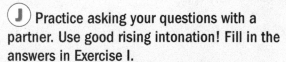 **Write five *yes/no* questions you can ask your partner about his or her housing preferences. Don't write the answers yet.**

Explain to students that they will be writing questions they want to ask their partners.

Evaluation 3

10–15 mins. ■

Ask volunteers to write their questions on the board. As a class, go over the grammar. Then have the whole class practice asking the questions with rising intonation.

Application

10–20 mins. ■■□

J Practice asking your questions with a partner. Use good rising intonation! Fill in the answers in Exercise I.

Go over the example with students, making sure they understand what to do. Walk around the classroom and help students as they complete the exercise. Encourage students to use good rising intonation!

Teaching Tip

Pairing students

Throughout the course, students will have many opportunities to work with partners. As a teacher, you can pair students in many ways based on the requirements of the activity; students' abilities and language level; or even the desire to build a stronger classroom community. Below are some suggestions for pairing students:

1. Let students choose who they would like to work with.
2. Have students work with the student sitting next to, in front of, or behind them.
3. Pair students with students who don't speak their native language.
4. Number the students—first half the class and then the other half—and have them find their matching number partner.

Activity Bank AB

Lesson 2, Worksheet 1: *Yes/No* Questions

Instructor's Notes

_____

_____

_____

_____

_____

_____

_____

_____

_____

_____

_____

AT-A-GLANCE PREP

Objective: Arrange and cancel utilities
Grammar: Information questions
Pronunciation: Falling intonation
Academic Strategy: Focused listening
Vocabulary: *utility, baseline, therms, arrange, cancel*

RESOURCES

Activity Bank: Lesson 3, Worksheets 1–2
Reading and Writing Challenge: Unit 3

Grammar Challenge 3: Unit 3, Challenge 3
Audio: CD 1, Tracks 8–9

 1.5 hour classes   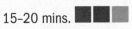 2.5 hour classes    3⁺ hour classes

AGENDA

Discuss utilities.
Interpret a gas bill.
Practice focused listening.
Identify information questions.
Arrange and cancel utilities.

Warm-up and Review   5 mins.

Review Lesson 2 by asking individual students about their housing preferences using *yes/no* questions.

Introduction   5-10 mins.

Write the word *utilities* on the board. Ask students if they know what this word means. Ask them to give you some examples of utilities. State the objective: *Today we will learn how to arrange and cancel utilities.*

Presentation 1   15-20 mins.

Have students open their books and look at the gas bill. Go over it with them, explaining all the parts and any new vocabulary they might not understand.

> **Therm:** a therm is 100,000 BTUs. It is a standard unit for measuring heat.
>
> **Baseline:** the amount of natural gas needed to meet the minimum basic needs of the average home. Gas companies are required to bill the baseline amount at their lowest residential rates. The goal is to encourage efficient use of natural gas.

Practice 1   10-15 mins.

A Discuss these questions with your classmates.

B Read the gas bill above and answer the questions below.

Evaluation 1   5 mins.

Go over the answers as a class.

Activity Bank

Lesson 3, Worksheet 2: Interpret a Gas Bill

STANDARDS CORRELATIONS

CASAS: 1.4.4, 1.5.3 (See CASAS Competency List on pages 169-175.)
SCANS: Information Acquire and evaluate information, organize and maintain information, interpret and communicate information
Interpersonal Participate as a member of a team, teach others, work with cultural diversity
Systems Monitor and correct performance
Basic Skills Reading, writing, arithmetic, listening, speaking

Thinking Skills Creative thinking, decision making
Personal Qualities Responsibility, sociability
EFF: Communication Reading with understanding, speak so others can understand, listen actively
Interpersonal Cooperate with others
Lifelong Learning Reflect and evaluate, learn through research, use information and communications technology (optional)

Paying the bills

GOAL ➤ **Arrange and cancel utilities**

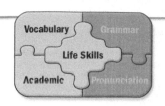

Vocabulary   Grammar
Life Skills
Academic   Pronunciation

A Discuss these questions with your classmates.

1. What are utilities? Utilities are extra costs for an apartment or house. Utilities include electricity, heat, gas, water, etc.

2. What utilities do you pay for? (Answers will vary.)

3. Does your landlord pay for any utilities? (Answers will vary.)

4. What information can you find on your (Answers will vary.) utility bills?

❈ S O U T H E R N   T E X A S   G A S ❈

P.O. Box D • Cedarville, TX 77014

Name Vu Nguyen
Service Address 3324 Maple Road, Cedarville, TX 77014
Account Number 891 007 1087 5   **Billing Period** 5/23/08-6/27/08

Readings: prev 4226   pres 4251

Summary of Charges

Customer Charge	33 days	x 0.16438=	5.42
Baseline	15 Therms	x0.65133=	9.77
Over Baseline	10 Therms	x0.82900=	8.29
Gas Charges			23.48
State Regulatory Fee	25 Therms	x0.00076=	.02
Taxes and Fees on Gas Charges			.02

Total Gas Charges Including Taxes and Fees	$23.50
Thank you for your payment Jun 06 2008	$27.65
Total Amount Due	**$23.50**

Current Amount Past Due if not paid by Jul 25, 2008
Next meter reading Jul 28, 2008

B Read the gas bill above and answer the questions below.

1. What is Vu's account number? 891 007 1087 5

2. How much is their gas bill this month? $23.50

3. How much did they pay last month? $27.65

4. Which bill was more expensive—this month's or last month's? last month's

5. Check the total amount of their bill. Is it correct? yes

6. When is the payment due? July 25, 2008

GOAL ➤ **Arrange and cancel utilities**

CD 1
TR 8

C Vu and his family are getting ready to move. Vu calls the electric company to speak to a customer service representative. Listen to the recording and write short answers for the following information.

1. Name of the company: Texas Electric

2. Name of the representative: Kristen

3. When Vu wants service turned off: Wednesday the 11th

4. When Vu wants service turned on: Monday the 9th

CD 1
TR 8

D Listen to the recording again and answer the questions.

1. The first voice is recorded and gives four choices. What are they?

   a. get new service or cancel existing service

   b. report a problem with service

   c. questions about billing

   d. all other questions

2. What information does Vu give to the gas company?

   a. his current address

   b. when he'd like the service turned off

   c. when he'd like the service turned on

   d. his new address

Pronunciation

Information Questions:
Rising and Falling Intonation

➤ What is your address?

➤ Where do you live?

➤ When will you be moving?

Presentation 2   10–15 mins.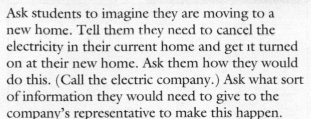

Ask students to imagine they are moving to a new home. Tell them they need to cancel the electricity in their current home and get it turned on at their new home. Ask them how they would do this. (Call the electric company.) Ask what sort of information they would need to give to the company's representative to make this happen.

Practice 2   5–10 mins.

Tell students they will be listening to Vu call the electric company to prepare for his family's move. Direct their attention to Exercise C and tell them they will be listening for four pieces of information.

Teaching Tip

Focused listening

The purpose of teaching focused listening is to help students learn how to understand the main ideas in a conversation even when they don't understand every word.

It's important to remind students that they will not understand every word each time they do a focused listening activity. Otherwise, they may become frustrated and stop listening all together. Preparing students for the listening activity will make them much more effective listeners.

1. Explain the context of the conversation.
2. Ask students what they think they might hear.
3. Show students specifically what they are listening for.

C Vu and his family are getting ready to move. Vu calls the electric company to speak to a customer service representative. Listen to the recording and write short answers for the following information.

 Listening Script   *CD 1, Track 8*

Recording: *Thank you for calling Texas Electric. Your call is very important to us. Please choose from the following options. For new service or to cancel your existing service, press 1. To report a problem with your service, press 2. If you have questions about your bill, press 3. For all other questions, press 4.*
(Vu presses 1.) Thank you. Just one moment.

Representative: *Hello, my name is Kristen. How may I help you?*
Vu: *Um, yes. My family is moving next week. We need to cancel our current service and get service in our new home.*
Representative: *What is your current address?*
Vu: *3324 Maple Road.*
Representative: *Are you Vu Nguyen?*
Vu: *Yes.*
Representative: *When would you like the service turned off?*
Vu: *Next Wednesday, please.*
Representative: *And what is your new address?*
Vu: *5829 Bay Road.*
Representative: *And when would you like the service turned on?*
Vu: *This Monday, please.*
Representative: *OK. Your current service will be turned off sometime between 8 and 12 on Wednesday the 11th. Your new service will be on before 9 on Monday morning the 9th. Is there anything else I can do for you?*
Vu: *No, that's it.*
Representative: *Thank you for calling Texas Electric. Have a nice day.*
Vu: *You, too.*

D Listen to the recording again and answer the questions.

Prepare students for the information they are to listen for.

Evaluation 2   5 mins.

Go over the answers with the class.

Pronunciation

Rising and falling intonation

Ask students a few information questions. Ask if your voice goes up or down at the end of each question. Students should be able to recognize the rising and falling intonation. Explain that this rising and falling intonation helps the listener know that you are asking a question that requires an answer.

Go over the examples in the box in the student book, emphasizing the intonation. Have students practice by repeating after you, first as a class and then individually.

Presentation 3   5–10 mins. ■■■

Go over the information questions in the chart and ask students how these questions are different from the *yes/no* questions they studied in the previous lesson. Point out that they start with information words (*who, what, why, when,* and *how*) as opposed to *do* or *does*.

Note: At this point, it is not important that students master the grammatical structure of information questions. It is more important that students recognize the difference between the two types of questions so they know how to answer them.

Practice 3   5–10 mins. ■

(E) Read the conversation as you listen to the recording. Underline the information questions.

 Listening Script   *CD 1, Track 9*

The listening script matches the conversation in Exercise E.

Evaluation 3   5–10 mins. ■

Have students share their answers with a partner. Then have them practice the conversation.

📖 Refer students to *Stand Out 3 Grammar Challenge*, Unit 3, Challenge 3 for more practice with information questions.

Application   15–25 mins. ■■■

(F) Imagine you are moving. Write down your current address and a new address. What date will you leave your old home? What date will you move to your new home? With a partner, practice Vu's conversation using your own information. Remember to practice rising and falling intonation!

(G) With a partner, discuss ways to reduce the cost of your electric bill. What can you do to save energy?

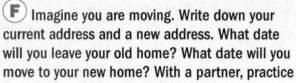

Activity Bank

Lesson 3, Worksheet 1: Arranging Utilities

Information Questions	
Question words	**Example questions**
How	*How* may I help you?
What	*What* is your current address?
When	*When* would you like your service turned off?

  E **Read the conversation as you listen to the recording. Underline the information questions.**

CD 1
TR 9

Recording: Thank you for calling Southern Texas Gas. Your call is very important to us. Please wait for the next available customer service representative.

Representative: Hello, my name is Liam. How may I help you?
Vu: Um, yes. My family is moving next week and we need to have our gas turned off here and get the gas turned on in our new home.
Representative: <u>What is your current address?</u>
Vu: 3324 Maple Road.
Representative: <u>What is your name sir?</u>
Vu: Vu Nguyen.
Representative: <u>When would you like the gas turned off?</u>
Vu: Next Thursday, please.
Representative: <u>And what is your new address?</u>
Vu: 5829 Bay Road.
Representative: <u>And when would you like the gas turned on in your new home?</u>
Vu: This Monday, please.
Representative: OK. Your current service will be turned off sometime between 7 and 9 A.M. on Thursday the 12th, and your new service will be on before 8 on Monday morning, the 9th. Is there anything else I can do for you?
Vu: No, that's it.
Representative: Thank you for calling Southern Texas Gas. Have a nice day.
Vu: Thanks. You, too.

 F **Imagine you are moving. Write down your current address and a new address. What date will you leave your old home? What date will you move to your new home? With a partner, practice Vu's conversation using your own information. Remember to practice rising and falling intonation!** (Answers will vary.)

 G **With a partner, discuss ways to reduce the cost of your electric bill. What can you do to save energy?** (Answers will vary.)

How much can we spend?

GOAL ➤ Make a budget

A What do you spend money on every month? Make a list. (Answers will vary.)

Monthly Expenses	
rent	

B Share your list with a partner. Add anything to your list that you forgot.

CD 1
TR 10

C Listen to Maryanne and Vu talk about their finances. Fill in the missing information.

INCOME

Vu's Salary	$3,000
Maryanne's Salary	$1,000
Total Income	$4,000

EXPENSES

Rent	$1,350
Utilities	
Electricity	$60
Gas	$40
Telephone	$65 (average)
Cable TV	$55
Internet	$45
Groceries	$450
Auto	
Gas and maintenance	$150
Car loan	$0
Total Expenses	$2,215

Math Practice

TOTAL means addition (+).

$$\begin{array}{r} \$5.00 \\ + \ \$7.00 \\ \hline \$12.00 \end{array} \qquad \begin{array}{r} \$47.00 \\ + \ \$36.00 \\ \hline \$83.00 \end{array}$$

$$\begin{array}{r} \$625.46 \\ + \ \$89.56 \\ \hline \$715.02 \end{array} \qquad \begin{array}{r} \$4,734.00 \\ + \ \$5,902.00 \\ \hline \$10,636.00 \end{array}$$

$$\begin{array}{r} \$3,500.00 \\ + \ \$2,250.00 \\ \hline \$5,750.00 \end{array}$$

Objective: Make a budget
Academic Strategies: Focused listening, reading a bar graph
Math: Budget arithmetic
Vocabulary: *budget, salary, total, average, addition, subtract, graph, maintenance*

RESOURCES

Activity Bank: Lesson 4, Worksheet 1
Reading and Writing Challenge: Unit 3

Grammar Challenge 3: Unit 3, Challenge 4
Audio: CD 1, Track 10

■ 1.5 hour classes ■ 2.5 hour classes ■ 3 hour classes

AGENDA

List monthly expenses.
Complete a budget.
Calculate a budget.
Make a bar graph.
Create a budget.

Warm-up and Review   10-15 mins. ■■■

Ask students if they have questions about utilities.

Introduction   5-10 mins. ■■■

(A) **What do you spend money on every month? Make a list.**

Have students make their lists by themselves.

(B) **Share your list with a partner. Add anything to your list that you forgot.**

When students have finished, make a class list on the board. Then write the word *budget* on the board. Ask students if they know what this term means. Ask about their experience with budgets. State the objective: *Today we will be making a budget.*

Presentation 1   10-15 mins. ■■■

Have students close their books. Play the conversation. Ask students what the couple is discussing. See if students can remember any details about the conversation.

Practice 1   10-15 mins. ■■■

(C) **Listen to Maryanne and Vu talk about their finances. Fill in the missing information.**

Have students open their books to page 50 and look at the couple's budget. Play the recording again. Have students listen for the information they need to complete the budget. Play the

recording as many times as necessary. When most of the students have all of the information, go over the budget as a class.

 Listening Script   *CD 1, Track 10*

Maryanne: *Now that you are making more money, I think we need to make a new budget.*
Vu: *OK, let's talk about income first. With the raise, my income will be $3,000 a month.*
Maryanne: *Great! And with my part-time job, I'm still making about $1,000 a month.*
Vu: *OK, that's it for income. The rent for our new apartment is going to be $1,350 a month. It's a bigger place so our utilities are going to go up.*
Maryanne: *Yeah, I was thinking our gas bill will probably be around $40 a month and our electricity will be about $60. Especially with that air-conditioning.*
Vu: *That sounds about right. What about the phone, cable, and Internet?*
Maryanne: *Well, if we use the same companies, they will be the same.*
Vu: *Is the phone bill really $65 a month?*
Maryanne: *Yes, it's an average. It includes long-distance calls to your mom in Vietnam.*
Vu: *I see. How much do you spend on groceries each month?*
Maryanne: *About $450. That shouldn't change. Um, what do we spend on the car?*
Vu: *Good news. We paid off the loan last month. Now the only expense is gas and maintenance.*
Maryanne: *Right. Let's budget $150 for that.*
Vu: *OK. Well, it looks like we've got some extra money. Let's talk about how we can use it.*

STANDARDS CORRELATIONS

CASAS: 1.5.1, 6.0.3, 6.0.5, 6.1.1, 6.1.2 (See CASAS Competency List on pages 169–175.)
SCANS: Resources Allocate money
Information Acquire and evaluate information, organize and maintain information, interpret and communicate information
Interpersonal Participate as a member of a team, teach others, exercise leadership, negotiate to arrive at a decision, work with cultural diversity
Systems Understand systems, monitor and correct performance, improve and design systems
Basic Skills Reading, writing, arithmetic, listening, speaking

Thinking Skills Creative thinking, decision making, problem solving, seeing things in the mind's eye
Personal Qualities Responsibility, sociability, self-management
EFF: Communication Speak so others can understand, listen actively
Decision Making Use math to solve problems and communicate, solve problems and make decisions, plan
Interpersonal Cooperate with others
Lifelong Learning Reflect and evaluate, learn through research, use information and communications technology (optional)

Addition

In order for students to complete their budgets, they must know how to add. Go over the examples in the math practice box on page 50 and help students find the totals of the addition problems.

Practice 1 *(continued)*

D Answer the following questions about the Nguyens' budget with a partner.

Evaluation 1   10-15 mins.

Go over the answers to Exercise D as a class. Make a list on the board of students' answers to items 4 and 5.

Presentation 2   5-10 mins.

Explain the bar graph to students, showing them how the Nguyens' budget information is represented. Ask students questions about the graph to make sure they understand it, such as: What does the first bar represent? How much did the Nguyens spend on electricity? What things are written at the bottom of the graph? What things are written on the left side of the graph?

Practice 2   10-15 mins.

E Look at the bar graph for the Nguyen family's expenses. Complete the graph with their expenses from page 50. For this exercise do not include rent.

F Now include on the graph the other items the Nguyen's should add to their budget and the budget amount of each.

Evaluation 2   10-15 mins.

Walk around the classroom and observe students.

D Answer the following questions about the Nguyens' budget with a partner.

1. What is their total income?

   $4,000

2. What are their total expenses?

   $2,215

3. How much extra cash do they have left after all the bills are paid? (*Hint:* Subtract total expenses from total income.)

   $1,785

4. In your opinion, what are some things they forgot to budget for?

   (Answers will vary.)

5. What do you think they should do with their extra money? (Answers will vary.)

E Look at the bar graph for the Nguyen family's expenses. Complete the graph with their expenses from page 50. For this exercise do not include rent.

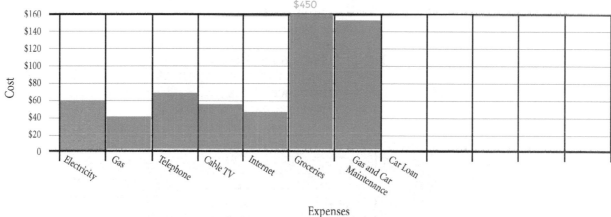

F Now include on the graph other items the Nguyen's should add to their budget and the budget amount for each.

G Work as a team to create a family budget. Use the following information: (Answers will vary)

➤ Your family has two adults and three children, ages two, five, and eight.

➤ You live in a four-bedroom house that you rent.

➤ Both adults have full-time jobs.

➤ You have two cars, one that you own (no payments) and the other that you lease.

Decide what your total household income is. Fill in the amounts that you would spend each month on expenses. Make a realistic budget based on your total income.

Monthly Budget	
_____ Salary	
_____ Salary	
_____ Total Income	
Expenses	
Rent	_____
Utilities	
Gas	_____
Telephone	_____
Cable TV	_____
Internet	_____
Food	
Groceries	_____
Dining out	_____
Entertainment	_____
Auto	
Gas and maintenance	_____
Car loan	_____
Insurance	_____
Registration	_____
Other	
_____	_____
_____	_____
_____	_____
Total Expenses	_____

H Prepare your own personal budget and make a bar graph.

Presentation 3   5-10 mins ▪▪▫

Set the stage for the practice activity by putting students into groups and presenting the following information from the student book to them:

1. You are a family with two adults and three children ages two, five, and eight.
2. You live in a four-bedroom house that you are renting.
3. Both adults in your household have full-time jobs.
4. You have two cars, one that you own (no payment) and the other that you are leasing.

Have each group decide what two jobs the adults have and how much each of them makes. Then have them decide how much per month they spend on the leased car.

Practice 3   15-20 mins. ▪

 Work as a team to create a family budget. Use the following information.

Walk around the classroom and help the teams as they work on their budgets.

Evaluation 3   10 mins. ▪

Ask for the groups to present their budgets to the class.

 Refer students to *Stand Out 3 Grammar Challenge*, Unit 3, Challenge 4 for practice with the past continuous.

Application   10-20 mins. ▪▪▫

 Prepare your own personal budget and make a bar graph.

> **Activity Bank** 💿
>
> Lesson 4, Worksheet 1: My Budget

Objective: Write a letter to a landlord
Grammar: Past continuous, past continuous with *while*
Academic Strategy: Writing a business letter
Vocabulary: *repairs, fix, repairperson, roaches, mouse, mice, electrician, plumber, exterminator*

AGENDA

Talk about household problems.
Identify repairpersons.
Use the past continuous with while.
Study the format of a business letter.
Write a letter to a landlord.

RESOURCES

Activity Bank: Lesson 5, Worksheets 1–2
Reading and Writing Challenge: Unit 3

Grammar Challenge 3: Unit 3, Challenge 5

 1.5 hour classes   2.5 hour classes   3⁺ hour classes

Warm-up and Review   5-10 mins.

Review the concept of budgets with students. Ask them why it is important to keep a monthly budget.

Introduction   5-10 mins.

Ask students what types of household repairs have to be done in their house or apartment. Ask them who does the repairs. Then ask them who pays for the repairs. State the objective: *Today we will learn how to write a letter to a landlord.*

Presentation 1   10-15 mins.

(A) Look at the pictures below. Do you ever have these problems in your home? Are you a do-it-yourself person or do you call someone?

Make sure students understand the four problems depicted in the pictures.

(B) Who can you call to fix each problem? Match the person with the problem.

Do this exercise as a class.

Preview the conversation in Exercise C with students. Practice it with a volunteer. Then ask two more volunteers to demonstrate the conversation.

Practice 1   10-15 mins.

(C) Practice the conversation with a partner. Then, practice with the situations Exercise A.

Have students use the examples in the pictures from Exercise A and then add two more problems they may themselves have run into.

Evaluation 1   10-15 mins.

Walk around the classroom. Help with vocabulary as needed.

STANDARDS CORRELATIONS

CASAS: 1.4.7 (See CASAS Competency List on pages 169–175.)
SCANS: Information Acquire and evaluate information, organize and maintain information, interpret and communicate information, use computers to process information (optional)
Interpersonal Participate as a member of a team, negotiate to arrive at a decision, work with cultural diversity
Systems Understand systems, monitor and correct performance
Technology Select technology, apply technology to a task, maintain and troubleshoot technology
Basic Skills Reading, writing, listening, speaking

Thinking Skills Creative thinking, decision making, problem solving, seeing things in the mind's eye
Personal Qualities Responsibility, sociability, self-management
EFF: Communication Speak so others can understand, listen actively, read with understanding, convey ideas in writing
Decision Making Solve problems and make decisions, plan
Interpersonal Cooperate with others
Lifelong Learning Reflect and evaluate, learn through research, use information and communications technology (optional)

Tenant rights

GOAL ➤ Write a letter to a landlord

 A Look at the pictures below. Do you ever have these problems in your home? Are you a do-it-yourself person or do you call someone?

a. The air conditioner isn't working.

c. There are roaches and mice in the kitchen.

b. The electricity went out.

d. The faucet is leaking.

 B Who can you call to fix each problem? Match the person with the problem.

1. __b__ electrician   3. __c__ exterminator
2. __a__ repairperson   4. __d__ plumber

 C Practice the conversation with a partner. Then, practice with the situations from Exercise A.

Tenant: Hello. This is <u>John</u> in Apartment 3B.
Landlord: Hi, <u>John</u>. What can I do for you?
Tenant: <u>The air-conditioning in our apartment isn't working</u>. (*State the problem.*)
Landlord: OK. I'll send <u>a repairperson over to fix it tomorrow</u>. (*State the solution.*)
Tenant: Thanks.

 **LESSON 5** **GOAL** ➤ **Write a letter to a landlord**

 D **Indira had a bad night in her apartment. Read about what happened.**

I had a terrible night. While I <u>was making</u> dinner, I saw a mouse. Then, the electricity went out while I <u>was studying</u>. It was dark, so I went to bed. But I couldn't sleep. The faucet <u>was dripping</u> all night. The neighbors <u>were shouting</u> and their dog <u>was barking</u>. Perhaps I should move!

E **Study the charts. Then, underline examples of the *past continuous* in the paragraph above.**

Past Continuous			
Subject	*be*	Verb + *ing*	Example sentence
I, he, she, it	was	making	I was making breakfast.
you, we, they	were	studying	She was taking a shower.
Use the past continuous to talk about things that started in the past and continued for a period of time.			

Past Continuous Using *While*			
Subject	*be*	Verb + *ing*	Example sentence
I, he, she, it	was	making	While I was making dinner, I saw a mouse.
you, we, they	were	studying	The electricity went out while we were studying.
To connect two events that happened in the past, use the past continuous with *while* for the longer event. Use the simple past for the shorter event.			
Note: You can reverse the two clauses, but you need a comma if the *while* clause comes first.			

F **Use *while* to combine the two sentences below. Read the sentences out loud.**

1. He was sleeping. The phone rang.

   <u>While he was sleeping, the phone rang.</u> OR <u>The phone rang while he was sleeping.</u>

2. Joshua was painting the cabinet. The shelf fell down.

   While Joshua was painting the cabinet, the shelf fell down. (or) The shelf fell down while Joshua was painting the cabinet.

3. I saw the crack in the wall. I was hanging a painting.

   While I was hanging a painting, I saw the crack in the wall. (or) I saw the crack in the wall while I was hanging a painting.

4. He was taking a shower. The water got cold.

   While he was taking a shower, the water got cold. (or) The water got cold while he was taking a shower.

5. The air-conditioning broke down. We were eating dinner.

   While we were eating dinner, the air-conditioning broke down. (or) The air-conditioning broke down while we were eating dinner.

Presentation 2   5–10 mins.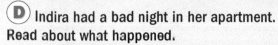

(D) Indira had a bad night in her apartment. Read about what happened.

Have students read the paragraph silently to themselves before you read it out loud to them. Ask them what four problems Indira had. Ask how they would have solved these problems.

(E) Study the charts. Then, underline examples of the *past continuous* in the paragraph above.

Explain that when one past event is interrupted by a more recent past event, we use the past continuous for the earlier, longer event and the simple past for the shorter, more recent event. Use the chart in the student book to explain the use of *while*.

Write example sentences from Indira's story labeling the parts *long* action *or short* action.

For example:

While I was making dinner, I saw a mouse.
      LONG   SHORT

Practice 2   15–20 mins.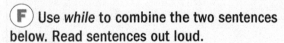

(F) Use *while* to combine the two sentences below. Read sentences out loud.

Have students work alone before they check their answers with a partner.

Refer students to *Stand Out 3 Grammar Challenge*, Unit 3, Challenge 5 for more practice using the past continuous tense with *while*.

Evaluation 2   10–20 mins.

Ask volunteers to read their combined sentences out loud. Evaluate them as a class.

Activity Bank

Lesson 5, Worksheet 1: Long Action/Short Action Cards

On the Activity Bank CD-ROM, there is a worksheet where students can practice creating sentences using the past continuous tense with *while*. The worksheet contains cards with longer and shorter events on them.

Distribute the cards with the long events on them to half the class and the cards with the short events to the other half. You will ask students to find their classmates who hold opposite cards. After students have found a match, they will create a combined sentence using the sentences from both cards. Demonstrate by borrowing a student's card and reading the sentence on it to the class. Ask if it is a long or short event. If is it a short event, say: *Then I need a long!* Find a student with a long card and create a combined sentence from the two cards.

Instructor's Notes

_____

_____

_____

_____

_____

_____

_____

_____

_____

_____

_____

_____

_____

_____

_____

_____

Presentation 3   5–10 mins. ■■□

Ask students what they would do if they had a problem with the place they were living that they couldn't fix themselves. Suggest the idea of writing a letter to their landlord or management company. Explain to them that although it might be easier to call their landlord or management company, having the problem in writing is a very good idea. In fact, it is a good idea to both call and write a letter.

(G) Vu Nguyen had a problem when his family first moved into their new apartment. Read the letter that he wrote to his landlord.

Have students read the letter to themselves and then ask them comprehension questions to make sure they understand it.

(H) What are the different parts of the letter? Discuss them with your teacher.

Practice 3   10–15 mins. ■

(I) Work with a partner to brainstorm problems you can have in an apartment. Write your ideas on a piece of paper and share them with the class.

Evaluation 3   10–15 mins. ■

As a class, make a list on the board of all the possible problems that can arise in a house or apartment.

Application   10–20 mins. ■■■

(J) Write a letter to your landlord about a problem that you had in the past or a current problem. Use Vu's letter as an example.

(K) Exchange letters with a partner. Check your partner's letter for grammar, spelling, and punctuation mistakes.

Optional Computer Activity: Have students type their letters on the computer. Show them how to use computer editor or a template.

Activity Bank

Lesson 5, Worksheet 2: Past Continuous with *While*

 Refer students to *Stand Out 3 Grammar Challenge*, Unit 3, Extension Challenges 1–2 for more practice with information questions and time clauses with *when* and *while*.

Instructor's Notes

_____

_____

_____

_____

_____

_____

_____

_____

_____

_____

_____

_____

_____

_____

_____

_____

_____

_____

_____

_____

G Vu Nguyen had a problem when his family first moved into their new apartment. Read the letter that he wrote to his landlord.

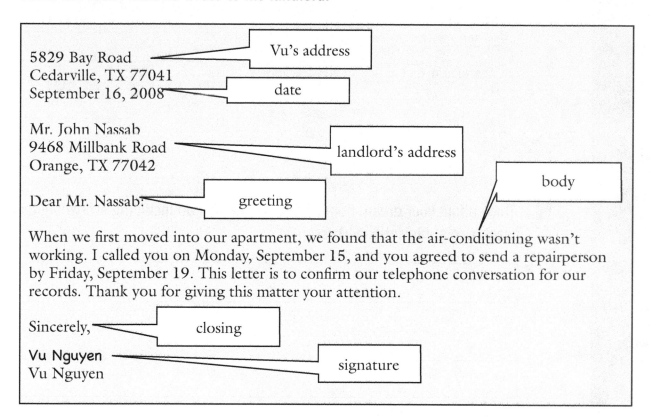

H What are the different parts of the letter? Discuss them with your teacher.

I Work with a partner to brainstorm problems you can have in an apartment. Write your ideas on a piece of paper and share them with the class. (Answers will vary.)

J Write a letter to your landlord about a problem that you had in the past or a current problem you are having. Use Vu's letter as an example. (Answers will vary.)

K Exchange letters with a partner. Check your partner's letter for grammar, spelling, and punctuation mistakes.

Review

A Read the classified ad. Rewrite the ad with the full form of the abbreviations. (Lesson 1)

3BR apt w/lg kitchen,
2 car gar, W/D, new
appl, **nr beach,**
$1,500/mo
+ $500 sec dep,
Avail 8/30

3-bedroom apartment with large kitchen,

2-car garage, washer/dryer, new appliances,

near beach, $1,500 per month plus $500

security deposit. Available August 30.

_____

_____

B Think about your dream home. Write a classified ad including everything that you would want. Use abbreviations. (Lesson 1)

(Answers will vary.)

C Complete the sentences with the correct word: *more* or *most* (+); or *fewer, less, fewest,* or *least* (−). (Lesson 1)

1. (+) Kim's house has _____**more**_____ entrances than Jen's house.

2. (+) The blue condo has _____more_____ bathrooms than the yellow one.

3. (+) Octavio's apartment gets the _____most_____ light.

4. (−) That condo has _____fewer_____ balconies than this one.

5. (−) Their house has the _____least_____ furniture.

6. (+) Andrew's place has _____more_____ rooms than Brad's place.

7. (−) The small apartment has _____less_____ patio space than the big one.

8. (+) The Jacksons' apartment has the _____most_____ appliances.

9. (+) That house has _____more_____ light than this one.

10. (−) His home has the _____fewest_____ bathrooms.

AGENDA
Discuss unit objectives.
Complete the review.
Do My Dictionary.
Evaluate and reflect on progress.

Objective: All unit objectives
Grammar: All unit grammar
Academic Strategy: Reviewing
Vocabulary: All unit vocabulary

RESOURCES

Activity Bank: Unit 3, Lesson 1–5,
Reading and Writing Challenge: Unit 3

Grammar Challenge 3: Unit 3, Challenges 1–5

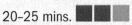 1.5 hour classes ■ 2.5 hour classes ■ 3⁺ hour classes

Warm-up and Review   5–10 mins.

Have students write two sentences that describe a past, present, or possible future problem pertaining to housing. Have them use *while* and the past continuous in their sentences. Tell them to memorize their sentences. Write the following conversation on the board:

Landlord: *What's the problem?*
Tenant: *First of all, ... Second of all, . . .*
Landlord: *I'll fix your . . . and . . . as soon as possible.*

Go through this conversation with students, showing them how to insert information from their own sentences. Demonstrate the activity with a volunteer. Have students practice this conversation with five other students, switching roles each time.

Introduction   5–10 mins.

Ask students as a class to try to recall the goals of this unit without looking at their books. Then remind them which goals they omitted, if any. (Unit goals: Interpret classified ads, make decisions about housing, arrange and cancel utilities, make a budget, and write a letter to a landlord.) Write the goals on the board. Show students the first page of the unit and mention the five objectives.

State the objective: *Today we will be reviewing everything you have learned in this unit.*

Presentation 1   10–15 mins.

This presentation will cover the first three pages of the review. Quickly go to the first page of each lesson. Discuss the objective of each. Ask simple questions to remind students of what they have learned.

Note: Since there is little presentation in the review, you can assign the review exercises for homework and go over them in class.

Practice 1   20–25 mins.

Note: There are two ways to do the review:
(1) Go through the exercises one at a time and, as students complete each one, go over the answers.
(2) Briefly go through the instructions of each exercise, allow students to complete all of the exercises at once, and then go over the answers.

A Read the classified ad. Rewrite the ad with the full form of the abbreviations. (Lesson 1)

B Think about your dream home. Write a classified including everything that you would want. Use abbreviations. (Lesson 1)

C Complete the sentences with the correct word: *more* or *most* (+); or *fewer, less, fewest,* or *least* (–). (Lesson 1)

Evaluation 1   20–25 mins.

Go around the classroom and check on students' progress. Help individuals as needed. If you see consistent errors among several students, interrupt the class and give a mini lesson or review to help students feel comfortable with the concept.

STANDARDS CORRELATIONS

CASAS: 7.2.1 (See CASAS Competency List on pages 169–175.)
SCANS: **Resources** Allocate time
Information Acquire and evaluate information
Interpersonal Participate as a member of a team, teach others, negotiate to arrive at a decision, work with cultural diversity
Systems Monitor and correct performance
Basic Skills Reading, writing, arithmetic, listening, speaking
Thinking Skills Creative thinking, decision making, problem solving, seeing things in the mind's eye
Personal Qualities Responsibility, sociability, self-management
EFF: **Communication** Convey ideas in writing, speak so others can understand, listen actively
Decision Making Solve problems and make decisions
Interpersonal Cooperate with others, guide others
Lifelong Learning Take responsibility for learning, reflect and evaluate, learn through research

Practice 1 (continued)   25-30 mins. ■■■□

D Write five *yes/no* questions to ask your partner about his or her dream home. Then, ask your partner the questions and write the answers. (Lesson 2)

E Now look at the ad for your dream home that you wrote in Exercise B and the answers you just got from your partner. Write four sentences comparing the two dream homes. (Lesson 1)

F Imagine you are moving to a new city. What utilities will you have to call and order? Write them below. With a partner, role-play a phone conversation with a customer service representative. (Lesson 3)

Evaluation 1 (continued)   25-30 mins. ■■■□

Go around the classroom and check on students' progress. Help individuals as needed. If you see consistent errors among several students, interrupt the class and give a mini lesson or review to help students feel comfortable with the concept.

Teaching Tip

Recycling/Review

The review process and the project that follows are part of the recycling/review process. Students at this level often need to be reintroduced to concepts to solidify what they have learned. Many concepts are learned and forgotten while learning other new concepts. This is because students learn but are not necessarily ready to acquire language concepts.

Therefore, it becomes very important to review and to show students how to review on their own. It is also important to recycle the new concepts in different contexts.

Instructor's Notes

D Write five *yes/no* questions to ask your partner about his or her dream home. Then, ask your partner the questions and write the answers. (Lesson 2) (Answers will vary.)

EXAMPLE: Q: <u>Do you want four bedrooms?</u>   A: <u>No, I don't.</u>

1. Q: _____   A: _____

2. Q: _____   A: _____

3. Q: _____   A: _____

4. Q: _____   A: _____

5. Q: _____   A: _____

E Now look at the ad for your dream home that you wrote in Exercise B and the answers you just got from your partner. Write four sentences comparing the two dream homes. (Lesson 1) (Answers will vary.)

EXAMPLE: <u>My partner's dream home has fewer bedrooms than my dream home.</u>

1. _____

_____

2. _____

_____

3. _____

_____

4. _____

_____

F Imagine you are moving to a new city. What utilities will you have to call and order? Write them below. With a partner, role-play a phone conversation with a customer service representative. (Lesson 3) (Answers will vary.)

_____gas_____   _____phone_____

_____electric_____   _____water_____

_____heat_____   _____cable_____

Review

G Think about your monthly expenses and complete the budget below. (Lesson 4)

(Answers will vary.)

_____	Salary
_____	Salary
_____	Total Income

Expenses

Rent	_____
Utitilites	_____
Gas	_____
Telephone	_____
Cable TV	_____
Internet	_____
Other	_____
Groceries	_____
Dining Out	_____
Entertainment	_____
Auto	
Gas and maintenance	_____
Car loan	_____
Insurance	_____
Registration	_____
Total Expenses	_____

H Use the simple past or the past continuous to complete the sentences. (Lesson 5)

1. The light _____**went out**_____ (go out) while Maryanne

   _____**was taking**_____ (take) a shower.

2. A spider _____**dropped**_____ (drop) onto my arm while I

   _____**was eating**_____ (eat) dinner.

3. While Marie _____**was studying**_____ (study), the landlord

   _____**called**_____ (call).

4. While Terry _____**was cleaning**_____ (clean) the window, he

   _____**hurt**_____ (hurt) his back.

5. Someone _____**broke**_____ (break) into their house

   while they _____**were visiting**_____ (visit) friends.

I Think of some problems you have had with the place that you are living in. On a piece of paper, use one of your ideas to write a letter to your landlord. (Lesson 5)

(Answers will vary.)

Practice 1 *(continued)*   25–30 mins. ■■■

(G) Think about your monthly expenses and complete the budget below. (Lesson 4)

(H) Use the simple past or the past continuous to complete these sentences. (Lesson 5)

(I) Think of some problems you have had with the place that you are living in. On a piece of paper, use one of your ideas to write a letter to your landlord. (Lesson 5)

Evaluation 1 *(continued)*   25–30 mins. ■■■

Go around the classroom and check on students' progress. Help individuals as needed. If you see consistent errors among several students, interrupt the class and give a mini lesson or review to help students feel comfortable with the concept.

Presentation 2   5-10 mins.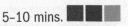

My Dictionary

Ask students to brainstorm new vocabulary items they learned in this unit. Have them do this without looking in their books.

Practice 2   15-20 mins.

Study with a partner.

Explain to students how to do this vocabulary activity and demonstrate the conversation with a few students.

Evaluation 2   5-10 mins.

Walk around the classroom and help students.

Presentation 3   5-10 mins.

Learner Log

In this unit, you learned many things about housing. How comfortable do you feel doing each of the skills listed below? Rate your comfort level on a scale of 1 to 4.

Go over the instructions with students and make sure they understand what to do. You may want to do the first one or two with the class to make sure they understand.

Teaching Tip

Learner Logs

Learner logs function to help students in many different ways:

1. They serve as part of the review process.
2. They help students to gain confidence and document what they have learned. Consequently, students see that they are making progress and want to move forward in learning.
3. They provide students with a tool that they can use over and over to check and recheck their understanding. In this way, students become independent learners.

Practice 3   5-10 mins.

Have students complete the Learner Log.

Evaluation 3   5-10 mins.

Walk around the classroom and help students.

Application   5-10 mins. ■■■

Go over the two reflection questions with students and have them complete the answers by themselves.

ᵀᴮ Assessment   ■■■

Use the Stand Out 3 Assessment CD-ROM with Exam*View*® to create a post-test for Unit 3.

My Dictionary

Study with a partner.

1. Go back through the unit. Highlight ten new words that you want to study.
2. Write each word on a 3-by-5 index card or on a small piece of paper.
3. Work in pairs. Your partner chooses one card and asks questions to help you guess the word on the card.
4. Switch roles and continue until all the words have been reviewed.

EXAMPLE: *Student A:* Who collects the rent? OR Who owns your apartment?
Student B: Tenant?
Student A: No, try again.
Student B: Landlord?
Student A: That's right.

Learner Log

In this unit, you learned many things about housing. How comfortable do you feel doing each of the skills listed below? Rate your comfort level on a scale of 1 to 4.

1 = Need more practice   **2** = OK   **3** = Good   **4** = Great!

Life Skill	Comfort Level				Page
I can interpret classified ads.	1	2	3	4	41
I can make decisions about housing.	1	2	3	4	44
I can arrange and cancel utilities.	1	2	3	4	47
I can interpret utility bills.	1	2	3	4	47
I can budget household expenses.	1	2	3	4	50
I can write a letter to a landlord.	1	2	3	4	53

If you circled 1 or 2, write down the page number where you can review this skill.

Reflection
1. What was the most useful skill you learned in this unit? _____

_____

2. How will this help you in life? _____

Create a housing plan.

With a team, you will create a housing plan, including a budget and classified ad of where you will live.

1. Form a team with four or five students. You are now a family. Choose positions for each member of your team.

POSITION	JOB DESCRIPTION	STUDENT NAME
Student 1: Leader	See that everyone speaks English. See that everyone participates.	
Student 2: Secretary	Write the classified ad.	
Student 3: Financial Planner	Create the budget.	
Students 4/5: Family Representatives	Plan a presentation of your housing plan.	

2. Think about your family's needs. Create your family budget. (Lesson 4)

3. Think of a place that will be perfect for your family. Create your classified ad. (Lessons 1–2)

4. Make a list of all the utilities you will need to arrange for. (Lesson 3)

5. Create a poster with artwork. Include your budget, classified ad, and list of utilities.

6. Present your poster to the class.

Create a housing plan.

With a team, you will create a housing plan, including a budget and classified ad of where you will live.

The team project is the final application for the unit. It gives students a chance to show that they have mastered all of the Unit 3 goals.

Note: Shorter classes can extend this project over two class meetings.

Stage 1   5 mins.

Form a team with four or five students. You are now a family. Choose positions for each member of your team.

Have students decide who will lead each step as described on the student page. Provide well-defined directions on the board for how teams should proceed. Explain that all the students do every step as a team. Teams shouldn't go to the next stage until the previous one is complete.

Stage 2   15–20 mins.

Think about your family's needs. Create your family budget. (Lesson 4)

Stage 3   10–15 mins.

Think of a place that will be perfect for your family. Create your classified ad. (Lessons 1–2)

Stage 4   5–10 mins.

Make a list of all the utilities you will need to arrange for. (Lesson 3)

Stage 5   25–30 mins.

Create a poster with artwork. Include your budget, classified ad, and list of utilities.

Stage 6   15–20 mins.

Present your poster to the class.

Help teams prepare for their presentations. Suggest that each member chooses a different part of the poster to present.

STANDARDS CORRELATIONS

CASAS: 4.8.1, 4.8.5, 4.8.6 (See CASAS Competency List on pages 169–175.)
SCANS: **Resources** Allocate time
Information Acquire and evaluate information, organize and maintain information, interpret and communicate information, use computers to process information
Systems Understand systems, improve and design systems
Technology Select technology, apply technology to exercise
Basic Skills Writing
Thinking Skills Creative thinking, decision making, problem solving, seeing things in the mind's eye, reasoning

Personal Qualities Responsibility, self-esteem, self-management, integrity/honesty
EFF: **Communication** Convey ideas in writing, speak so others can understand
Decision Making Solve problems and make decisions, plan
Interpersonal Guide others, resolve conflict and negotiate, advocate and influence, cooperate with others
Lifelong Learning Take responsibility for learning, reflect and evaluate, use information and communication technologies (optional)

Objective: Ask for information
Grammar: Information questions
Pronunciation: Rising and falling intonation
Academic Strategy: Focused listening
Vocabulary: *DMV, checking account, car registration, class registration*

AGENDA

Identify things to do.
Ask and answer information questions.
Use rising and falling intonation.
Write questions.
Complete information conversations.
Make a to-do list.

RESOURCES

Activity Bank: Lesson 1, Worksheet 1
Reading and Writing Challenge: Unit 4

■ 1.5 hour classes ■ 2.5 hour classes ■ 3⁺ hour classes

Grammar Challenge 3: Unit 4, Challenge 1
Audio: CD 1, Track 11
Stand Out 3 Assessment CD-ROM with Exam*View*®

 Preassessment *(optional)*

Use the Stand Out 3 Assessment CD-ROM with Exam*View*® to create a pretest for Unit 4.

Warm-up and Review 5-10 mins.

Write *community resources* on the board. Ask students what it means. Go over some examples with them.

Introduction 1 min.

State the objective: *Today we will ask for information using information questions.*

Presentation 1 10-15 mins.

Ask students to look at the picture and discuss what Gloria is doing. Then, ask them to close their books, take out a piece of paper, and number it 1–6. Tell them to listen for the tasks Gloria needs to do. Play the recording. Have them write down the six tasks. Play the recording several times, pausing as necessary. After students have written down the six tasks, have them open their books and compare their lists to Gloria's to-do list.

Practice 1 10-15 mins.

Ⓐ **Gloria and her family are new to the community. Read her list of things to do. Where does Gloria need to go for each one? Listen and write the names of the places below.**

Have students work in pairs to fill in Gloria's list after they listen to the recording again.

 Listening Script CD 1, Track 11

Gloria is new to the community. First of all, she needs to go to a bank to open a checking account so she can pay her bills. Second, she needs to go the Department of Motor Vehicles to register her car and renew her driver's license. For now, she will need to use public transportation, but she doesn't know where to get a bus schedule. She'll have to ask at the bus station. Also, she would like to take some ESL classes to improve her English. There is a community college nearby; maybe she could try there. Her children would like to play sports so she needs to find a place for them to do that. Perhaps she can call the Department of Parks and Recreation. Also, the kids want to use computers to e-mail their friends from the old neighborhood. They'll probably have the Internet at the public library.

Ⓑ **Practice the conversation with a partner, using the information from Exercise A.**

Go over the conversation as a class and show students how to substitute information. Then have students practice on their own.

Evaluation 1 5 mins. ■■■

Observe the activity. Ask volunteers to demonstrate the conversation for the class.

STANDARDS CORRELATIONS

CASAS: 0.1.2 (See CASAS Competency List on page pages 169–175.)
SCANS: Information Acquire and evaluate information, organize and maintain information, interpret and communicate information
Interpersonal Participate as a member of a team, teach others, work with cultural diversity
Systems Monitor and correct performance

Basic Skills Reading, writing, arithmetic, listening, speaking
Thinking Skills Creative thinking, decision making, problem solving
EFF: Communication Speak so others can understand, listen actively
Interpersonal Cooperate with others
Lifelong Learning Reflect and evaluate

Our Community

GOALS

> Ask for information
> Interpret charts and compare information

> Interpret a road map
> Identify daily activities
> Write about a place

LESSON 1

Places in your community

GOAL > Ask for information

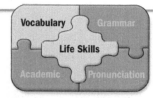

Vocabulary — Grammar — Life Skills — Academic — Pronunciation

CD 1
TR 11

A Gloria and her family are new to the community. Read her list of things to do. Where does Gloria need to go for each one? Listen and write the names of the places below.

Things to Do

1. Find a place for my children to play sports _Department of Parks and Recreation_

2. Register for an ESL class _community college_

3. Open a checking account _bank_

4. Register my car and get a new license _Department of Motor Vehicles_

5. Find a place for my children to use computers _public library_

6. Pick up some bus schedules _bus station_

B Practice the conversation with a partner, using the information from Exercise A.

EXAMPLE: *Student A:* Where can I get a new driver's license?
Student B: At the DMV.

DMV = Department of Motor Vehicles

C Study the chart.

Information Questions		
Location	Where	is the bank?
	How far	is the school from here?
	What	is the address?
Time	When	does the library open?
	What time	does the restaurant close?
	How often	do the buses run?
Cost	How much	does it cost?

D Match the questions you could ask when calling a local business with the correct answers.

Questions

_g_ 1. How often do the buses run?

_f_ 2. Where is your restaurant?

_h_ 3. How much does it cost?

_e_ 4. What is your address?

_c_ 5. What time do you close?

_b_ 6. How far is the store from here?

_a_ 7. When do you open?

_d_ 8. What time do you close on Sunday?

Answers

a. We open at 10 A.M.

b. Our store is about five miles away.

c. We close at 10 P.M.

d. We're open from 10 to 6 on Sunday.

e. We are located at 71 South Pine Ave.

f. We're on the corner of 7th and Pine.

g. They run every 20 minutes.

h. It costs $50 to service your computer.

E Practice asking and answering the questions above with a partner. Remember to use rising and falling intonation.

Pronunciation

Information Questions:
Rising and Falling Intonation

➤ What time does the bank open?

➤ How much does it cost?

➤ What is the address?

Presentation 2   5-10 mins. ■■■

C) Study the chart.

Present the basic formation of information questions to students. Ask them to help you think of questions that aren't in the chart. Write students' ideas on the board.

Teaching Tip

Presenting grammar

You will often present students with an aspect of grammar; however, you will not present all of the rules associated with that aspect. For many students, it can be overwhelming to be presented with too much information at once. In many cases, students only need the basics to complete the task at hand. The information presented to students in the Student Book is enough for them to complete the assigned tasks. They will get additional practice and rules on the Activity Bank CD-ROM and in *Stand Out 3 Grammar Challenge*.

In this lesson, students will have practice asking and answering information questions, an aspect they were exposed to in Unit 3. Point out that certain verbs are used with certain types of information. For example, *to be* is often used in questions pertaining to location.

Practice 2   10-15 mins. ■■

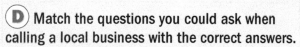

D) Match the questions you could ask when calling a local business with the correct answers.

Go over the directions with students and do the first item as a class.

E) Practice asking and answering the questions above with a partner. Remember to use rising and falling intonation.

Evaluation 2   10-15 mins. ■■

Go over the answers to Exercise D as a class. Walk around the classroom and listen to students practicing their intonation. When students have finished, ask for volunteers to ask and answer the questions for the class, emphasizing intonation as they do so.

Presentation 3   5-10 mins.

Practice 3   15-20 mins. ▪

F Help Gloria think of questions she needs to ask when she calls local businesses. Write questions to match the answers below.

When students have finished, have them compare their answers with a partner. If they get ideas for additional questions from their partner, tell them to write them down. Select a few students to write their information questions on the board. Go over them as a class.

Evaluation 3   5-10 mins. ▪

Have students walk around the classroom and practice asking the questions they wrote. Have them only ask one question per classmate so that they will talk to at least seven classmates.

 Refer students to *Stand Out 3 Grammar Challenge,* Unit 4, Challenge 1 for more practice with information questions.

Application   10-20 mins. ▪▪▪

G Complete the conversations below with a logical question or answer. When you are finished, practice the conversations with a partner.

Ask volunteers to practice their conversations for the class.

H On a piece of paper, make your own to-do list like the one Gloria made on page 61. Next to each item, write the place where you can go in your community to get the task done. Also, write some questions to ask. Look at the example below.

Have volunteers write their questions on the board. Then have students practice asking one another the questions they wrote about community resources.

Activity Bank

Lesson 1, Worksheet 1: Information Questions

GOAL ➤ Ask for information

 Help Gloria think of questions she needs to ask when she calls local businesses. Write questions to match the answers below.

1. What time does the bank open?   The bank opens at 9:00 A.M.

2. How much does a driver's license cost?   A driver's license costs $25.

3. How far is the library from here?   The library is about a mile from here.

4. How often does the train run?   The trains run every ten minutes.

5. When can you return books?   You can return books anytime.

6. Where is the DMV?   The DMV is at 112 Main Street.

7. Where is the children's book section?   The children's book section is upstairs.

 Complete the conversations below with a logical question or answer. When you are finished, practice the conversations with a partner.

Conversation 1
A: Good morning. This is Food Mart.

B: When do you open?
A: We're open now.
B: Great! Thank you.

Conversation 2
A: Thank you for calling The Book Stop. How can I help you?

B: What is your address?
A: 4635 Broadway.
B: And when do you close?

A: (Answers will vary.)
B: Thanks!

 On a piece of paper, make your own to-do list like the one Gloria made on page 61. Next to each item, write the place where you can go in your community to get the task done. Also, write some questions to ask. Look at the example below.
(Answers will vary.)

To Do	Place	Question
get information about ESL classes	an adult-education center	When do classes start? Where is the school?

The bank, the library, and the DMV

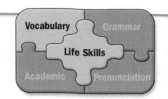

GOAL ➤ Interpret charts and compare information

A Write the places.

1. open an account _____bank_____

4. get a driver's license _____DMV_____

2. register your car _____DMV_____

5. make a deposit _____bank_____

3. check out books _____library_____

6. use a computer _____library_____

B What is the name of your bank? What kind of bank account do you have? Discuss the following words with your classmates and teacher. (Answers will vary.)

service fee	direct deposit	unlimited check writing	ATM
transactions	minimum balance	teller	

C Riverview Bank offers three kinds of checking accounts. Read the brochure below.

RIVERVIEW BANK	Premiere	Express	Standard
Service Fee with direct deposit	$22	$0	$8
without direct deposit	$20	$7	$10
Check Writing	unlimited	20 per month	unlimited
ATM Transactions	unlimited	unlimited	unlimited
Teller Transactions	unlimited	$2 for each transaction	$4 fee per month
Other Information	no service fee if account balance is over $10,000	no minimum balance	no minimum balance

D With a partner, practice asking questions about the bank brochure above.
(Answers will vary.)

1. What is the service fee without direct deposit for the _____ account?

2. How many checks can you write per month with the _____ account?

3. How many ATM transactions can you have per month with the _____ account?

Objective: Interpret charts and compare information
Academic Strategies: Making inferences, reading charts
Vocabulary: *service fee, direct deposit, check writing, transactions, minimum balance, ATM, teller, unlimited, circulation, reference, librarian, check out, borrow, loan, fine, overdue, loss, public library, branch, main, commercial, valid, permit, disabled, renewal, replacement*

AGENDA
Talk about bank services.
Talk about library services.
Talk about DMV services.
Create a school brochure.

RESOURCES

Activity Bank: Lesson 2, Worksheets 1–2
Reading and Writing Challenge: Unit 4

Grammar Challenge 3: Unit 4, Challenge 2

■ 1.5 hour classes　■ 2.5 hour classes　■ 3· hour classes

Warm-up and Review　5–10 mins. ■■■

Review Lesson 1 by calling out the name of a place and asking a volunteer to come up with a question to ask about it. For example:

> **Teacher:** post office
> **Student:** What time does it open?

Introduction　5–10 mins. ■■■

Write *bank, DMV,* and *library* on the board. Ask students what they can do at each of these places. State the objective: *In this lesson, we will interpret charts and compare information.*

 Write the places.

Do this exercise as a class. Then have students write the answers in their books.

Presentation 1　10–15 mins. ■■■

 What is the name of your bank? What kind of bank account do you have? Discuss the following words with your classmates and teacher.

Have students open their books and discuss the words in the box. Ask volunteers to give you an example or definition of each term.

 **Riverview Bank offers three kinds of checking accounts. Read the brochure below.**

Go over the information with students. Ask them questions to make sure they understand, such as: *What is the service fee for the Express account if you have direct deposit? How many checks can you write with the Standard account?*

Practice 1　10–15 mins. ■■■

 With a partner, practice asking questions about the bank brochure above.

Go over the example with students before they begin working with their partners.

Evaluation 1　5 mins. ■■■

Observe students as they practice.

 Activity Bank

> Lesson 2, Worksheet 1: Automated Bank Information

STANDARDS CORRELATIONS

CASAS: 1.8.5, 2.5.6 (See CASAS Competency List on pages 169–175.)
SCANS: **Information** Acquire and evaluate information, organize and maintain information, interpret and communicate information
Interpersonal Participate as a member of a team, teach others, negotiate to arrive at a decision, work with cultural diversity
Systems Understand systems, monitor and correct performance
Basic Skills Reading, writing, arithmetic, listening, speaking
Thinking Skills Decision making, seeing things in the mind's eye

Personal Qualities Responsibility, sociability, self-management
EFF: **Communication** Read with understanding, speak so others can understand, listen actively
Decision Making Solve problems and make decisions
Interpersonal Cooperate with others
Lifelong Learning Reflect and evaluate, learn through research, use information and communication technology (optional)

Presentation 2

Ask students the following questions: *Do you like to go to your public library? What can you do at a library?* Have students turn to page 65 and look at the bold headings on the brochure. Ask them what sort of information they might find in this brochure.

E Read the following brochure about library services. You may not understand every word or phrase, but see if you can get the general idea.

Ask students not to use dictionaries for words they don't understand. Have them read the brochure more than once if they need to.

Practice 2

5–15 mins.

F Decide if these statements are true or false based on the information in the library brochure. Fill in the circle. Then, change each false statement and make it true.

Explain the difference between *true* and *false*. Remind students that when they answer true or false questions, their answer should be based on what they have read or heard, not on what they think is true or false. Go over the example in Exercise F, showing them how to make a false statement true.

Evaluation 2

10–20 mins.

Go over the answers as a class.

Activity Bank

Lesson 2, Worksheet 2: The Library

LESSON 2

GOAL ➤ Interpret charts and compare information

E Read the following brochure about library services. You may not understand every word or phrase, but see if you can get the general idea.

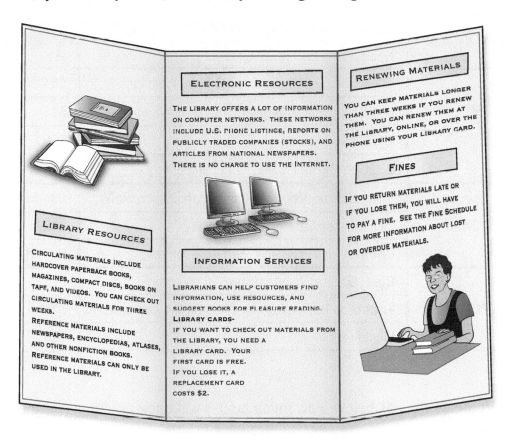

ELECTRONIC RESOURCES

THE LIBRARY OFFERS A LOT OF INFORMATION ON COMPUTER NETWORKS. THESE NETWORKS INCLUDE U.S. PHONE LISTINGS, REPORTS ON PUBLICLY TRADED COMPANIES (STOCKS), AND ARTICLES FROM NATIONAL NEWSPAPERS. THERE IS NO CHARGE TO USE THE INTERNET.

RENEWING MATERIALS

YOU CAN KEEP MATERIALS LONGER THAN THREE WEEKS IF YOU RENEW THEM. YOU CAN RENEW THEM AT THE LIBRARY, ONLINE, OR OVER THE PHONE USING YOUR LIBRARY CARD.

FINES

IF YOU RETURN MATERIALS LATE OR IF YOU LOSE THEM, YOU WILL HAVE TO PAY A FINE. SEE THE FINE SCHEDULE FOR MORE INFORMATION ABOUT LOST OR OVERDUE MATERIALS.

LIBRARY RESOURCES

CIRCULATING MATERIALS INCLUDE HARDCOVER PAPERBACK BOOKS, MAGAZINES, COMPACT DISCS, BOOKS ON TAPE, AND VIDEOS. YOU CAN CHECK OUT CIRCULATING MATERIALS FOR THREE WEEKS.
REFERENCE MATERIALS INCLUDE NEWSPAPERS, ENCYCLOPEDIAS, ATLASES, AND OTHER NONFICTION BOOKS. REFERENCE MATERIALS CAN ONLY BE USED IN THE LIBRARY.

INFORMATION SERVICES

LIBRARIANS CAN HELP CUSTOMERS FIND INFORMATION, USE RESOURCES, AND SUGGEST BOOKS FOR PLEASURE READING.
LIBRARY CARDS-
IF YOU WANT TO CHECK OUT MATERIALS FROM THE LIBRARY, YOU NEED A LIBRARY CARD. YOUR FIRST CARD IS FREE. IF YOU LOSE IT, A REPLACEMENT CARD COSTS $2.

F Decide if these statements are true or false based on the information in the library brochure. Fill in the circle. Then, change each false statement to make it true.

	True	False
1. You ~~can~~ **cannot** check out reference materials.	○	●
2. Librarians can suggest books to read.	●	○
3. You can check out circulating materials.	●	○
4. The library has a database of phone listings ~~from all over the world~~ **U.S.**	○	●
5. Your first library card ~~costs $2.~~ **is free.**	○	●
6. You can renew materials over the phone using ~~a driver's license.~~ **your library card.**	○	●
7. You can check out library materials for three weeks.	●	○
8. If a book is late, it is overdue and you must pay a fine.	●	○
9. There ~~is~~ **is not** a fee to use the Internet.	○	●

GOAL ➤ Interpret charts and compare information

G Have you been to the DMV in your city? If so, why did you go there? Did you have to pay for services? Look at the chart of DMV fees below.

	DMV Fees		
	Type	**Fee**	**Valid**
NEW	Driver License, Regular Class C (non-commercial)	$54.50	8 years
	Instruction Permit, Regular Class C (non-commercial)	$18	2 years
	Identification Card	$29	8 years
	Disabled Person Parking Permit, Temporary	No Fee	8 years
RENEWAL	Driver License, Regular Class C (non-commercial)	$34.50	NA
	Identification Card	$25	NA
	Disabled Person Parking Permit, Temporary	No Fee	
REPLACEMENT	Driver License, Regular Class C (non-commercial)	$21	NA
	Instruction Permit, Regular Class C (non-commercial)	$18	NA
	Identification Card	$24	NA

H Read the sentences below. How much money will each person have to pay at the DMV?

1. Enrico needs to get a new ID card. $_29_

2. Liza lost her instruction permit and she needs to get a new one. $_18_

3. Peter's driver's license expired and he needs to get a new one. $_34.50_

4. Kim and Claudia just learned how to drive and they both need to get new driver's licenses. $_109_

5. Gertrude needs a disabled person parking permit. $_No fee_

I Imagine that you have to create a brochure for new students at your school. Work with a group to list all the important information to include. (Answers will vary.)

Presentation 3

10-15 mins. ■■■■

G Have you been to the DMV in your city? If so, why did you go there? Did you have to pay for services? Look at the chart of DMV fees below.

Go over the chart with students, helping them understand each type of fee.

Practice 3

5-10 mins. ■

H Read the sentences below. How much money will each person have to pay at the DMV?

Evaluation 3

10-15 mins. ■

Have students share their answers with a partner and then go over the answers as a class.

Application

10-20 mins. ■■■

I Imagine that you have to create a brochure for new students at your school. Work with a group to list all the important information to include.

Put students in small groups and get the class started by brainstorming a few ideas together.

GC Refer students to *Stand Out 3 Grammar Challenge*, Unit 4, Challenge 2 for more practice with information questions.

Objectives: Interpret a road map
Grammar: Imperatives
Academic Strategy: Map reading
Vocabulary: *run, north, south, east, west, northeast, northwest, southeast, southwest, far*

RESOURCES

Activity Bank: Lesson 3, Worksheet 1
Reading and Writing Challenge: Unit 4

Grammar Challenge 3: Unit 4, Challenge 3

AGENDA

Read a map.
Understand and use map vocabulary.
Giving directions using imperatives.
Use a street map.
Give and receive directions.

Warm-up and Review   5 mins.

Review Lesson 2 by asking students questions about the bank, library, and DMV. Have pairs or small groups make lists of the things they can do at each of these places. Have the groups share their lists with the class and make a comprehensive list on the board.

Introduction   5-10 mins.

Write the word *map* on the board and ask students what a map is. Ask them what information they can find on a map. Ask if any of them use maps to find places in the United States. If some do, ask them to name those places. State the objective: *Today we will learn how to interpret a road map.*

Presentation 1   15-20 mins.

Present map-reading vocabulary and symbols to students using the information in Exercises A and B. Go over the questions and draw simple maps of your area on the board to help students understand the geographic concepts.

Ⓐ Discuss these questions with your classmates.

Ⓑ Gloria and her family lived in Lindon. They decided to move to Victoria because Victoria has better schools and safer neighborhoods. This is a map of the area where they live. Look at the map. Then, answer the questions on page 68.

Discuss Gloria's situation with the class before going over the map.

STANDARDS CORRELATIONS

CASAS: 2.2.1, 2.2.5 (See CASAS Competency List on pages 169–175.)
SCANS: **Information** Acquire and evaluate information, interpret and communicate information
Interpersonal Participate as a member of a team, teach others, exercise leadership, work with cultural diversity
Systems Understand systems, monitor and correct performance
Basic Skills Reading, writing, arithmetic, listening, speaking
Thinking Skills Creative thinking, decision making, problem solving, seeing things in the mind's eye

Personal Qualities Responsibility, sociability, self-management
EFF: **Communication** Speak so others can understand, listen actively, observe critically
Decision Making Solve problems and make decisions, plan
Interpersonal Cooperate with others, guide others
Lifelong Learning Reflect and evaluate, use information and communication technology (optional)

LESSON 3 Finding Places

GOAL ➤ Interpret a road map

 A Discuss these questions with your classmates. (Answers will vary.)

1. How far do you live from your school in miles?

2. What are some major freeways or interstates in your area? What directions do they run?

3. Where is your school located? What are the nearest towns or cities? Where are they in relation to your school?

 B Gloria and her family lived in Lindon. They decided to move to Victoria because Victoria has better schools and safer neighborhoods. This is a map of the area where they live. Look at the map. Then, answer the questions on page 68.

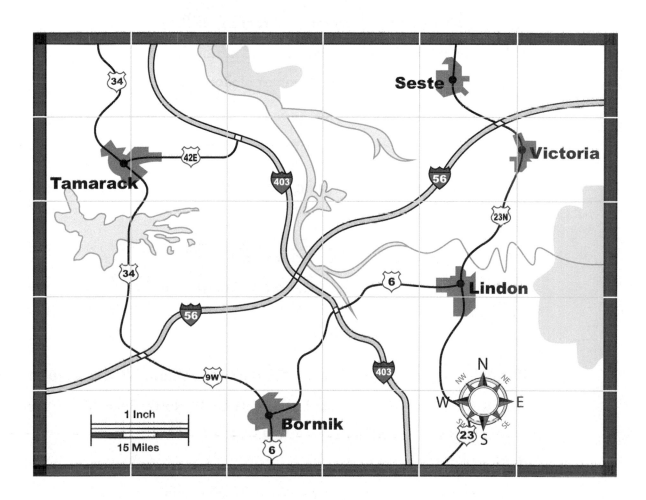

C Work in pairs. Answer the questions below using the map on page 67. Then, ask two more questions of your own.

EXAMPLE: *Student A:* Where is Lindon in relation to Victoria?
            Student B: It is southwest of Victoria.

1. How far is Lindon from Victoria? _____30_____ miles

2. What freeway is Victoria closest to? _____56_____ What direction does this
   freeway run? _____east-west_____

3. Gloria also considered moving her family to Tamarack. Where is this city
   located in relation to Lindon? _____northwest_____

4. Which direction does Interstate 403 run? _____north-south_____

5. How far is Bormik from Lindon? _____45_____ miles

6. Where is Bormik located in relation to Lindon? _____southwest_____

7. _____

8. _____

D Study these expressions for giving directions on a road map. Practice pointing with your finger on the map on page 67.

Go north on 403.	**Exit at** Seste.
Take 56 West.	**Get off at** Exit 48 in Bormik.
Get on 34 North.	

E Using the map on page 67, follow the directions below. What city are you near?

1. Take 403 North to 6 East. At Lindon, get on 23 North. Take 23 North and go
   past Highway 56. What city are you in? _____Seste_____

2. Take 403 South to 42 East. At Tamarack, take 34 South. Take 56 East to 403 South.
   Get on Highway 6 going south. What city are you in? _____Bormick_____

3. Take 6 North until it turns into 9 West. Then get on 56 East. Cross 403 and
   go about 40 miles. What city is to the south? _____Victoria_____

Practice 1   10–15 mins.

C Work in pairs. Answer the questions below using the map on page 67. Then, ask two more questions of your own.

Go over the example with students. Encourage students to take turns asking and answering the questions.

Evaluation 1   5 mins.

Go over the answers as a class.

Presentation 2   10–15 mins.

Explain to students that when we give directions we use imperatives. Give them some examples: *Turn left. Go to the next street. Go two blocks and turn right.* Have a volunteer stand up and give him or her directions to a specific spot in the room.

D Study these expressions for giving directions on a road map. Practice pointing with your finger on the map on page 67.

Practice 2   5–10 mins.

E Using the map on page 67, follow the directions below. What city are you near?

Give students an example first by having them all look at the map. Read them the following directions and ask them where they are: *From Tamarack, take 34 East. Then take 403 South to 56 West. Then take 6 West. What city are you near?* (Bormik)

 Refer students to *Stand Out 3 Grammar Challenge*, Unit 4, Challenge 3 for more practice with imperatives.

Evaluation 2   3 mins.

Go over the answers as a class.

Instructor's Notes

Presentation 3   5–10 mins.

F Look at the city map. How is it different from the state map on page 67?

Make a list of the differences on the board.

G Study these expressions for giving directions in a city.

Remind students that imperatives are used when giving directions.

Practice 3   5–10 mins. ■

H Read the directions below and follow them on the map with your finger.

For additional practice, have students take out a sheet of paper or give them each a note card. Give students a starting point. Ask them to choose a specific location from the map, such as the intersection of two streets, and write directions from the starting point to the location they chose. Ask two volunteers to read out the locations they wrote down. Now ask Student A to give directions to his or her specified location to Student B. Student B then gives directions on how to get to his or her specified location. Have a few students demonstrate this exchange until the whole class understands. Then have students walk around and talk to others. They must take their maps with them so they can practice giving and taking directions.

Evaluation 3   5–10 mins. ■

Go over the answers to Exercise H.

Application   15–25 mins.

I Give your partner directions to different places on the two maps. Start your conversations using the questions below.

Model a conversation with a volunteer. Show students how they will have to decide which map to use.

In pairs, have students give one another directions from school to their homes. Each person must write down the directions they are given by their partners. Then they must draw a map showing those directions. Have pairs compare maps.

Note: If your students are uncomfortable sharing their home addresses, have them substitute directions to a store or another location in the community.

Activity Bank

Lesson 3, Worksheet 1: Giving Directions

Instructor's Notes

_____

_____

_____

_____

_____

_____

_____

_____

_____

_____

_____

_____

_____

_____

_____

_____

_____

_____

_____

_____

F Look at the city map. How is it different from the map on page 67?

G Study these expressions for giving directions in a city.

Go straight for three blocks.	It's **next to** the bank.
Turn left. / **Make a** left.	It's **across from** the park.
Take Second Avenue to Oak Street.	It's **on the corner of** First and Main.

H Read the directions below and follow them on the map with your finger.

Start at the subway station on Fifth Avenue. Take a right out of the station. Turn left on Main Street. Go straight for three blocks. Take a left on Second Avenue. It's at the corner of Oak and Second Avenue. What's the name of the building? _____Oak Street Hotel_____

I Give your partner directions to different places on the two maps. Start your conversations using the questions below.

	Tarmack		Seste?
How can I get to	Bormik	from	Victoria?
	the subway station		the post office?
	the art museum		the Japanese restaurant?

Getting things done!

GOAL ➤ **Identify daily activities**

A Look at the picture and read about Gloria's busy day.

Yesterday was a busy day! After I woke up, I got the kids ready for school. Before my husband left for work, I ironed his shirt. When everyone left the house, I made my list of errands and off I went. First, I returned some books to the library. I stopped by the bank to make a deposit after I returned the books. Then, I went to the post office to mail a package to my family back in Brazil. The next errand on my list was grocery shopping. But before I went grocery shopping, I remembered to go to the cleaners and pick up some skirts. Finally, when I finished shopping, I went home. It was a long morning!

B Number in the correct order.

___9___ picked up dry cleaning

___2___ got the kids ready for school

___3___ ironed husband's shirt

___5___ left the house

___7___ made a deposit at the bank

___1___ woke up

___4___ made a list of errands

___8___ mailed a package at the post office

___6___ returned books to the library

___10___ went grocery shopping

Objective: Identify daily activities
Grammar: Adverbial time clauses
Pronunciation: Phrasing
Vocabulary: *Iron, errands, deposit, dry cleaning*

AGENDA

What did you do yesterday?
Read about Gloria's day.
Use adverbial time clauses.
Use phrasing in speech.
Write about your day.

RESOURCES

Activity Bank: Lesson 4, Worksheet 1
Reading and Writing Challenge: Unit 4

Grammar Challenge 3: Unit 4, Challenge 4

■ 1.5 hour classes   ■ 2.5 hour classes   ■ 3+ hour classes

Warm-up and Review   10–15 mins.

Have volunteers tell you how to get to their house. As they give you directions, draw a corresponding map on the board. If you have time, let another student come up and draw a map while a different student gives directions.

Introduction   5–10 mins.   ■■■

Ask a volunteer to tell you five things they did yesterday in order. Make a list on the board. Then describe to the class what the student did, using *before* and *after*. For example: *Before you went to the bank, you took your daughter to school.* Do this with as many students as you feel is necessary to demonstrate the concept. State the objective: *Today we will identify daily activities.*

Presentation 1   10–15 mins.   ■■■

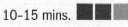 **Look at the picture and read about Gloria's busy day.**

Have students open their books and look at the picture of Gloria. Ask them what she is doing. Have them read the paragraph quietly to themselves. When they have finished, check if they have any vocabulary questions.

Practice 1   5–10 mins.

B **Number in the correct order.**

Evaluation 1   5 mins.   ■■■

Go over the answers as a class.

Presentation 2   10–20 mins.   ■■■

Using the paragraph about Gloria, present adverbial time clauses to students. Read them the second sentence: *After I woke up, I got the kids ready for school.* Ask students what Gloria did first. Continue by asking this about each sentence in the paragraph that has two actions. Now write the sentences on the board. Ask students what happened first in each sentence. Put numbers above the actions so students can see which actions occurred first, and which occurred second. Ask students to help you find a pattern.

STANDARDS CORRELATIONS

CASAS: 7.2.6 (See CASAS Competency List on pages 170–177.)
SCANS: Information Acquire and evaluate information, interpret and communicate information
Interpersonal Participate as a member of a team, teach others, exercise leadership, work with cultural diversity
Systems Monitor and correct performance
Basic Skills Reading, writing, listening, speaking

Thinking Skills Decision making
Personal Qualities Responsibility, sociability, self-management
EFF: Communication Read with understanding, speak so others can understand, convey ideas in writing
Decision Making Solve problems and make decisions, plan
Interpersonal Cooperate with others
Lifelong Learning Take responsibility for learning, reflect and evaluate

Presentation 2 *(continued)*   10–20 mins.

C *Before, after,* and *when* are used to connect two ideas and show their relationship in time. These words begin adverbial time clauses.

Study the chart with students. Explain the rules using the examples in the chart.

Practice 2   15–20 mins. ■■

D In each of these sentences, underline the action that happened first.

E Rewrite each sentence above, switching the order of the two actions.

Go over the example with students. Remind them of the no-comma rule.

F Talk with your partner. In the sentences you wrote above, which action happened first?

Evaluation 2   5–10 mins. ■■

Ask volunteers to write their sentences on the board. Go over the answers as a class.

 Before, after, and *when* are used to connect two ideas and show their relationship in time. These words begin adverbial time clauses.

Adverbial Clauses with *Before, After,* and *When*	
Example	**Rule**
After I returned the books, I stopped by the bank to make a deposit.	The action closest to *after* happened first. (First, she returned the books. Second, she went to the bank.)
Before I went grocery shopping, I stopped by the cleaners to pick up some skirts.	The action closest to *before* happened second. (First, she went to the cleaners. Second, she went grocery shopping.)
When everyone left the house, I made my list of errands and off I went.	The action closest to *when* is completed and then next act begins. (First, everyone left. Second, she made her list.)
I went home **when** I finished shopping. **When** I finished shopping, I went home.	You can reverse the two clauses and the meaning stays the same. You need a comma if the adverbial clause goes first.

 In each of these sentences, underline the action that happened first.

EXAMPLE: After <u>I woke up</u>, I made breakfast.

1. <u>I stopped by the bank to make a deposit</u> before I returned the books.

2. Before Wendy went shopping, <u>she went to the gym.</u>

3. <u>When my kids came home,</u> I made dinner.

 Rewrite each sentence above, switching the order of the two actions.

EXAMPLE: **After** I woke up, I made breakfast.
           I made breakfast after I woke up.

1. Before I returned the books, I stopped by the bank to make a deposit.

2. Wendy went to the gym before she went shopping.

3. I made dinner when my kids came home.

F   Talk with your partner. In the sentences you wrote above, which action happened first?

Pronunciation

Phrasing
➤ **Phrasing** is taking a pause or breath in the middle of a sentence.
➤ **We usually pause between two thoughts or when there is a comma.**
                    pause
➤ When my kids came home, I made dinner.
                ∨ pause
➤ She went to the store before she picked up the dry cleaning.

G Write sentences with adverbial clauses. Use the words in parentheses. Then, rewrite the sentences, reversing the clauses.

EXAMPLE: Ali finished work. He went out with his friends. (when)

a. When Ali finished work, he went out with his friends.

b. Ali went out with his friends when he finished work.

1. Yasu saved enough money. He bought a new bicycle. (after)

   a. After Yasu saved enough money, he bought a new bicycle.

   b. Yasu bought a new bicycle after he saved enough money.

2. The alarm went off. Maya jumped out of bed. (when)

   a. When the alarm went off, Maya jumped out of bed.

   b. Maya jumped out of bed when the alarm went off.

H List five things you did yesterday in the order in which you did them. Then, write three sentences using *before, after,* or *when* to talk about your day. (Answers will vary.)

1. _____

   _____

2. _____

   _____

3. _____

   _____

Yesterday

1. _____

2. _____

3. _____

4. _____

5. _____

Presentation 3   5–10 mins.

Pronunciation

Phrasing

Explain to students that it is not only important to pronounce words correctly, but pausing in the correct place in the sentence is also important to be better understood.

Read the sentences in the box to students twice, once without any pause and then with a pause in the correct place. Ask them if they can hear the difference between the two. Have them repeat the sentences after you.

Once students understand the concept, have them practice some more by reading Gloria's paragraph as well as the sentences from Exercises D and E out loud.

Practice 3   5–10mins.

(G) **Write sentences with adverbial clauses. Use the words in parentheses. Then, rewrite the sentences, reversing the clauses.**

Go over the example with students, making sure they understand what they are supposed to do.

Evaluation 3   5 mins.

Ask for volunteers to write their sentences on the board. Go over the answers as a class.

 Refer students to *Stand Out 3 Grammar Challenge*, Unit 4, Challenge 4 for more practice with adverbial time clauses.

Application   10–20 mins.

(H) **List five things you did yesterday in the order in which you did them. Then, write three sentences using *before, after,* or *when* to talk about your day.**

For further application, have students describe two actions they did yesterday on a sheet of paper. Write the following question on the board: *What did you do yesterday?* Explain to students that they should answer with the information on their paper and use *after, before,* or *when* to combine the two actions they described. Ask a few volunteers to present their

sentences out loud so the class gets the idea. Make any necessary corrections on the board to help the whole class write correct sentences.

Have students again write down two actions that took place yesterday. Now ask them to make a sentence combining the two events and to exchange the sentence with a partner. Have students peer-edit their sentences.

Activity Bank

Lesson 4, Worksheet 1: Adverbial Time Clauses

Instructor's Notes

_____
_____
_____
_____
_____
_____
_____
_____
_____
_____
_____
_____
_____
_____
_____
_____
_____
_____
_____

Objective: Write about a place
Grammar: Editing
Academic Strategy: Paragraph writing
Vocabulary: *brainstorm, neighborhoods, affordable*

AGENDA
Read brainstorming notes.
Order sentences in a paragraph.
Use transitions.
Brainstorm as a pre-writing tool.
Write a paragraph.

RESOURCES

Activity Bank: Templates Folder: Editing
Reading and Writing Challenge: Unit 4

Grammar Challenge 3: Unit 4, Challenge 5

■ 1.5 hour classes   ■ 2.5 hour classes   ■ 3+ hour classes

Warm-up and Review   5–10 mins.

If you didn't have students complete the activity for further application after Exercise H on page 72, you can do it now as a review of Lesson 4. If you did do it, repeat the activity, having students write new information.

Introduction   5 mins.

Ask students what they would say about their community if asked to write a paragraph about it. Write some of their answers on the board. State the objective: *Today we will be writing about a place.*

Presentation 1   5–10 mins.

Ⓐ Gloria is writing a paragraph about Victoria. Read her brainstorming notes below.

Ask the class if they remember what it means to brainstorm. If they have forgotten, remind them by going over Gloria's notes in Exercise A as an example. Tell them that while brainstorming, they should write down everything that comes

to mind. They can cross out ideas that they don't like later. Go over the following terms: *topic sentence, support sentences,* and *conclusion sentence.* Remind them of their basic definitions.

Practice 1   5–10 mins.

Ⓑ Gloria decided to focus on a few of the ideas for her paragraph. She wrote the six sentences below, but they are not in the correct order. Choose the best topic sentence and write *1* in front of it. Choose the best conclusion sentence and write *6* in front of it. Then, choose the order of the support sentences and number them 2–5. (Look at page 8 to review the different parts of a paragraph.)

Have students complete the exercise alone. Then, have them compare answers with a partner.

Evaluation 1   5 mins.

Go over the answers as a class.

LESSON 5 **My town**

GOAL ➤ **Write about a place**

A Gloria is writing a paragraph about Victoria. Read her brainstorming notes below.

Reasons I love Victoria

safe neighborhoods (kids play in park)   affordable housing (can buy new house)

good schools (nationally recognized)   ~~good shopping~~

~~mild weather (never gets too cold or hot)~~   good job opportunities (computer industry)

> *Brainstorm:* to write a list of ideas you might use in your paragraph

B Gloria decided to focus on a few of the ideas for her paragraph. She wrote the six sentences below, but they are not in the correct order. Choose the best topic sentence and write *1* in front of it. Choose the best conclusion sentence and write *6* in front of it. Then, choose the order of the support sentences and number them 2–5. (Look at page 8 to review the different parts of a paragraph.) (Order of sentences 2–5 will vary.)

____ Thanks to the great job market in Victoria, my husband got an excellent position in a computer company.

____ Our family can buy a nice house because the housing prices are very affordable here.

_6_ I love Victoria so much that I can't imagine moving.

____ The neighborhoods are very safe and so I can let my children play in the park with other children.

____ The excellent schools in this area are nationally recognized.

_1_ There are many reasons I love my new hometown Victoria.

C Now compose a paragraph, using Gloria's sentences in Exercise B. Use transitions from the box below to connect your support sentences. Write a title for Gloria's paragraph on the top line.

First of all,	Second,	Also,
First,	Third,	Finally,
Second of all,	Furthermore,	

(Answers will vary.)

_____

_____

_____

_____

_____

_____

_____

_____

_____

_____

_____

D Now think about your town. Follow each step below. (Answers will vary.)

1. Brainstorm at least six reasons why you like your town.

EXAMPLE: _____ friendly people _____

Reasons I love _____

friendly people

Presentation 2   5–10 mins. ■■■

Remind students that when they write a paragraph, they need to connect their ideas with transitions. Go over the list of transitions in the box. Give them a few examples of how the transitions might be used.

Practice 2   15–20 mins. ■■

(C) Now compose a paragraph, using Gloria's sentences in Exercise B. Use transitions from the box below to connect your support sentences. Write a title for Gloria's paragraph on the top line.

Evaluation 2   15–20 mins. ■■

Observe students as they write.

Presentation 3   15–20 mins. ■■■

Choose a city that no one in your class lives in but that everyone knows something about. It could be a neighboring city or another large city in your state or country.

1. Ask students to help you come up with a list of reasons why this is a good city. Remind students that this is part of the brainstorming process.
2. Now ask students which reasons they think are the best and cross out the others.
3. Have the class help you write a topic sentence for this paragraph.

These steps will prepare students to write their own paragraphs about a town or city of their choice.

Practice 3   15–20 mins. ■

(D) Now think about your town. Follow each step below.

Before students begin, go through each step with them, making sure they understand what they are supposed to do.

Evaluation 3   15–20 mins. ■

Walk around the classroom and help students as necessary.

Instructor's Notes

Application

15-25 mins. ◼◼◼◻

E On a piece of paper, write a paragraph about your town or city, using your work in Exercise D. Use transitions to connect your ideas.

Technology Extension: Have students type their paragraph on the computer. Have them insert a picture of their city from the Internet.

Refer students to *Stand Out 3 Grammar Challenge*, Unit 4, Challenge 5 for more practice with editing.

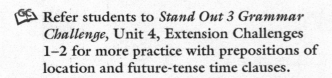

Activity Bank

Templates: Editing

Refer students to *Stand Out 3 Grammar Challenge*, Unit 4, Extension Challenges 1–2 for more practice with prepositions of location and future-tense time clauses.

2. Choose four of your reasons about why you like your town to include in your paragraph.

3. Write a topic sentence for your paragraph. (Answers will vary.)

_____

_____

_____

4. Write four support sentences based on the four reasons you chose.

a. _____

_____

_____

b. _____

_____

_____

c. _____

_____

_____

d. _____

_____

_____

5. Write a conclusion sentence.

_____

_____

_____

E **On a piece of paper, write a paragraph about your town or city, using your work in Exercise D. Use transitions to connect your ideas.** (Answers will vary.)

Review

A Where can you do the following things in your community? (Lesson 1)

1. have lunch   restaurant

2. get medicine   pharmacy/drugstore

3. mail a letter   post office

4. get cash   bank

B What are some questions you might ask at the places you wrote in Exercise A? Write a question for each place. (Lesson 1) (Answers will vary.)

1. _____

2. _____

3. _____

4. _____

C Look back at the Riverview Bank brochure on page 64. Read about the following people and decide which checking account would be best for each. Write the account name on the line. (Lesson 2)

1. Vu likes to do all of his banking at an ATM machine. He rarely goes inside the bank. His company deposits his paycheck automatically. He writes about 15 checks a month. Which account is best for Vu?

Express

2. Mario likes to go inside the bank and do his transactions with a teller. He doesn't trust ATM machines. He also writes a lot of checks, so he's looking for an account that allows him unlimited check writing. He likes to keep at least $2,500 in his account. Which account is best for Mario?

Standard

3. Gloria and her husband want to buy a new house. They currently have $15,600 in the bank. They pay a lot of bills each month by check, so they want unlimited check writing. Gloria likes to do her banking with a teller. However, her husband works during banking hours and needs to use an ATM machine. Which account is best for Gloria and her husband?

Premiere

AT-A-GLANCE PREP

Objectives: All unit objectives
Grammar: All unit grammar
Academic Strategy: Reviewing
Vocabulary: All unit vocabulary

AGENDA
Discuss unit objectives.
Complete the review.
Do My Dictionary.
Evaluate and reflect on progress.

RESOURCES

Activity Bank: Unit 4, Lessons 1–5
Reading and Writing Challenge: Unit 4

Grammar Challenge 3: Unit 4, Challenges 1–5

 1.5 hour classes ■ 2.5 hour classes ■ 3⁺ hour classes

Stand Out 3 Assessment CD-ROM with Exam*View*®

Warm-up and Review   5-10 mins.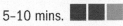

In groups, have students read their paragraphs from Lesson 5.

Introduction   5-10 mins. ■■■

Ask students as a class to try to recall (in general) all the goals of this unit without looking at their books. Then remind them which goals they omitted, if any. (Unit goals: Ask for information, interpret charts and compare information, interpret a road map, identify daily activities, and write about a place) Write all the objectives on the board. Show students the first page of the unit and mention the five objectives. State the objective: *Today we will be reviewing everything you have learned in this unit.*

Presentation 1   10-15 mins. ■■■

This presentation will cover the first three pages of the review. Quickly go to the first page of each lesson. Discuss the objective of each. Ask simple questions to remind students of what they have learned.

Note: Since there is little presentation in the review, you can assign Exercises A–E for homework and go over them in class the next day.

Practice 1   20-25 mins. ■■■

Note: There are two ways to do the review: (1) Go through the exercises one at a time and, as students complete each one, go over the answers. (2) Briefly go through the instructions of each exercise, allow students to complete all of the exercises at once, and then go over the answers.

A Where can you do the following things in your community? (Lesson 1)

B What are some questions you might ask at the places you wrote in Exercise A? Write a question for each place. (Lesson 1)

C Look back at the Riverview Bank brochure on page 64. Read about the following people and decide which checking account would be best for each. Write the account name on the line. (Lesson 2)

Evaluation 1   20-25 mins.

Go around the classroom and check on students' progress. Help individuals as needed. If you see consistent errors among several students, interrupt the class and give a mini lesson or review to help students feel comfortable with the concept.

STANDARDS CORRELATIONS

CASAS: 7.2.1 (See CASAS Competency List on pages 169–175.)
SCANS: Resources Allocate time
Information Acquire and evaluate information
Interpersonal Participate as a member of a team, teach others, negotiate to arrive at a decision, work with cultural diversity
Systems Monitor and correct performance
Basic Skills Reading, writing, arithmetic, listening, speaking
Thinking Skills Creative thinking, decision making, problem solving, seeing things in the mind's eye

Personal Qualities Responsibility, sociability, self-management
EFF: Communication Convey ideas in writing, speak so others can understand
Decision Making Solve problems and make decisions
Interpersonal Cooperate with others, guide others
Lifelong Learning Take responsibility for learning, reflect and evaluate, learn through research

Practice 1 *(continued)*   20-25 mins. ■■■

D Draw a map showing the way from your school to a nearby restaurant. Then, write the directions. Read the directions to your partner and see if your partner can draw a map. (Lesson 3)

E Write sentences with adverbial clauses. Use *before, after,* or *when.* (Lesson 4)

Evaluation 1 *(continued)*   20-25 mins. ■■■

Go around the classroom and check on students' progress. Help individuals as needed. If you see consistent errors among several students, interrupt the class and give a mini lesson or review to help students feel comfortable with the concept.

Teaching Tip

Recycling/Review

The review exercises and the project that follows are part of the recycling/review process. Students at this level often need to be reintroduced to concepts to solidify what they have learned. Many concepts are learned and forgotten while learning other new concepts. This is because students learn but are not necessarily ready to acquire language concepts.

Therefore, it becomes very important to review and to show students how to review on their own. It is also important to recycle the new concepts in different contexts.

Instructor's Notes

D Draw a map showing the way from your school to a nearby restaurant. Then, write the directions. Read the directions to your partner and see if your partner can draw a map. (Lesson 3) (Answers will vary.)

Draw your map here:

Write your directions here:

_____

_____

_____

_____

_____

_____

_____

_____

_____

_____

E Write sentences with adverbial clauses. Use *before, after,* or *when.* (Lesson 4)

EXAMPLE: I woke up. I made breakfast. (Answers will vary.)

After I woke up, I made breakfast. _____

1. The children finished breakfast. I got them ready for school.

_____

2. I got some money out of the ATM. I bought some groceries.

_____

3. Mala finished work. She went to the movies.

_____

4. Luigi graduated from college. He got a job in a computer company.

_____

Review

F Ask your partner why he or she likes the city he or she lives in. Write four reasons below. **(Lesson 5)** (Answers will vary.)

Reasons I love _____

G Write a short paragraph about your partner's city. Don't forget to use transitions. **(Lesson 5)**

_____ (Answers will vary.)

_____

_____

_____

_____

_____

_____

_____

_____

_____

_____

_____

_____

H Share the paragraph with your partner. Have your partner find the topic sentence, support sentences, and conclusion sentence. **(Lesson 5)**

Practice 1 *(continued)* 20–25 mins. ■■■□

F Ask your partner why he or she likes the city he or she lives in. Write four reasons below. (Lesson 5)

G Write a short paragraph about your partner's city. Don't forget to use transitions. (Lesson 5)

H Share the paragraph with your partner. Have your partner find the topic sentence, support sentences, and conclusion sentence. (Lesson 5)

Evaluation 1 *(continued)* 20–25 mins. ■■■□

Go around the classroom and check on students' progress. Help individuals as needed. If you see consistent errors among several students, interrupt the class and give a mini lesson or review to help students feel comfortable with the concept.

Presentation 2   5-10 mins.

My Dictionary

Ask students to brainstorm new vocabulary items they learned in this unit. Have them do this without looking in their books. Then, as a class, put these items on the board in alphabetical order.

Practice 2   15-20 mins.

(Shorter classes can do these exercises for homework.)

Write down ten new words you learned in this unit. Put them in alphabetical order. Then, look up the words in your dictionary to see if you were correct. Write sentences to help you remember the most difficult words.

Evaluation 2   15-20 mins.

Walk around the classroom and help students.

Presentation 3   5-10 mins.

Learner Log

Write the word *log* on the board. Ask students to explain what this word means. Explain to them that it is a journal, notebook, or place where you keep track of information. In this case, they will be keeping track of what they learned.

In this unit, you learned many things about communities. How comfortable do you feel doing each of the skills listed below? Rate your comfort level on a scale of 1 to 4.

Go over the instructions with students and make sure they understand what to do. You may want to do the first one or two with the class to make sure they understand.

Practice 3   5-10 mins.

Have students complete the Learner Log.

Evaluation 3   5-10 mins.

Walk around the classroom and help students.

Application   5-10 mins.

Go over the two reflection questions with students and have them complete the answers by themselves.

Assessment *(optional)*

Use the *Stand Out 3 Assessment* CD-ROM with *ExamView*® to create a post-test for Unit 4.

My Dictionary

Write down ten new words you learned in this unit. Put them in alphabetical order. Then, look up the words in your dictionary to see if you were correct. Write sentences to help you remember the most difficult words.

(Answers will vary.)

1.   6.
2.   7.
3.   8.
4.   9.
5.   10.

Sentences: _____

_____

_____

Learner Log

In this unit, you learned many things about communities. How comfortable do you feel doing each of the skills listed below? Rate your comfort level on a scale of 1 to 4.

1 = Need more practice   **2** = OK   **3** = Good   **4** = Great!

Life Skill	Comfort Level	Page
I can ask for information.	1 2 3 4	61
I can interpret charts.	1 2 3 4	64
I can compare information.	1 2 3 4	64
I can interpret road and street maps.	1 2 3 4	67
I can give and receive directions.	1 2 3 4	67
I can identify daily activities.	1 2 3 4	70
I can write about my town.	1 2 3 4	73

If you circled 1 or 2, write down the page number where you can review this skill.

Reflection

1. What was the most useful skill you learned in this unit?

_____

2. How will this help you in life?

_____

Create a community brochure.

Imagine that a new family has moved into your neighborhood and you want to tell them all about your community. With your team, you will create a brochure about your community.

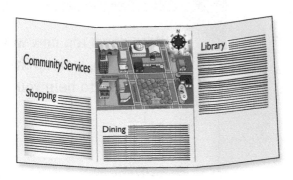

1. Form a team with four or five students. Choose a position for each member of your team.

POSITION	JOB DESCRIPTION	STUDENT NAME
Student 1: Leader	See that everyone speaks English. See that everyone participates.	
Student 2: Writer	Write information for brochure.	
Student 3: Designer	Design brochure layout and add artwork.	
Students 4/5: City Representatives	Help writer and designer with their work.	

2. Make a list of everything you want to include in your brochure, for example, information about the library, banks, and other local services. (Lessons 1–2)

3. Create the text for your community brochure. (Lessons 1–2, 5)

4. Create a map of your community. (Lesson 3)

5. Create artwork for your community brochure.

6. Present your brochure to the class.

Create a community brochure.

Each team will create a brochure for new neighbors in their community.

The team project is the final application for the unit. It gives students a chance to show that they have mastered all of the Unit 4 goals.

Note: Shorter classes can extend this project over two class meetings.

Stage 1   5 mins.

Form a team with four or five students. Choose a position for each member of your team.

Have students decide who will lead each step as described on the student page. Provide well-defined directions on the board for how teams should proceed. Explain that all the students do every step as a team. Teams shouldn't go to the next stage until the previous one is complete.

Stage 2   15-20 mins.

Make a list of everything you want to include in your brochure, for example, information about the library, banks, and other local services. (Lessons 1–2)

Help students get started by brainstorming a few ideas of things they might include in their brochure.

Stage 3   10-15 mins.

Create the text for your community brochure. (Lessons 1–2, 5)

Stage 4   10-15 mins.

Create a map of your community. (Lesson 3)

Stage 5   5 mins.

Create artwork for your community brochure.

Optional Computer Activity: Students may want to use the computer to design their final brochures.

Stage 6   15-20 mins.

Present your brochure to the class.

Help teams prepare for their presentations. Suggest that each member choose a different part of the brochure to present.

STANDARDS CORRELATIONS

CASAS: 4.8.1, 4.8.5, 4.8.6 (See CASAS Competency List on pages 169–175.)
SCANS: **Resources** Allocate time
Information Acquire and evaluate information, organize and maintain information, interpret and communicate information, use computers to process information (optional)
Systems Understand systems, improve and design systems
Technology Select technology, apply technology to exercise
Basic Skills Writing
Thinking Skills Creative thinking, decision making, problem solving, seeing things in the mind's eye, reasoning

Personal Qualities Responsibility, self-esteem, self-management, integrity/honesty
EFF: **Communication** Convey ideas in writing, speak so others can understand
Decision Making Solve problems and make decisions, plan
Interpersonal Guide others, resolve conflict and negotiate, advocate and influence, cooperate with others
Lifelong Learning Take responsibility for learning, reflect and evaluate, use information and communication technologies (optional)

Objective: Identify parts of the body
Grammar: Modal *should*
Vocabulary: *organs, condition, disease,*
parts of the body (internal and external)

AGENDA

Identify parts of the body.
Match doctors and their specializations.
Use should to make recommendations.
Identify internal organs.
Talk about conditions and diseases.

RESOURCES

Activity Bank: Lesson 1, Worksheets 1–2
Reading and Writing Challenge: Unit 5

Grammar Challenge 3: Unit 5, Challenge 1

 1.5 hour classes ■ 2.5 hour classes ■ 3⁺ hour classes

Stand Out 3 Assessment CD-ROM with Exam*View*®

Preassessment *(optional)*

Use the Stand Out 3 Assessment CD-ROM with
Exam*View*® to create a pretest for Unit 5.

Warm-up and Review   5 mins.

Begin by pointing to some basic body parts (leg,
arm, head, hand) and asking: *What's this?* Use
yourself or a volunteer as a model. Write what
students say on the board.

Introduction   10 mins.

Have students get in small groups and make a list
of as many parts of the body as they can. Do not
allow them to use dictionaries. Allow about ten
minutes for this activity. State the objective:
Today we will be identifying parts of the body.

Presentation 1   10–15 mins.

Have students call out the different body
parts their groups wrote down. List them on
the board. Go through the class list and have
volunteers point to the parts on their own bodies
as you name them. Have students repeat the
names. Help them with any parts they don't
know the names of.

Practice 1   10–15 mins.

(A) Label the parts of the human body using
the words from the box.

Let students help one another with this exercise
as they work.

(B) What other parts of the body can you
name? Work with a partner. Label other parts
of the body by drawing a line from the body part
and writing its name.

Evaluation 1   5 mins.

Observe pairs as they work. Help with spelling
as necessary.

Activity Bank

Lesson 1, Worksheet 1: Parts of the Body

STANDARDS CORRELATIONS

CASAS: 3.1.1, 3.1.3, 3.2.1 (See CASAS Competency List on pages 169–175.)
SCANS: **Information** Acquire and evaluate information, organize and
maintain information, interpret and communicate information
Interpersonal Participate as a member of a team, teach others, exercise
leadership, negotiate to arrive at a decision, work with cultural diversity
Systems Monitor and correct performance

Basic Skills Reading, writing, listening, speaking
Thinking Skills Creative thinking, seeing things in the mind's eye
Personal Qualities Responsibility, sociability
EFF: **Communication** Speak so others can understand
Interpersonal Cooperate with others
Lifelong Learning Reflect and evaluate

Health

GOALS

> Identify parts of the body
> Communicate symptoms to a doctor
> Identify health habits

> Interpret nutrition information
> Interpret fitness information

LESSON **1**

The human body

GOAL > Identify parts of the body

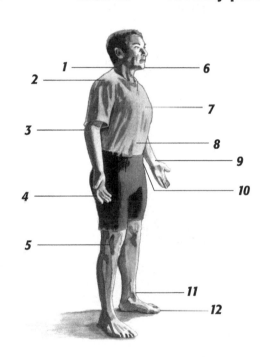

wrist	~~neck~~	shoulder
ankle	chest	toe
hip	stomach	elbow
knee	finger	chin

A Label the parts of the human body using the words from the box.

1. __neck__
2. __shoulder__
3. __elbow__
4. __finger__
5. __knee__
6. __chin__
7. __chest__
8. __stomach__
9. __wrist__
10. __hip__
11. __ankle__
12. __toe__

B What other parts of the body can you name? Work with a partner. Label other parts of the body by drawing a line from the body part and writing its name.

(Answers will vary.)

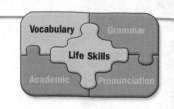

C Match the doctor with the specialization. Ask your teacher for help with answers and pronunciation. Write your answers in the chart below. Add one more to the list.

Doctors   **Specialization**

1. __c__ podiatrist   a. allergies and asthma

2. __i__ dermatologist   b. children

3. __h__ gynecologist/obstetrician   c. feet

4. __f__ cardiologist   d. teeth

5. __g__ ophthalmologist   e. mental illness

6. __b__ pediatrician   f. heart

7. __d__ dentist   g. eyes

8. __a__ allergist   h. women and childbirth

9. __e__ psychiatrist   i. skin

10. __j__ (Answers will vary.)   j. (Answers will vary.)

D Talk with a partner. Use the statements below to make recommendations about which type of doctor to see.

EXAMPLE: *Student A:* My mother's feet hurt.
         Student B: She should see a podiatrist.

1. My father is worried about his heart.   He should see a cardiologist.

2. My six-year-old son has a fever.   He should see a pediatrician.

3. My nose is running and my eyes are itchy.   You should see an allergist.

4. My eyes hurt when I read.   You should see an ophthalmologist.

5. I feel depressed.   You should see a psychiatrist.

6. I have a rash on my neck.   You should see a dermatologist.

7. I think I have a cavity.   You should see a dentist.

8. My sister thinks she is pregnant.   She should see a gynecologist/obstetrician.

9. (Answers will vary.)

Presentation 2 5-10 mins.

Write *hospital* and *doctor's office* on the board. Ask students for examples of when they might need to go to each place. Write their answers on the board. Now ask them for the names of specialists they know about. Write what they say on the board while trying not to elicit or reveal any information about what each doctor does.

Practice 2 5-10 mins.

(C) Match the doctor with the specialization. Ask your teacher for help with answers and pronunciation. Write your answers in the chart below. Add one more to the list.

Have students complete Exercise C with a partner. This exercise may be difficult but try not to give students the answers.

Evaluation 2 5 mins.

Help students with the pronunciation of the medical specialists found in Exercise C as you go over the answers.

Presentation 3 5-10 mins.

Discuss the word *special* and then *specialization*. Write this sentence on the board: *A dentist specializes in teeth.* Show students that, in this type of sentence, a noun or gerund follows the word *in*. Have students help you make sentences using the rest of the items in the chart. Write them on the board. Now erase the names of the doctors from the sentences. Rewrite the names in a list on the board, but in a different order. Write this question at the top of the list: *What does a _____ do?* Pose this question to students, inserting each kind of doctor. For example: *What does a cardiologist do?* Encourage them to answer by pointing to the sentence on the board that now reads: *A _____ specializes in the heart.* Do one or two more examples with students.

Have students practice this question-and-answer exchange with a partner, taking turns asking the question. Make sure their books are closed.

Practice 3 10-15 mins.

(D) Talk with a partner. Use the statements below to make recommendations about which type of doctor to see.

With a partner, students should practice the example conversation, substituting symptoms and doctors from the numbered items.

Evaluation 3 10-15 mins.

Observe students while they practice conversations with their partners.

Activity Bank

Lesson 1, Worksheet 2: Doctors

Instructor's Notes

Presentation 4   5–10 mins. ■■■

Do a quick review of external body parts by pointing to some of your own and asking students to name them. Then point to your head and ask students what's inside. (brain) Point to your neck and ask what's inside. (throat)

In groups, have students make a list of all the internal body parts they can think of. Have one group come to the board and write down everything on its list. Then have each group add to the list until all groups have had a chance to contribute.

E Look at the illustration of the internal parts of the human body. Review the pronunciation of new words with your teacher.

Practice 4   15–20 mins. ■

F Can you talk to your doctor about your medical history? Match the condition or disease with the correct part of the body. Then, add one idea of your own.

 Refer students to *Stand Out 3 Grammar Challenge*, Unit 5, Challenge 1 for more practice with the modal *should*.

Evaluation 4   5–10 mins. ■

Go over the answers as a class. Ask students what they wrote for Item 6 and make a list of students' ideas on the board.

Application   10–20 mins. ■■■

Have students take out a sheet of paper and number it for as many body parts as you want to quiz them on. For the quiz, point to body parts on your own body and ask students to write the names of the parts on their paper. Have students check their answers with a partner and then go over them as a class. You can also extend the quiz by pointing to a body part and asking them to write down the kind of doctor that specializes in that part.

Variation: Do the same quiz orally, calling on individual students to say the name of the body part.

E Look at the illustration of the internal parts of the human body. Review the pronunciation of new words with your teacher.

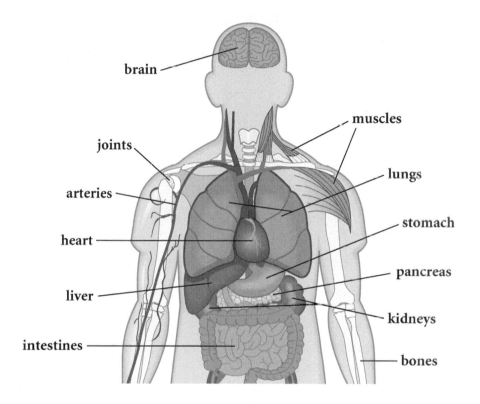

brain

muscles

joints

lungs

arteries

stomach

heart

pancreas

liver

kidneys

intestines

bones

F Can you talk to your doctor about your medical history? Match the condition or disease with the correct part of the body. Then, add one idea of your own.

Condition or disease	Part of body
1. _b_ high blood pressure	a. brain
2. _e_ asthma	b. heart and arteries
3. _d_ ulcers	c. joints
4. _a_ stroke	d. stomach
5. _c_ arthritis	e. lungs
6. _f_ (Answers will vary.)	f. (Answers will vary.)

Illnesses and symptoms

GOAL ➤ **Communicate symptoms to a doctor**

 A Read the conversation and answer the questions.

Doctor: What seems to be the problem?
Ali: I have a terrible backache.
Doctor: I see. How long have you had this backache?
Ali: I've had it for about a week.
Doctor: Since last Monday?
Ali: Yes, that's right.

1. What is the matter with Ali? _____ He has a backache. _____

2. When did his problem start? _____ It started last Monday. _____

B Make similar conversations using the information below.

EXAMPLES:
Student A: What's the matter?
Student B: I <u>feel dizzy</u>.
Student A: How long <u>have you felt dizzy</u>?
Student B: <u>For two days</u>.

Student A: What's the matter?
Student B: <u>My back hurts</u>.
Student A: How long <u>has your back hurt</u>?
Student B: <u>Since yesterday</u>.

Base Verb	Past Participle
be	been
have	had
feel	felt
hurt	hurt

1. I have a headache.
   (five hours)

2. My eyes are red.
   (last night)

3. My shoulder hurts.
   (two weeks)

4. I feel tired. (Monday)

5. My throat is sore.
   (three days)

AT-A-GLANCE PREP

Objective: Communicate symptoms to a doctor
Grammar: Present perfect
Vocabulary: *backache, headache, dizzy, sore, allergies, ill, sick, cold*

AGENDA
Talk about illnesses and symptoms.
Use the present perfect.
Use for and since.
Role play a conversation with a doctor.

RESOURCES

Activity Bank: Lesson 2, Worksheets 1–2
Reading and Writing Challenge: Unit 5

Grammar Challenge 3: Unit 5, Challenge 2

 1.5 hour classes █ 2.5 hour classes █ 3· hour classes

Warm-up and Review   5 mins.

Review Lesson 1 by pointing to body parts and having students identify them.

Introduction   5-10 mins.

Ask students why they go to the doctor or why they take their children to the doctor. Write some of their reasons on the board. Ask them if they have to explain their symptoms in English or if their doctor speaks their native language. Remind them that it is important to be able to explain what is wrong in English in case of an emergency or if they must see a doctor who speaks only English. State the objective: *Today we will practice communicating symptoms to a doctor.*

Presentation 1   10-15 mins.

(A) Read the conversation and answer the questions.

Have students open their books, look at the picture, and go over the conversation. If the present perfect is new to them, explain that we use it to talk about an action that started in the past and is still occurring. (You don't need to give an in-depth explanation at this point since you will be going over the grammar chart that deals with the present perfect in Presentation 2.)

Practice 1   10-15 mins.

(B) Make similar conversations using the information below.

Evaluation 1   5 mins.

Observe the students as they practice the conversations. Ask volunteers to demonstrate for the class.

STANDARDS CORRELATIONS

CASAS: 3.1.1 (See CASAS Competency List on pages 169–175.)
SCANS: Information Acquire and evaluate information, interpret and communicate information
Interpersonal Participate as a member of a team, exercise leadership, negotiate to arrive at a decision, work with cultural diversity
Systems Monitor and correct performance
Basic Skills Reading, writing, listening, speaking

Thinking Skills Creative thinking, decision making
Personal Qualities Responsibility, sociability, self-management
EFF: Communication Convey ideas in writing, speak so others can understand, listen actively
Decision Making Solve problems and make decisions
Interpersonal Cooperate with others
Lifelong Learning Reflect and evaluate

Presentation 2   10–15 mins. ■■□

C Study the charts with your teacher.

Explain the charts to students.

Practice 2   5–15 mins. ■□

D Complete the sentences with the present perfect of the verb in parentheses and *for* or *since*.

Evaluation 2   10–20 mins. ■□

Have students share their answers with a partner before you go over the answers with the class.

Activity Bank

Lesson 2, Worksheet 1: Present Perfect

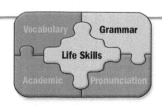

LESSON 2 **GOAL** ➤ **Communicate symptoms to a doctor**

C Study the charts with your teacher.

Present Perfect					
Subject	**have**	**Past participle**		**Time**	**Example sentence**
I, you we, they	have	been	sick	since Tuesday	I *have been* sick since Tuesday.
she, he, it	has	had	a backache	for two weeks	She *has had* a backache for two weeks.
Use the present perfect for events starting in the past and continuing up to the present.					

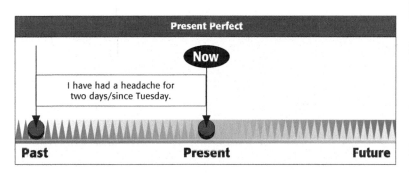

Length of Time	Point in Time
for ...	*since ...*
five minutes	last night
three days	Thursday
one week	November
two years	1998
a long time	I was a child

D Complete the sentences with the present perfect of the verb in parentheses and *for* or *since*.

1. She ___has been___ (be) tired ___since___ last week.

2. John's leg ___has been___ (be) sore ___for___ three days.

3. Karen ___has had___ (have) a sore throat ___since___ last night.

4. I ___have felt___ (feel) sick ___since___ Monday.

5. The girl's arm ___has hurt___ (hurt) ___for___ two days.

6. The twins ___have been___ (be) sick ___for___ a week.

Unit 5   Lesson 2 **85**

LESSON **2** GOAL ➤ **Communicate symptoms to a doctor**

E Make sentences using the present perfect and *for* or *since*.

EXAMPLE: Ali has a backache / Monday

Ali has had a backache since Monday.

1. I have a cold / three days

   I have had a cold for three days.

2. my leg hurts / last night

   My leg has hurt since last night.

3. Julie feels dizzy / a week

   Julie has felt dizzy for a week.

4. Peter is sick / two weeks

   Peter has been sick for two weeks.

5. they are ill / a long time

   They have been ill for a long time.

6. our allergies are bad / we were five years old

   Our allergies have been bad since we were five years old.

F Work in pairs. Write symptoms for each illness below.

Illness	Symptoms
a cold	runny nose, coughing, sneezing
the flu	fever, sore throat, coughing, muscle aches, headache, feeling very tired
a cough	sore throat, coughing
allergies	runny nose, coughing, sneezing
depression	feeling very sad

G With your partner, role-play a conversation between a doctor and a patient. Choose an illness from the chart above and ask questions about the symptoms. Remember to use *how long* and the present perfect.

Presentation 3   5-10 mins.

Write the following sentences and their clarifying phrases on the board:

I have had asthma since 1973.
(started in the past and I still have it)

I have had a backache for two days.
(started in the past and I still have it)

I had a cold last year.
(in the past; I no longer have it)

I have a cough right now.
(now)

Explain the grammar of each of the sentences briefly.

Practice 3   5-10 mins. ■

(E) **Make sentences using the present perfect and *for* or *since*.**

Evaluation 3   10-15 mins.

Ask volunteers to write their sentences on the board. Go over them as a class.

Application   10-20 mins. ■■■

(F) **Work in pairs. Write symptoms for each illness below.**

If students are having trouble with this exercise, it can be done as a class. Either way, make sure students have the chart filled out before they begin Exercise G.

(G) **With your partner, role-play a conversation between a doctor and a patient. Choose an illness from the chart above and ask questions about the symptoms. Remember to use *how long* and the present perfect.**

Model this exercise with a few students.

Activity Bank

Lesson 2, Worksheet 2: What's the Matter?

 Refer students to *Stand Out 3 Grammar Challenge*, Unit 5, Challenge 2 for more practice with the present perfect.

Teaching Tip

Role play

Doing a role play is different from practicing dialogs given in the book. Students are given a situation, but they have to create the conversation on their own. Encourage students to think about the situation first and what they might say. Then have them converse without writing anything down. This activity will be difficult for students at first, but the more practice they get, the easier it will become.

Instructor's Notes

_____

_____

_____

_____

_____

_____

_____

_____

_____

_____

_____

_____

_____

_____

_____

_____

AT-A-GLANCE PREP

Objective: Identify health habits
Academic Strategy: Future conditional
Vocabulary: *cause, effect, habit, lungs, liver, sunscreen, stress, cavity*

AGENDA

Identify healthy and unhealthy habits.
Match habit causes and effects.
Use future conditionals.
Write about your habits.

RESOURCES

Activity Bank: Lesson 3, Worksheets 1–2
Reading and Writing Challenge: Unit 5

Grammar Challenge 3: Unit 5, Challenge 3

 1.5 hour classes   2.5 hour classes   3⁺ hour classes

Warm-up and Review   5 mins.

Have students take out a sheet of paper and think about all the illnesses, symptoms, or conditions they currently have or have had in the past. Ask them to write five sentences about these problems. Ask volunteers to share one of their sentences out loud.

Introduction   5-10 mins.

Write the word *habit* on the board. Ask students to help you define it. Write *Good Health Habits* and *Bad Health Habits* on the board. Ask student to list examples of each kind of habit in groups. When they finish, ask each group to report its answers to the class. Write everything students say on the board. State the objective: *Today we will be identifying health habits.*

Presentation 1   10-15 mins.

(A) Look at the picture. What are the people doing? What is healthy and what is unhealthy?

Make two lists on the board titled *healthy* and *unhealthy*. Ask students to help you complete

the lists with ideas from the picture. Take a few items on the list and ask students what will happen if this habit continues. For example: If the young girl keeps sunbathing and getting sunburned, what will happen? Answer: *She will get skin cancer.*

Practice 1   10-15 mins.

(B) Health habits are actions that affect your health, such as drinking water (a good habit) or smoking (a bad habit). Read and match each health habit to an effect below. There may be more than one answer. Compare answers with a partner.

Go over the instructions and the example. Have students complete the exercise by themselves. When they have finished, have them check their answers with a partner.

Evaluation 1   5 mins.

Go over the answers as a class.

STANDARDS CORRELATIONS

CASAS: 3.4.2, 3.5.9 (See CASAS Competency List on pages 169–175.)
SCANS: **Information** Acquire and evaluate information, organize and maintain information, interpret and communicate information
Interpersonal Participate as a member of a team, develop leadership skills, negotiate to arrive at a decision, work with cultural diversity
Systems Monitor and correct performance
Basic Skills Reading, writing, listening, speaking
Thinking Skills Creative thinking, decision making, problem solving, seeing things in the mind's eye

Personal Qualities Responsibility, sociability, self-management
EFF: **Communication** Convey ideas in writing, speak so others can understand
Decision Making Solve problems and make decisions, plan
Interpersonal Cooperate with others
Lifelong Learning Reflect and evaluate

Health habits

GOAL > Identify health habits

A Look at the picture. What are the people doing? What is healthy and what is unhealthy?

healthy = good for your mind and body

unhealthy = bad for your mind and body

B Health habits are actions that affect your health, such as drinking water (a good habit) or smoking (a bad habit). Read and match each health habit to an effect below. There may be more than one answer. Compare answers with a partner.

Health habit (Cause)

1. _j_ be very stressed

2. _c_ drink too much alcohol

3. _g_ stay in the sun too long

4. _i_ eat junk food every day

5. _h_ exercise at least three times a week

6. _d_ don't get enough calcium

7. _b_ don't sleep eight hours every night

8. _e_ smoke too much

9. _a_ stay away from smoking

10. _f_ wear sunscreen

Effect

a. have healthy lungs

b. not be well rested

c. destroy your liver

d. not have strong bones

e. get lung cancer

f. protect your skin

g. get skin cancer

h. be fit and healthy

i. gain weight

j. have high blood pressure

GOAL ➤ **Identify health habits**

C Study the chart with your teacher.

Future Conditional Statements	
Cause: *If* + present tense	**Effect: future tense**
If you *are* very stressed,	you *will have* high blood pressure.
If you *don't eat* enough calcium,	you *won't have* strong bones.
We can connect a cause and an effect by using a *future conditional* statement. The *if*-clause (or the *cause*) is in the present tense and the *effect* is in the future tense.	
Effect: future tense	**Cause: *if* + present tense**
You *will have* high blood pressure	*if* you *are* very stressed.
You can reverse the clauses, but use a comma only when the *if*-clause comes first.	

D Complete the sentences with the correct forms of the verbs in parentheses.

1. If you _____wash_____ (wash) your hands a few times a day, you _____won't get_____ (not get) so many colds.

2. If Ann _____gets_____ (get) her teeth cleaned regularly, she _____won't have_____ (not have) so many cavities.

3. My dad _____won't lose_____ (not lose) weight if he _____keeps_____ (keep) eating foods that are high in fat.

4. My skin _____will burn_____ (burn) if I _____don't use_____ (not use) sunscreen.

5. If people _____don't stretch_____ (not stretch) before they exercise, they _____will have_____ (have) sore muscles.

6. If you _____drink_____ (drink) too much beer, you _____will get_____ (get) a big stomach.

7. If Susan _____doesn't eat_____ (not eat) before she runs her race, she _____will pass out_____ (pass out).

8. Araceli _____will lose_____ (lose) the weight she gained when she was pregnant if she

   _____walks_____ (walk) with her baby every day.

9. Bang Vu _____won't be able to_____ (not be able to) talk tomorrow if he _____doesn't rest_____ (not rest) his voice.

Presentation 2

10–15 mins. ■■□

Write the following sentence on the board: *If you stay in the sun too long, you will get skin cancer.* Explain the concept of cause and effect and the grammar of this conditional statement.

C **Study the chart with your teacher.**

Once students understand the information in the chart, have them turn back to page 87 and work with a partner. Have the pairs make conditional statements from the information in Exercise B.

Practice 2

5–10 mins. ■■□

D **Complete the sentences with the correct forms of the verbs in parentheses.**

Go over the example as a class and then have students complete the exercise on their own.

Activity Bank

Lesson 3, Worksheet 1: Future Conditional

Refer students to *Stand Out 3 Grammar Challenge*, Unit 5, Challenge 3 for more practice with future conditional statements.

Evaluation 2

3 mins. ■■□

Go over the answers as a class.

Presentation 3

5-10 mins.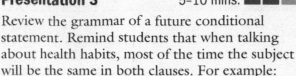

Review the grammar of a future conditional statement. Remind students that when talking about health habits, most of the time the subject will be the same in both clauses. For example: *If we eat unhealthy food every day, we will get fat.* Contrast this sentence with the following incorrect sentence: *If we eat unhealthy food every day, you will get fat.*

Practice 3

10-15 mins.

(E) **With a partner, practice making conditional statements with the information from Exercise B on page 87. Use different subjects (*I, you, we, they, he, she, it*).**

Evaluation 3

5 mins.

Ask volunteers to write their sentences on the board. Go over them as a class.

Application

15-25 mins.

(F) **Think about your good and bad health habits. Make two lists.**

(G) **Write four future conditional statements about good health habits you would like to have. Then, read them to your partner.**

Go over the example with students before they begin the exercise.

 Activity Bank

Lesson 3, Worksheet 2: Health Cause and Effect Cards

For the activity with the health cause-and-effect cards, you will need to print out and cut up the cards. Give half the students a cause card and the other half an effect card. (Ideally, you can print the cause cards and the effect cards on different colored paper so it will be easy for students to distinguish between the two types of cards.) Tell students that they will need to find a match with a student who has an opposite type of card that makes sense when combined with their card. Practice with a few students first. Show them the difference between a good match and one that is not as good.

Good match: *When I retire, I will work less and get some rest.*

Bad match: *When I retire, I will have a heart attack.*

Have students walk around and look for a good match. Tell students that when they find a good match, the two of them should sit down. (Some students will be left at the end, unable to find a good match.)

Ask each pair to read their future conditional statement aloud. Ask the students who couldn't find a good match to read their card out loud and ask the class to think of a good match.

Instructor's Notes

_____
_____
_____
_____
_____
_____
_____
_____
_____
_____
_____
_____
_____
_____
_____
_____
_____
_____
_____
_____
_____
_____
_____
_____
_____
_____
_____

GOAL ➤ Identify health habits

E With a partner, practice making conditional statements with the information from Exercise B on page 87. Use different subjects (*I, you, we, they, he, she, it*).

EXAMPLE: If we smoke cigarettes, we will get lung cancer.   (Answers will vary.)

1. _____

2. _____

3. _____

4. _____

5. _____

6. _____

F Think about your good and bad health habits. Make two lists. (Answers will vary.)

My Good Health Habits	My Bad Health Habits

G Write four future conditional statements about good health habits you would like to have. Then, read them to your partner. (Answers will vary.)

EXAMPLE: If I get more sleep, I will concentrate better on my work.

1. _____

2. _____

3. _____

4. _____

Nutrition labels

GOAL ➤ Interpret nutrition information

MyPyramid
STEPS TO A HEALTHIER YOU
MyPyramid.gov

| GRAINS | VEGETABLES | FRUITS | MILK | MEAT & BEANS |

GRAINS Make half your grains whole	VEGETABLES Vary your veggies	FRUITS Focus on fruits	MILK Get your calcium-rich foods	MEAT & BEANS Go lean with protein
Eat at least 3 oz. of whole-grain cereals, breads, crackers, rice, or pasta every day 1 oz. is about 1 slice of bread, about 1 cup of breakfast cereal, or ½ cup of cooked rice, cereal, or pasta	Eat more dark-green veggies like broccoli, spinach, and other dark leafy greens Eat more orange vegetables like carrots and sweet potatoes Eat more dry beans and peas like pinto beans, kidney beans, and lentils	Eat a variety of fruit Choose fresh, frozen, canned, or dried fruit Go easy on fruit juices	Go low-fat or fat-free when you choose milk, yogurt, and other milk products If you don't or can't consume milk, choose lactose-free products or other calcium sources such as fortified foods and beverages	Choose low-fat or lean meats and poultry Bake it, broil it, or grill it Vary your protein routine — choose more fish, beans, peas, nuts, and seeds

For a 2,000-calorie diet, you need the amounts below from each food group. To find the amounts that are right for you, go to MyPyramid.gov.

| Eat 6 oz. every day | Eat 2½ cups every day | Eat 2 cups every day | Get 3 cups every day;
for kids aged 2 to 8, it's 2 | Eat 5½ oz. every day |

A The food pyramid can help you make good decisions about daily food choices. It tells you how much of each food group you should eat every day. Skim the information in the pyramid and answer the questions below.

1. Which foods should you eat the most of? _____ grains (or) milk

2. Which foods should you eat the least of? _____ meat & beans

3. How much fruit should you eat every day? _____ 2 cups

4. What food group is rice in? _____ grains

5. What is an example of an orange vegetable? _____ carrot (or) sweet potato

Objective: Interpret nutrition information

Grammar: Imperatives

Academic Strategies: Active listening, active reading

Vocabulary: *variety, maintain, ideal weight, healthy weight, balance, fat, saturated fat, cholesterol, starch, fiber, grain, avoid, moderation, sodium, sugar, amount, serving size, calories, % daily value, carbohydrate, protein, vitamins, nutrients, digestion*

RESOURCES

Activity Bank: Lesson 4, Worksheet 1

Reading and Writing Challenge: Unit 5

Grammar Challenge 3: Unit 5, Challenge 4

Audio: CD 1, Track 12

■ 1.5 hour classes   ■ 2.5 hour classes   ■ 3⁺ hour classes

AGENDA

Talk about the food pyramid.
Read tips for healthy eating.
Interpret nutrition labels.
Understand dietary guidelines.
Plan meals based on guidelines.

Warm-up and Review   10-15 mins.

Ask students to look at the sentences they wrote in Lesson 3, Exercise G. Have them share their sentences with a partner. Then ask volunteers to share their sentences with the class.

Introduction   5-10 mins.

Write the word *nutrition* on the board. Ask students what this word means to them. State the objective: *Today we will be learning how to interpret nutrition information.*

Presentation 1   10-15 mins.

A The food pyramid can help you make good decisions about daily food choices. It tells you how much of each food group you should eat every day. Skim the information in the pyramid and answer the questions below.

Go over the pyramid and do Exercise A as a class.

STANDARDS CORRELATIONS

CASAS: 3.5.1, 3.5.3, 3.5.5, 3.5.9, 6.7.3 (See CASAS Competency List on pages 169–175.)

SCANS: Information Acquire and evaluate information, interpret and communicate information

Interpersonal Participate as a member of a team, teach others, exercise leadership, negotiate to arrive at a decision, work with cultural diversity

Systems Monitor and correct performance

Basic Skills Reading, writing, arithmetic, listening, speaking

Thinking Skills Creative thinking, decision making, problem solving, seeing things in the mind's eye

Personal Qualities Responsibility, sociability, self-management

EFF: Communication Read with understanding, speak so others can understand, listen actively

Decision Making Use math to solve problems and communicate, solve problems and make decisions

Interpersonal Cooperate with others

Lifelong Learning Learn through research

Practice 1   10–15 mins.

B Read the tips for healthy eating. Put a check mark (✓) next to the tips you follow or would like to follow. Then, discuss your answers with a partner.

Evaluation 1   5 mins.

Take a class poll to determine how many students follow each of the healthy eating tips.

Presentation 2   5–10 mins.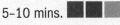

C Reading nutrition labels can help you make smart eating choices. Read the nutrition label for macaroni and cheese.

Explain what everything on the label means and how to find certain information, such as *percent (%) of daily value* and *amount per serving*. Ask students some basic questions, such as: *How much iron is in one serving?*

Practice 2   15–20 mins.

D Listen to Darla explain nutritional information to her grandmother.

Play the recording with student books closed. Tell students just to listen.

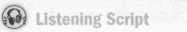

Listening Script   *CD 1, Track 12*

Part 1

Grandma: *Darla, I need your help.*
Darla: *Sure. What can I do, Grandma?*
Grandma: *Well, my doctor says I need to pay attention to nutrition, but I don't understand nutritional labels.*
Darla: *Oh, sure, I can help. Let's look at this box of macaroni and cheese. What's your first question?*
Grandma: *Well, I have high blood pressure. I shouldn't have a lot of salt. I don't see salt on this label.*
Darla: *Oh, you need to look at sodium. The sodium amount tells you how much salt there is.*
Grandma: *So, there is 470 mg of sodium in this box?*
Darla: *No, the amount they give you is the amount in each serving.*
Grandma: *How do I know how much a serving is?*
Darla: *They tell you on the label. See the serving size?*
Grandma: *OK. I see there are two servings in this box, one for me and one for Grandpa.*
Darla: *What's next?*
Grandma: *I need to watch calories if I want to lose weight. How many calories should I have each day?*
Darla: *About 2,000. You can have more calories if you are active.*

Part 2

Grandma: *What should I eat if I want to have a healthy heart?*
Darla: *You should avoid cholesterol and saturated fat.*
Grandma: *OK. Grandpa is diabetic. He needs to limit sugar.*
Darla: *Yes, sugar is on the nutritional label.*
Grandma: *Now, Grandpa and I both need something to help digestion.*
Darla: *You need a lot of fiber.*
Grandma: *One last question. Why do older women need to have a lot of calcium?*
Darla: *Oh, that's because women need calcium to protect them against bone disease.*
Grandma: *That's really helpful. Thanks, Darla.*

B Read the tips for healthy eating. Put a check mark (✓) next to the tips you follow or would like to follow. Then, discuss your answers with a partner. (Answers will vary.)

Tips for healthy eating	Follow	Would like to follow
1. Keep raw vegetables in the refrigerator to eat as a snack.		
2. Eat a variety of foods to get all the nutrients you need.		
3. Eat lean meats like fish and chicken.		
4. Choose fat-free or low-fat dairy products.		
5. Try not to drink beverages with a lot of sugar such as soft drinks.		
6. Flavor foods with herbs and spices instead of salt.		
7. Pay attention to serving sizes.		
8. Choose foods that have less saturated fat.		

C Reading nutrition labels can help you make smart eating choices. Read the nutrition label for macaroni and cheese.

Macaroni & Cheese Nutrition Facts

Amount Per Serving
Calories 250   Calories from Fat 110

	% Daily Value*
Total Fat 12g	18%
Saturated Fat 3g	15%
Cholesterol 30mg	10%
Sodium 470mg	20%
Total Carbohydrate 31g	10%
Dietary Fiber 0g	0%
Sugars 5g	
Protein 5g	
Vitamin A	4%
Vitamin C	2%
Calcium	20%
Iron	4%

*Percent Daily Values are based on a 2,000 calorie diet. Your Daily Values may be higher or lower depending on your calorie needs.

  D Listen to Darla explain nutritional information to her grandmother.

CD 1
TR 12

CD 1
TR 12

E Listen to each part of the conversation again and answer the questions below. Fill in the circle next to the correct answer.

Part 1

1. What does Grandma need to look at if she wants to watch her salt intake?
   ● sodium   ○ saturated fat

2. How many servings are in this box of macaroni and cheese?
   ● two   ○ four

3. How many calories should an average adult have each day?
   ○ 200   ● 2,000

Part 2

1. What should Grandma avoid to have a healthy heart?
   ● cholesterol and saturated fat
   ○ carbohydrates and saturated fat

2. What should a diabetic look for on a food label?
   ● sugar   ○ salt

3. What nutrient helps digestion?
   ○ iron   ● fiber

4. What nutrient is good for bones?
   ● calcium   ○ vitamin A

F Read the nutritional guidelines.

Recommended Amount of Calories and Fat Per Day
- 2,000 calories per day
- 20 or less grams saturated fat
- 65 grams total fat

Quick Guide to % Daily Value* for Nutrients
5% or less is LOW   20% or more is HIGH

*Percent Daily Values are based on a 2,000-calorie diet. Your Daily Values may be higher or lower depending on your calorie needs.

G Now look at the macaroni and cheese label on page 91. Answer the questions below.

1. Is macaroni and cheese high in fat? ___Yes._____

2. Is macaroni and cheese low in sodium? ___No._____

3. Does it contain any protein? How much? ___Yes, 5 grams._____

4. What vitamins does it contain? Is it high in vitamins? _Vitamins A and C; no._

5. Is macaroni and cheese a good source of calcium? _Yes._____

6. Do you think macaroni and cheese is a healthy food choice? Why or why not?
   (Answers will vary.)_____

H Work with a partner and plan three meals based on the food pyramid on page 90. Share your plan with your class. Whose menu is the most delicious and nutritious?

Practice 2 (continued)   15–20 mins. ■■□

E Listen to each part of the conversation again and answer the questions below. Fill in the circle next to the correct answer.

Evaluation 2   5–10 mins. ■■□

Go over answers as a class and address any more questions that come up about nutrition labels.

Presentation 3   5–10 mins. ■■□

F Read the nutritional guidelines.

Discuss the guidelines with students. Ask them to estimate how many calories and how many grams of fat they eat per day.

Practice 3   5–10 mins. ■

G Now look at the macaroni and cheese label on page 91. Answer the questions below.

Evaluation 3   3 mins. ■

Go over the answers to Exercise G as a class.

Activity Bank

Lesson 4, Worksheet 1: Nutrition Label Quiz

Refer students to *Stand Out 3 Grammar Challenge*, Unit 5, Challenge 4 for more practice with imperatives.

Application   10–20 mins. ■■□

H Work with a partner and plan three meals based on the food pyramid on page 90. Share your plan with your class. Whose menu is the most delicious and nutritious?

Have students work in pairs. When they have finished, have them share their work with another pair. Ask different pairs to share their meal plans with the class. As a class, vote on whose plan is the most nutritious.

Instructor's Notes

Objective: Interpret fitness information
Academic Strategy: Active reading
Vocabulary: *physical fitness, exercise, routine, recreational, aerobics, cardiovascular, stroller*

AGENDA

Read a fitness article.
Identify routine vs. recreational activities.
Discuss the health benefits of physical activity.

RESOURCES

Activity Bank: Lesson 5, Worksheets 1–2
Reading and Writing Challenge: Unit 5

Grammar Challenge 3: Unit 5, Challenge 5

■ 1.5 hour classes   ■ 2.5 hour classes   ■ 3⁺ hour classes

Warm-up and Review   5-10 mins. ■■■

Have students write down everything they can remember about healthy eating from Lesson 4. After five minutes, have students share what they wrote and make a list on the board.

Introduction   5-10 mins. ■■■

Ask students questions about fitness, such as: *Do you exercise? What types of exercise do you do? How often do you exercise?* State the objective: *Today we will be interpreting fitness information.*

Presentation 1   10-15 mins. ■■■

Emphasize to students that as they read an article from a magazine, they will not understand every word of the article. Ask them not to use their dictionaries and not to worry about every word they don't understand.

Practice 1   10-15 mins. ■■■

 You are going to read part of an article about physical fitness. Before you read, write one piece of advice that you think the article will contain. Then, read the article.

Ask students to also read the statements that follow in Exercise B. Have them think about whether the statements are true or false as they read.

 Decide if the statements are true or false. Bubble in the correct answer.

 Discuss these questions with your partner.

Evaluation 1   5-10 mins. ■■■

Have students form groups and go over the answers to the questions. Walk around the classroom and talk with each group.

Healthy living

GOAL ➤ Interpret fitness information

A You are going to read part of an article about physical fitness. Before you read, write one piece of advice that you think the article will contain. Then, read the article.

Be Physically Active Each Day

Being physically active and maintaining a healthy weight are necessary for good health. Children, teens, adults, and the elderly can improve their health by including moderate physical activity in their daily lives.

Try to get at least 30 minutes (adults) or 60 minutes (children) of moderate physical activity most days of the week, preferably daily. No matter what activity you choose, you can do it all at once, or spread it out over the day.

Make Physical Activity a Regular Part of Your Routine

Choose activities that you enjoy and that you can do regularly. Some people prefer activities that fit into their daily routine, like gardening or taking extra trips up and down stairs. Others prefer a regular exercise program, such as a physical activity program at their worksite. Some do both. The important thing is to be physically active every day.

Adapted from: Dietary Guidelines for Americans 2000 Center for Nutritional Policy and Promotion, USDA.

B Decide if the statements are true or false. Bubble in the correct answers.

	True	False
1. Physical exercise is necessary for good health.	●	○
2. Elderly people do not need to exercise.	○	●
3. Adults should exercise every day.	●	○
4. It is better to exercise throughout the day.	○	●
5. Climbing stairs is a good way to exercise regularly.	●	○
6. The most important thing is to exercise regularly.	●	○

C Discuss these questions with your partner. (Answers will vary.)

1. Do you exercise more or less than recommended in the article? _____

2. Does your workplace offer physical activity programs? What are they? _____

_____

GOAL ➤ **Interpret fitness information**

D Look at the examples of physical activities. Which is an example of a routine activity? Which is an example of a recreational activity?

Ana plays tennis
twice a week
with her friend.

Mike rides his bicycle
to the office every day.

E Read the list of routine activities. Put a check mark (✓) next to the activities you have tried. Put an *X* next to the activities you would like to try. Add two more activities.

(Answers will vary.)

- ❑ Walk or ride a bike to work.
- ❑ Walk up stairs instead of taking an elevator.
- ❑ Get off the bus a few stops early and walk the remaining distance.
- ❑ Garden.
- ❑ Push a stroller.

- ❑ Clean the house.
- ❑ Play actively with children.
- ❑ Take a brisk ten-minute walk or bike ride in the morning, at lunch, and after dinner.
- ❑ _____
- ❑ _____

F Read the list of recreational activities. Put a check mark (✓) next to the activities you have tried. Put an *X* next to the activities you would like to try. Add two more activities.

(Answers will vary.)

- ❑ Walk, jog, or bicycle.
- ❑ Swim or do water aerobics.
- ❑ Play tennis or racquetball.
- ❑ Golf (pull cart or carry clubs).
- ❑ Canoe.
- ❑ Cross-country ski.

- ❑ Play basketball.
- ❑ Dance.
- ❑ Take part in an exercise program at work, home, school, or gym.
- ❑ _____
- ❑ _____

Presentation 2   5–10 mins. ■■□

Write *physical activity* on the board. Have students call out different physical activities they know of and write them on the board as they say them. Ask students what part of their everyday routine could be considered physical activity, such as walking to class, cleaning the house, and so on.

(D) Look at the examples of physical activities. Which is an example of a routine activity? Which is an example of a recreational activity?

Practice 2   15–20 mins. ■■

(E) Read the list of routine activities. Put a check mark (✓) next to the activities you have tried. Put an X next to the activities you would like to try. Add two more activities.

(F) Read the list of recreational activities. Put a check mark (✓) next to the activities you have tried. Put an X next to the activities you would like to try. Add two more activities.

Evaluation 2   5–10 mins. ■■

Have students discuss with a partner where they can best pursue each recreational activity. Have them share their ideas with the class.

Presentation 3   5-10 mins.

For the next two exercises, students will be reading some information and discussing the questions that follow the information in groups. You may wish to assign each group one exercise, either G or H, and then have them report what they learn to the class. As an extension (if you have time) or for homework students can write out the answers to the questions they discussed.

Practice 3   10-15 mins. ■

G Read the paragraph. Then, discuss the questions below with a partner.

H Read about more benefits of physical activity. Then, discuss the questions with a partner.

Evaluation 3   10-15 mins.

Have a class discussion about physical activity. Ask for students' personal opinions.

Application   10-15 mins. ■■■

Have students make a list of all the physical activities—both routine and recreational—that they do in a week.

Activity Bank

Lesson 5, Worksheet 1: Fitness Q & A

Lesson 5, Worksheet 2: Fitness Chart

📖 Refer students to *Stand Out 3 Grammar Challenge*, Unit 5, Challenge 5 for practice with imperatives *vs.* declaratives.

📖 Refer students to *Stand Out 3 Grammar Challenge*, Unit 5, Extension Challenges 1–2 for practice with the present perfect and *for* or *since*.

GOAL ➤ **Interpret fitness information**

G Read the paragraph. Then, discuss the questions below with a partner.

Health Benefits of Physical Activity

Being physically active for at least 30 minutes on most days of the week reduces the risk of developing or dying of heart disease. It has other health benefits as well. No one is too young or too old to enjoy the benefits of regular physical activity. Two types of physical activity are especially beneficial: 1) Aerobic activities. These are activities that speed your heart rate and breathing. They help cardiovascular fitness. 2) Activities for strength and flexibility. Developing strength may help build and maintain your bones. Carrying groceries and lifting weights are two strength-building activities. Gentle stretching, dancing, or yoga can increase flexibility.

1. Why are aerobic activities good for you? They reduce the risk of heart disease and strengthen bones.
2. What are some examples of aerobic activities? running, swimming, walking
3. Why are activities for strength good for your bones? Developing strength may help build and maintain your bones.
4. What are some examples of strength-building activities? lifting weights, carrying groceries
5. What types of activities can increase your flexibility? stretching, dancing, yoga
6. What are some activities you do for strength and flexibility? (Answers will vary.)

H Read about more benefits of physical activity. Then, discuss the questions with a partner.

More Health Benefits of Physical Activity	
➤ Increases physical fitness	➤ Lowers risk factors for cardiovascular disease, colon cancer, and type 2 diabetes
➤ Helps build and maintain healthy bones, muscles, and joints	
	➤ Helps control blood pressure
➤ Builds endurance and muscular strength	➤ Promotes psychological well-being and self-esteem
➤ Helps manage weight	➤ Reduces feelings of depression and anxiety

1. What diseases can exercise help prevent? cardiovascular disease, colon cancer, type 2 diabetes
2. How does exercise help your circulatory system? It helps control blood pressure.
3. How does exercise affect your mood and your mental health? It reduces feelings of depression and anxiety, and it promotes psychological well-being and self-esteem.
4. What are some other benefits of exercise? (Answers will vary.)

Review

A **Match each condition with the doctor who treats it. Then, use this information to practice the conversation below with a partner.**

Condition

1. __b__ My skin is very red and itchy.
2. __d__ My heart is beating quickly.
3. __h__ My husband is always sneezing.
4. __e__ My baby is coughing.
5. __g__ My mother's toe hurts.
6. __f__ There is something in my eye.
7. __a__ My brother has a cavity.
8. __i__ I feel nervous all the time.
9. __c__ My sister is pregnant.

Doctor

a. dentist
b. dermatologist
c. gynecologist/obstetrician
d. cardiologist
e. pediatrician
f. ophthalmologist
g. podiatrist
h. allergist
i. psychiatrist

EXAMPLE: *Student A:* <u>My skin is very red and itchy</u>. What should I do?
            Student B: You should see a <u>dermatologist</u>.

B **Make sentences using the present perfect and *for* or *since*. (Lesson 2)**

1. Ali has a backache / Monday

   <u>Ali has had a backache since Monday.</u>

2. my neck hurts / two days

   <u>My neck has hurt for two days.</u>

3. Maria feels dizzy / yesterday

   <u>Maria has felt dizzy since yesterday.</u>

4. my children have a cold / Friday

   <u>My children have had a cold since Friday.</u>

5. Peter is sick / two weeks

   <u>Peter has been sick for two weeks.</u>

6. I have an earache / 10:00 A.M.

   <u>I have had an earache since 10:00 A.M.</u>

7. they are absent from work / one month

   <u>They have been absent from work for one month.</u>

Objectives: All unit objectives
Grammar: All unit grammar
Academic Strategy: Reviewing
Vocabulary: All unit vocabulary

AGENDA
Discuss unit objectives.
Complete the review.
Do My Dictionary.
Evaluate and reflect on progress.

RESOURCES

Activity Bank: Unit 5, Lessons 1–5
Reading and Writing Challenge: Unit 5

Grammar Challenge 3: Unit 5, Challenges 1–5

 1.5 hour classes   2.5 hour classes   3· hour classes

Stand Out 3 Assessment CD-ROM with Exam*View*®

Warm-up and Review   5–10 mins.

With books closed, have groups list all the parts of the body they can. Have a competition to see who can list the most.

Introduction   5–10 mins.

Ask the class to recall the unit goals without looking at their books. Remind them of any goals they omitted. (Unit goals: identify parts of the body, communicate symptoms to a doctor, identify health habits, interpret nutrition information, and interpret fitness information) Write the goals on the board. Show students the first page of the unit and mention the five goals. State the objective for the review: *Today we will review everything you have learned in this unit.*

Presentation 1   10–15 mins.

This presentation will cover the first three pages of the review. Quickly go to the first page of each lesson. Discuss the goal of each. Ask simple questions to remind students of what they have learned.

Note: Since there is little presentation in the review, you can assign Exercises A–E for homework and go over them in class.

Practice 1   20–25 mins.

Note: There are two ways to do the review: (1) Go through the exercises one at a time and, as students complete each one, go over the answers. (2) Briefly go through the instructions of each exercise, allow students to complete them all at once, and then go over the answers.

 A Match each condition with the doctor who treats it. Then, use this information to practice the conversation below with a partner.

B Make sentences using the present perfect and *for* or *since*. (Lesson 2)

Evaluation 1   20–25 mins.

Go around the classroom and check on students' progress. Help individuals when needed. If you see consistent errors among several students, interrupt the class and give a mini lesson or review to help students feel comfortable with the concept.

Practice 1 *(continued)*   25–30 mins. ■■■□

C Complete the sentences with a future conditional verb.

D Read the information. Then, decide if the statements below are true or false. Bubble in the correct answer.

Evaluation 1 *(continued)*   25–30 mins. ■■■□

Go around the classroom and check on students' progress. Help individuals when needed. If you see consistent errors among several students, interrupt the class and give a mini lesson or review to help students feel comfortable with the concept.

Teaching Tip

Recycling/Review

The review exercises and the project that follows are part of the recycling/review process. Students at this level often need to be reintroduced to concepts to solidify what they have learned. Many concepts are learned and forgotten while learning other new concepts. This is because students learn but are not necessarily ready to acquire language concepts.

Therefore, it becomes very important to review and to show students how to review on their own. It is also important to recycle the new concepts in different contexts.

Instructor's Notes

C Complete the sentences with a future conditional verb. (Answers will vary.)

1. If you eat out every night, ___you will spend a lot of money.___

2. _____ if he goes to the best doctors in the country.

3. If _____, they will look and feel great.

4. If Paulo smokes a pack of cigarettes a day, _____.

5. If _____, you will get sick.

6. If _____, you will improve your flexibility.

7. If you read nutritional labels, _____.

8. If _____, you will have a lot of cavities.

D Read the information. Then, decide if the statements below are true or false. Bubble in the correct answer.

Find your balance between food and physical activity

- Be sure to stay within your daily calorie needs.
- Be physically active for at least 30 minutes most days of the week.
- About 60 minutes a day of physical activity may be needed to prevent weight gain.
- For sustaining weight loss, at least 60 to 90 minutes a day of physical activity may be required.
- Children and teenagers should be physically active for 60 minutes every day, or most days.

Know the limits on fats, sugars, and salt (sodium)

- Make most of your fat sources from fish, nuts, and vegetable oils.
- Limit solid fats like butter, stick margarine, shortening, and lard, as well as foods that contain these.
- Check the Nutrition Facts label to keep saturated fats, *trans* fats, and sodium low.
- Choose food and beverages low in added sugars. Added sugars contribute calories with few, if any, nutrients.

	True	False
1. Children only need to exercise for 20 minutes a day.	○	●
2. Choose foods that are low in added sugar.	●	○
3. If you want to lose weight, you should exercise between 60 and 90 minutes a day.	●	○
4. Fish and nuts are good fats.	●	○

Review

 With a partner, ask and answer questions about the nutritional information on the package of frozen peas. Decide if the frozen peas are a healthy choice. (Lesson 4)

Frozen Peas Nutrition Facts	Amount/Serving	%DV*
Ingredients: green peas, salt	Total Carbohydrate 12g	4%
Serving size 2/3 cup (88g)	Fiber 4g	16%
Servings Per Container About 5	Sugars 6g	
	Protein 5g	
Calories 70	Vitamin A	6%
Calories from Fat 5	Vitamin C	15%
Total Fat 0.5g	1%	Calcium 0%	0%
Sat. Fat 0g	0%	Iron 4%	4%
Cholesterol 0mg	0%	*Percent Daily Values are based on a 2,000 calorie diet. Your Daily Values may be higher or lower depending on your calorie needs.	
Sodium 100mg	4%		

Home Style
Frozen Peas

1. Are the peas high in fat? No.
2. Are the peas low in sodium? Yes.
3. Do they contain any protein? How much? Yes; 5 grams.
4. What vitamins do they contain? Are they high in vitamins? Vitamins A and C; no.
5. Are the peas a good source of calcium? No.
6. Do you think peas are a healthy food choice? Yes.

 Look back at the articles on pages 93 and 95. Write four pieces of advice that you would like to follow. (Lesson 5) (Answers will vary.)

1. _____

2. _____

3. _____

4. _____

Practice 1 *(continued)*   25–30 mins. ■■■

E With a partner, ask and answer questions about the nutritional information on the package of frozen peas. Decide if the frozen peas are a healthy choice. (Lesson 4)

F Look back at the articles on pages 93 and 95. Write four pieces of advice you would like to follow. (Lesson 5)

Evaluation 1 *(continued)*   25–30 mins. ■■■

Go around the classroom and check on students' progress. Help individuals when needed. If you see consistent errors among several students, interrupt the class and give a mini lesson or review to help students feel comfortable with the concept.

Presentation 2   5–10 mins.

My Dictionary

Ask students to brainstorm new vocabulary items they learned in this unit. Have them do this without looking in their books.

If you want to use a new word, it's important to know what part of speech it is. Is it a person, place, or thing (a noun); an action (verb); or a word that describes a noun (adjective)?

Go over the parts of speech with students, making sure they understand the differences.

Practice 2   15–20 mins.

(Shorter classes can do these exercises for homework.)

Look at the words from Unit 5 in the box below. Make a chart like the one below. Put each word into the correct category in the chart. Use a dictionary to check your answers.

Evaluation 2   15–20 mins.

Walk around the classroom and help students.

Presentation 3   5–10 mins.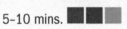

Learner Log

In this unit, you learned many things about health. How comfortable do you feel doing each of the skills listed below? Rate your comfort level on a scale of 1 to 4.

Make sure that students understand what to do. You may want to read the skills with the class in case students have questions about them.

Practice 3   5–10 mins.

Have students complete the Learner Log.

Evaluation 3   5–10 mins.

Walk around the classroom and help students.

Application   5–10 mins.

Go over the two reflection questions with students and have them complete the answers by themselves.

TB Assessment *(optional)*

Use the Stand Out 3 Assessment CD-ROM with Exam*View*® to create a post-test for Unit 5.

My Dictionary

If you want to use a new word, it's important to know what part of speech it is. Is it a person, place, or thing (a noun); an action (a verb); or a word that describes a noun (an adjective)?

Look at the words from Unit 5 in the box below. Make a chart like the one below. Put each word into the correct category in the chart. Use a dictionary to check your answers.

| ankle | ophthalmologist | | dentist | worry | | itchy | | sore | | cavity |
| stay | hospital | tired | | cough | diabetes | | stress | | sore | protect | gain |

NOUN		VERB		ADJECTIVE	
ophthalmologist		worry		itchy	
ankle	cough	stay	maintain	sore	healthy
dentist	diabetes	protect	stretch	tired	active
cavity	stress	gain		raw	gentle
hospital	cholesterol				

Learner Log

In this unit, you learned many things about health. How comfortable do you feel doing each of the skills listed below? Rate your comfort level on a scale of 1 to 4.

1 = Need more practice   **2** = OK   **3** = Good   **4** = Great!

Life Skill	Comfort Level	Page
I can identify parts of the body.	1 2 3 4	81
I can identify doctors and their specializations.	1 2 3 4	82
I can communicate my symptoms to a doctor.	1 2 3 4	84
I can interpret food labels.	1 2 3 4	91
I can identify healthy and unhealthy habits.	1 2 3 4	87
I can interpret information on dietary guidelines.	1 2 3 4	90
I can interpret information on fitness.	1 2 3 4	93

If you circled 1 or 2, write down the page number where you can review this skill.

Reflection

1. What was the most useful skill you learned in this unit? _____

2. How will this help you in life? _____

Team Project

Create a healthy living plan.

You are a team of doctors and health-care professionals who have decided to make a healthy living plan to give patients when they leave the hospital.

1. Form a team with four or five students. Choose a position for each member of your team.

POSITION	JOB DESCRIPTION	STUDENT NAME
Student 1: Health Advisor	See that everyone speaks English. See that everyone participates.	
Student 2: Writer	Write down information for plan.	
Student 3: Designer	Design plan layout and add artwork.	
Students 4/5: Health Representatives	Help writer and designer with their work.	

2. Make a list of all the information you want to include in your plan (healthy habits, fitness and nutrition advice, etc.). (Lessons 3–5)

3. Create the different sections of your plan, for example, a guide to reading nutritional labels, a guide to exercise, a list of doctors and their specializations, and a guide to common symptoms and diseases. (Lessons 1–5)

4. Add artwork to the plan, for example, maps of parks and gyms in your area or a drawing of the food pyramid.

5. Make a collage of all your information.

6. Share your healthy living plan with the class.

Team Project

Create a healthy living plan.

Each team will create a healthy living plan to give patients when they leave the hospital.

The team project is the final application for the unit. It gives students a chance to show that they have mastered all of the Unit 5 objectives.

Note: Shorter classes can extend this project over two class meetings.

Stage 1   5 mins.

Form a team with four or five students. Choose a position for each member of your team.

Have students decide who will lead each step as described on the student page. Provide well-defined directions on the board for how teams should proceed. Explain that all the students do every step as a team. Teams shouldn't go to the next stage until the previous one is complete.

Stage 2   15-20 mins.

Make a list of all the information you want to include in your plan (healthy habits, fitness and nutrition advice, etc.). (Lessons 3–5)

Stage 3   10-15 mins.

Create the different sections of your plan, for example, a guide to reading nutritional labels, a guide to exercise, a list of doctors and their specializations, and a guide to common symptoms and diseases. (Lessons 1–5)

Stage 4   10-15 mins.

Add artwork to the plan, for example, maps of parks and gyms in your area or drawings of the food pyramid.

Stage 5   5 mins.

Make a collage of all your information.

Optional Computer Activity: Students may want to use the computer to design their plans.

Stage 6   15-20 mins.

Share your healthy living plan with the class.

Help teams prepare for their presentations. Suggest that each member choose a different part of the plan to present.

STANDARDS CORRELATIONS

CASAS: 4.8.1, 4.8.5, 4.8.6. (See CASAS Competency List on pages 169–175.)
SCANS: Resources Allocate time
Information Acquire and evaluate information, organize and maintain information, interpret and communicate information, use computers to process information (optional)
Systems Understand systems, improve and design systems
Technology (optional) Select technology, apply technology to exercise
Basic Skills Writing
Thinking Skills Creative thinking, decision making, problem solving, seeing things in the mind's eye, reasoning

Personal Qualities Responsibility, self-esteem, self-management, integrity/honesty
EFF: Communication Convey ideas in writing, speak so others can understand
Decision Making Solve problems and make decisions, plan
Interpersonal Guide others, resolve conflict and negotiate, advocate and influence, cooperate with others
Lifelong Learning Take responsibility for learning, reflect and evaluate, use information and communication technologies (optional)

Objective: Identify job titles and skills
Grammar: Simple present
Vocabulary: *job, career, title, skills,* job titles

AGENDA

Identify job titles.
Identify job skills.

RESOURCES

Activity Bank: Lesson 1, Worksheet 1
Reading and Writing Challenge: Unit 6

Grammar Challenge 3: Unit 6, Challenge 1

■ 1.5 hour classes   ■ 2.5 hour classes   ■ 3⁺ hour classes

Stand Out 3 Assessment CD-ROM with Exam*View*®

 Preassessment *(optional)*

Use the Stand Out 3 Assessment CD-ROM with
Exam*View*® to create a pretest for Unit 6.

Warm-up and Review   5–10 mins.

Write *job titles* on the board. Ask students, one
at a time: *What do you do?* If a student doesn't
understand, ask different students until someone
gives you an appropriate answer. If students
continue to have difficulty, say: *I am a teacher.
What do you do?* Once students start telling you
what they do, write their responses on the board.

Introduction   5–10 mins.

Ask students the difference between a job
and a career. *The Newbury House Dictionary
of American English* defines *career* as "a life's
work, especially in business or in a profession."
Job is defined as "work that one is paid to do;
everyday, permanent employment." *Profession* is
defined as "an occupation requiring an advanced
degree." Discuss these terms and ask students if
they consider their work a job or a career. State
the objective: *Today we will be discussing job titles
and skills.*

Presentation 1   10–15 mins.

A **Look at the pictures and write the correct
letter next to each job title below.**

Have students fill in the blanks by themselves.
When they have finished, go over each job. See if
they know what the person in each picture does
before you explain. Ask if they know anyone who
holds a job like the ones shown. When you have
finished, ask them if they can think of any jobs
that are not listed.

Practice 1   15–20 mins.

B **Talk to your partner about the four jobs.
Which job is the most interesting? Which job is
the most difficult? Why?**

Have students, in pairs, discuss the questions.
Ask each pair to take notes on the answers.

Evaluation 1   10–15 mins.

Ask each pair to report what they discussed.
Write their response and reasons on the board.
See if you can come up with a consensus on
which is the most interesting job and which is
the most difficult job.

STANDARDS CORRELATIONS

CASAS: 4.1.8 (See CASAS Competency List on pages 169–175.)
SCANS: **Information** Acquire and evaluate information, organize and
maintain information, interpret and communicate information
Interpersonal Participate as a member of a team, teach others, exercise
leadership, negotiate to arrive at a decision, work with cultural diversity
Systems Monitor and correct performance
Basic Skills Reading, writing, listening, speaking
Thinking Skills Creative thinking, decision making

Personal Qualities Responsibility, sociability, self-management
EFF: **Communication** Convey ideas in writing, speak so others can
understand, listen actively
Decision Making Solve problems and make decisions
Interpersonal Resolve conflict and negotiate, cooperate with others
Lifelong Learning Reflect and evaluate

Getting Hired

GOALS

- ➤ **Identify job titles and skills**
- ➤ **Identify job skills and preferences**
- ➤ **Interpret job advertisements**
- ➤ **Fill out a job application**
- ➤ **Interview for a job**

LESSON 1

Jobs and careers

GOAL ➤ **Identify job titles and skills**

A Look at the picures and write the correct letter next to each job title below.

a.

c.

b.

d.
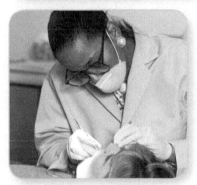

__c__ 1. graphic artist

__d__ 2. dental hygienist

__a__ 3. home health-care aide

__b__ 4. bookkeeper

B Talk to your partner about the four jobs. Which job is the most interesting? Which job is the most difficult? Why? (Answers will vary.)

GOAL ➤ **Identify job titles and skills**

 Match the job with the description.

_e_	1. graphic artist	a. cleans teeth
_i_	2. repair technician	b. takes care of children
_f_	3. administrative assistant	c. designs and maintains yards
_a_	4. dental hygienist	d. writes programs for computers
_c_	5. landscaper	e. designs artwork for companies
_h_	6. bookkeeper	f. types, files, and does general office work
_j_	7. home health-care aide	g. uses equipment in a factory or on a construction site
_d_	8. computer programmer	h. keeps financial records
_b_	9. nanny	i. fixes appliances and equipment
_g_	10. machine operator	j. takes care of sick people in their own homes

D **Look at the pictures below. What do you think each person does? Write a job title from the box below each picture.**

cashier	custodian	doctor	electrician	food server	judge
lawyer	nurse	plumber	scientist	~~teacher~~	postal worker

1. __teacher__

2. _food server_

3. _custodian_

4. _nurse_

5. _plumber_

6. _judge_

7. _cashier_

8. _scientist_

Presentation 2   5–10 mins. ■■■

Ask students: *What does a dental hygienist do?*
Ask a few other questions about different jobs
until students understand that you are asking for
a job description. Go over the instructions for
Exercise C.

Practice 2   10–15 mins. ■■

C Match the job with the description.

D Look at the pictures below. What do you
think each person does? Write a job title from
the box below each picture.

Evaluation 2   5–10 mins. ■■

Have students share their answers with a partner.
Then go over the answers as a class.

Presentation 3
5-10 mins.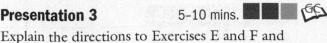

Explain the directions to Exercises E and F and go over a few examples if students need help.

Practice 3
15-20 mins. ▪

E Work with a small group to write one skill for each job title below.

F Work with a small group to write the job title for each skill below. (*Hint*: The job titles are from Exercise D.)

Evaluation 3
5-10 mins. ▪

Go over the answers to Exercises E and F as a class.

Application
10-20 mins. ▪▪▪

G Practice the conversation with a partner. Use the job titles and skills from this lesson.

Write the conversation on the board but omit the job title in the question and the job description in the answer. Go back over the job titles and job descriptions in Exercise C, asking the class to verbally fill in the blanks in the conversation. Make sure they understand when to use *a* or *an*.

Have volunteer pairs go through each item in Exercise C and perform the conversation that you wrote on the board. Have them take turns being Student A and Student B, allowing the pair to go through each of the ten examples twice.

H Work with a partner. Think of four more jobs and write what each person does.

Write the following question on the board: *What do you do?* Tell students to write a statement that answers the question. Under the question, write: *I am a teacher. I teach English to students and help them with their reading, writing, listening, and speaking.* Give students a few minutes to write out their own job titles and descriptions. Walk around the classroom and help students with vocabulary. When students have finished, have the class get in a circle. Explain that you will select a student and then the whole class must ask in unison: *What do you do?* The selected student will respond with his or her job title and description. Allow time to do this exchange with each student in the class. (Remind students that *homemaker* and *student* are job titles.)

 Refer students to *Stand Out 3 Grammar Challenge*, Unit 6, Challenge 1 for practice with the simple present tense.

Activity Bank

Lesson 1, Worksheet 1: Job Titles

Instructor's Notes

_____

_____

_____

_____

_____

_____

_____

_____

_____

_____

_____

_____

_____

_____

_____

_____

_____

_____

_____

_____

_____

_____

_____

GOAL ➤ **Identify job titles and skills**

Vocabulary | Grammar
Life Skills
Academic | Pronunciation

E Work with a small group to write one skill for each job title below.

Job title	Skill
1. custodian	cleaning
2. teacher	helps students learn
3. doctor	helps sick people, gives medicines, diagnoses illnesses
4. food server	delivers food to tables in restaurants
5. judge	makes decisions in court cases
6. nurse	takes care of sick patients

F Work with a small group to write the job title for each skill below. (*Hint:* The job titles are from Exercise D.)

Job title	Skill
1. plumber	fixes leaking pipes
2. postal worker	delivers mail and packages
3. electrician	fixes electrical problems
4. cashier	rings up the total for purchased items
5. lawyer	defends crime victims
6. scientist	invents new medicine

G Practice the conversation with a partner. Use the job titles and skills from this lesson.

EXAMPLE: *Student A:* What does a graphic artist do?
   Student B: A graphic artist designs artwork for companies.

H Work with a partner. Think of four more jobs and write what each person does.

EXAMPLE: A farmer grows fruits and vegetables. (Answers will vary.)

1. _____

2. _____

3. _____

4. _____

LESSON 2

What can you do?

GOAL ➤ Identify job skills and preferences

A What are your special job skills? Put a check mark (✓) next to the things you are good at. Add two skills to the list. (Answers will vary.)

❑ answer phones and take messages
❑ assemble things
❑ cook
❑ draw
❑ drive a car or truck
❑ fix machines
❑ order supplies
❑ balance accounts
❑ operate machines
❑ talk to customers
❑ read maps
❑ sew
❑ speak other languages
❑ take care of children
❑ take care of the elderly
❑ type
❑ repair computers
❑ use computers

❑ _____

❑ _____

B Are there any skills you want to improve? Are there any skills you want to learn? List them below. (Answers will vary.)

Improve: _____

Learn: _____

C Exchange your list with a partner. Think of ways your partner can learn or improve the skills he or she wrote down. Use ideas from the box below.

volunteer	ask a friend to teach you	practice at home
take a class	find a job training program	get trained at your company

EXAMPLE: *Student A:* I want to learn to <u>take care of the elderly</u>.
          Student B: Maybe you can <u>volunteer at a hospital or nursing home</u>.

Objective: Identify job skills and preferences
Grammar: Infinitives and gerunds
Academic Strategy: Paragraph writing
Vocabulary: *operate, job training program, supplies, practice, skills, assemble, sew, elderly, nursing home*

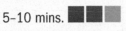

AGENDA

Identify your job skills.
Talk about job preferences.
Use infinitives and gerunds.
Write about your skills.

RESOURCES

Activity Bank: Lesson 2, Worksheet 1
Reading and Writing Challenge: Unit 6

Grammar Challenge 3: Unit 6, Challenge 2

 1.5 hour classes   2.5 hour classes   3⁺ hour classes

Warm-up and Review   5–10 mins. ■■■

Review the application activity from Lesson 1. Have students answer the question without looking at their papers. Ask each student individually: *What do you do?*

Introduction   5–10 mins. ■■■

Write the word *skills* on the board. Ask students if they know what the word means. If they don't, define it by giving concrete examples, such as *typing* or *painting*. State the objective: *In this lesson, you will identify your job skills (what you can do) and your preferences (what you would like to do).*

Presentation 1   10–15 mins. ■■■

(A) What are your special job skills? Put a check mark (✓) next to the things you are good at. Add two skills to the list.

Go through each skill with students. Have them put a check mark next to the skills they can do. At the end of the list, have them write two skills they have that don't appear on the list.

(B) Are there any skills you want to improve? Are there any skills you want to learn? List them below.

Give students a few minutes to work on this on their own.

Practice 1   10–15 mins. ■■■

(C) Exchange your list with a partner. Think of ways your partner can learn or improve the skills he or she wrote down. Use ideas from the box below.

Have students work with the list they made in Exercise B. Go through the conversation with students and talk about some possible responses. Then have students talk with a partner about the skills on their lists.

Evaluation 1   5 mins. ■■✓

Observe the activity. Ask a few volunteers to perform the conversation for the class.

STANDARDS CORRELATIONS

CASAS: 4.1.9 (See CASAS Competency List on pages 169–175.)
SCANS: **Resources** Allocate human resources
Information Acquire and evaluate information, organize and maintain information, interpret and communicate information
Interpersonal Participate as a member of a team, teach others, work with cultural diversity
Systems Monitor and correct performance
Basic Skills Reading, writing, listening, speaking

Thinking Skills Creative thinking, decision making, seeing things in the mind's eye
Personal Qualities Responsibility, sociability, self-management
EFF: **Communication** Reading with understanding, convey ideas in writing, speak so others can understand, listen actively
Decision Making Solve problems and make decisions
Interpersonal Guide others, advocate and influence, cooperate with others
Lifelong Learning Reflect and evaluate

Presentation 2 10-15 mins.

D Claude needs a job. Can you suggest a good job for him?

Have students silently read the paragraph about Claude and then ask them if they can think of a good job for him. Have them give reasons for their suggestions.

Write *want, enjoy,* and *like* on the board. Ask students to look at the paragraph about Claude again and to underline each instance of these three verbs. Tell them that the tense doesn't matter. Now write the words *infinitive* and *gerund* on the board and ask students if they know the difference. Explain the difference with a few examples.

E Study the chart with your classmates and teacher. Then, underline examples of infinitives and gerunds in the paragraph above.

Practice 2 5-10 mins.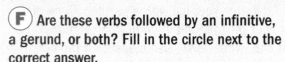

F Are these verbs followed by an infinitive, a gerund, or both? Fill in the circle next to the correct answer.

Evaluation 2 10-20 mins.

Go over the answers to Exercise F as a class.

Ask students to write down three sentences about themselves—one using *want*, one using *enjoy*, and one using *like*. Give them a few minutes to finish and then ask volunteers to either read their sentences out loud or write them on the board.

Activity Bank

Lesson 2, Worksheet 1: Infinitives and Gerunds

LESSON 2

GOAL ➤ Identify job skills and preferences

D Claude needs a job. Can you suggest a good job for him?

Claude is quiet and shy. He is friendly, but he doesn't really like to talk to customers. He is very good at assembling things. When he was a teenager, he enjoyed fixing bicycles. He likes to be busy. He wants to get a job where he can use his technical skills.

E Study the chart with your classmates and teacher. Then, underline examples of infinitives and gerunds in the paragraph above.

Infinitives and Gerunds Infinitive = *to* + verb Gerund = verb + *ing*			
Verb	**Infinitive or Gerund?**	**Example sentence**	**Other verbs that follow the same rule**
want	infinitive	He wants *to get* a job.	plan, decide
enjoy	gerund	He enjoys *fixing* bicycles.	finish, give up
like	both	He likes *to talk*. He likes *talking*.	love, hate

F Are these verbs followed by an infinitive, a gerund, or both? Fill in the circle next to the correct answer.

	Infinitive	Gerund	Both
1. I like _____ on a team.	○ to work	○ working	● to work/working
2. I enjoy _____ problems.	○ to solve	● solving	○ to solve/solving
3. I want _____ to customers.	● to talk	○ talking	○ to talk/talking
4. I decided _____ math.	● to study	○ studying	○ to study/studying
5. I hate _____ decisions.	○ to make	○ making	● to make/making
6. I gave up _____ two years ago.	○ to smoke	● smoking	○ to smoke/smoking
7. I love _____ machines.	○ to repair	○ repairing	● to repair/repairing

G What are your special job skills? Put a check mark (✓) next to the things you are good at. Add two skills to the list. (Answers will vary.)

❑ solve problems
❑ work under pressure
❑ work in a fast-paced environment
❑ work on a team
❑ make decisions
❑ pay attention to details
❑ work with my hands
❑ read and follow directions

❑ help people
❑ organize information
❑ work with money
❑ talk to customers
❑ _____
❑ _____

H Study the chart with your classmates and teacher.

			Gerunds and Nouns after Prepositions		
Subject	**Verb**	**Adjective**	**Preposition**	**Gerund/Noun**	**Example sentence**
I	am	good	at	calculating	I am good at *calculating*.
she	is	good	at	math	She is good at *math*.
A gerund or a noun follows an adjective + a preposition. Some other examples of adjectives + prepositions are *interested in, afraid of, tired of, bad at,* and *worried about*.					

I Tell your partner about your skills and interests. What things are you *good at, bad at, interested in, tired of,* and *afraid of*? Your partner will suggest a good job for you.

EXAMPLE: *Student A*: I am good at paying attention to details. I'm interested in organizing information.
           Student B: Maybe you should be a bookkeeper.

J Write a paragraph about your job skills on a piece of paper. What are you good at? What are you interested in learning? How do you plan to learn or practice these skills?

(Answers will vary.)

Presentation 3   15-20 mins. ■■■

G What are your special job skills? Put a check mark (✓) next to the things you are good at. Add two skills to the list.

Go over the skills on the list with students and have them put a check next to the things that they are good at. Help them come up with other skills that are not on the list.

H Study the chart with your classmates and teacher.

Introduce this chart by asking students questions, such as: *Are you good at solving problems? Are you good at talking to customers?* At first, they may give a one-word answer of *yes* or *no*. Eventually, encourage them to answer in a complete sentence. For example: *Yes, I am good at solving problems. No, I am not good at talking to customers.*

Go over the chart and explain that either a gerund or a noun follows an adjective + preposition combination. Ask students to write six sentences about their skills and interests, using the adjective + preposition combinations listed in the chart. Ask volunteers to read their sentences out loud.

Practice 3   5-10 mins. ■

I Tell your partner about your skills and interests. What things are you *good at, bad at, interested in, tired of,* and *afraid of?* Your partner will suggest a good job for you.

Have students refer to the sentences they wrote just prior to this exercise.

Evaluation 3   5-10 mins. ■

Observe students as they do this activity.

Application   10-20 mins. ■■■

J Write a paragraph about your job skills on a piece of paper. What are you good at? What are you interested in learning? How do you plan to learn or practice these skills?

Suggest that students try to incorporate some of the phrases they have learned in this lesson in their paragraphs.

Refer students to *Stand Out 3 Grammar Challenge,* Unit 6, Challenge 2 for more practice with gerunds and infinitives.

Objective: Interpret job advertisements

Academic Strategy: Reading for understanding

Vocabulary: abbreviations in job ads, *technician, proof of car insurance, insurance forms, fax, licensed, custodian*

RESOURCES

Activity Bank: Lesson 3, Worksheets 1–2

Reading and Writing Challenge: Unit 6

Grammar Challenge 3: Unit 6, Challenge 3

■ 1.5 hour classes ■ 2.5 hour classes ■ 3⁺ hour classes

AGENDA

Read job ads.
Understand classified abbreviations.
Match jobs with skills and preferences.
Write an ad for your dream job.

Warm-up and Review   5 mins. ■■■

Ask students to take out the job skills paragraph they wrote in Exercise J of Lesson 2 and share it with a partner. Ask a few volunteers to read their paragraphs out loud.

Introduction   5-10 mins. ■■■

Write the phrase *How to find a job* on the board. Ask students to think of some different ways to find a job. Write their responses on the board. Your list may look something like this:

How to find a job
Ask friends or family
Respond to Help Wanted signs
Answer ads in the newspaper or on the Internet

State the objective: *Today we will read and interpret job advertisements.*

Presentation 1   15-20 mins. ■■■

 **Read the following job advertisements.**

Look at the first ad together. Explain the word *abbreviation*. Then write *Jobs Offered* and *Abbreviations* on the board. Ask students what

job the second ad offers. Write the job title on the board. Ask them what abbreviations appear in this ad and note them on the board. Now ask students for the meaning of each abbreviation. Have them guess if they don't know. Write their ideas on the board.

Have students get in groups of three or four and go through all eight ads on the page, making a list of the jobs offered and another list of the abbreviations used in each ad. Call on different people to come up to the board and fill in information under the two headings. You may have to help them with the abbreviations list.

 Are there any words or abbreviations that are new to you? List them below and discuss them with your classmates and teacher.

CASAS: 4.1.3 (See CASAS Competency List on pages 169-175.)

SCANS: **Resources** Allocate human resources

Information Acquire and evaluate information, organize and maintain information, interpret and communicate information

Interpersonal Participate as a member of a team, teach others, exercise leadership, negotiate to arrive at a decision, work with cultural diversity

Systems Monitor and correct performance

Basic Skills Reading, writing, listening, speaking

Thinking Skills Creative thinking, decision making, problem solving, seeing things in the mind's eye

Personal Qualities Responsibility, sociability, self-management

EFF: **Communication** Reading with understanding, convey ideas in writing, speak so others can understand

Decision Making Solve problems and make decisions, plan

Interpersonal Cooperate with others

Lifelong Learning Reflect and evaluate, learn through research, use information and communications technology (optional)

Help wanted

GOAL ➤ Interpret job advertisements

Vocabulary | Grammar
Life Skills
Academic | Pronunciation

A Read the following job advertisements.

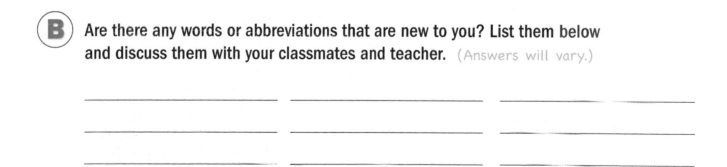

24 NewsObserver   Sunday, October 1

HELP WANTED

① **Auto technician:** Do you like to work on cars? Do you have an excellent attitude, good mechanical skills, & the ability to learn fast? Strong electronics background preferred. Call Chrissy at (310) 555-9078.

④ **Photographer.** Reliable? Enjoy children? Join our team taking school pictures. A cheerful personality is a plus. We offer paid training. Must have car & proof of insurance. Fax resume to Lifetouch Studios 318-555-7440.

⑦ Need caring, **Licensed Nurse's Aide** to care for elderly couple. Housing on site. Competitive salary. Send resume with references to: P.O. Box 2728 Morgan City, LA 70381.

② Acme Construction, **Administrative Assistant.** Min. 2 yrs. exp in clerical. Good computer skills req. Ability to work under pressure and type 40 wpm. Fax res. 818-555-3141.

⑤ Fast-growing supermarket chain seeks bright, motivated **managers** for meat & produce. Prior management experience, required. Excellent salary and benefits. Fax resume to: 626-555-1342.

⑧ Dependable **custodian** for 3 apartment buildings. Min. 2 yrs exp. plumbing, carpentry, painting, repair. Must have own tools and car $12-14/hr+benes 818-555-3500x523.

③ **Receptionist,** weekends: 10am-6pm. Requires HS diploma (or equiv) and 1 year experience. Excellent phone & organizational skills along with a pleasant attitude a must! Please apply in person to: 396 Marcasel Avenue, Los Angeles, CA 90066.

⑥ Detail-oriented **pharmacy clerk** needed to process insurance forms & assist customer. Must be biling/Spanish. Strong commun & org skills. Great bene. Call: Armine (605) 555-6613

WA

B Are there any words or abbreviations that are new to you? List them below and discuss them with your classmates and teacher. (Answers will vary.)

_____ _____ _____

_____ _____ _____

_____ _____ _____

C   Read the ads in Exercise A again and answer the questions below.

1. What experience should the auto technician have? __electronics background__

2. Which employer wants someone who can work under pressure? _administrative assistant_

3. Which job provides training? _photographer_

4. Which job requires references? _licensed nurse's aide_

5. Which jobs require a friendly personality? _receptionist, photographer_

6. Which jobs require a car? _custodian, photographer_

7. Which jobs require someone who likes details? _pharmacy clerk_

8. Which job requires someone who is bilingual? _pharmacy clerk_

9. Which job offers housing? _licensed nurse's aide_

10. What are ways to apply for these jobs? _in person, call, fax resume, send resume_

D   What skills are required for each job advertised in Exercise A? Complete the chart.

Job	Skills required or preferred
1. Photographer	reliable, enjoy children, cheerful personality
2. Custodian	dependable, 2 years experience in plumbing, carpentry, painting, repair
3. Pharmacy clerk	bilingual/Spanish, communication skills, organizational skills, detail-oriented
4. Auto technician	electronics background, mechanical skills, ability to learn fast, excellent attitude, like to work on cars
5. Receptionist	phone skills, organizational skills, pleasant attitude, 1 year experience
6. Manager	motivated, prior management experience, bright

Practice 1   10-15 mins.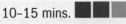

C Read the ads in Exercise A again and answer the questions below.

Go over the first item with students. Make sure students know to look back at page 107. Have students complete the rest of the exercise by themselves. When they have finished, they can check their answers with a partner.

Evaluation 1   5 mins.

Go over the answers as a class.

 Refer students to *Stand Out 3 Grammar Challenge*, Unit 6, Challenge 3 for more practice with gerunds after prepositions.

Presentation 2   5 mins.

Write the phrase *Licensed Nurse's Aide* on the board. Ask students what skills are needed for this job title. Have them look back at page 107 for help. Make a list of their ideas on the board. Then ask them what job preferences the person who applies for this job should have. Make another list on the board.

Practice 2   10-15 mins.

D What skills are required for each job advertised in Exercise A? Complete the chart.

Students can do this exercise alone or with a small group.

Evaluation 2   5-10 mins.

Assign a pair or small group of students one of the job titles and have them write their lists on the board.

Presentation 3   5-10 mins.

Present this scenario to students: *You recently lost your job at a restaurant. It was a nice restaurant and you had been a food server there for five years. The restaurant decided to move to a new location, too far from your home. Now you need a new job. What job can you apply for?* Ask students to look at the job openings on page 107 and give you an answer.

Practice 3   5-10 mins. ■

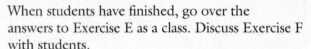

(E) Read the descriptions and decide which job or jobs from page 107 each person should apply for. Write the job titles.

Students can do this alone or in groups.

(F) Answer the following questions about yourself.

Evaluation 3   5 mins. ■

When students have finished, go over the answers to Exercise E as a class. Discuss Exercise F with students.

Application   15-20 mins.

Ask students what different items are included in a job advertisement. Make a list on the board. They might suggest such items as job title, qualifications, hours needed, pay, benefits, contact person, and contact number. As a class, decide what items are most important to include in a job advertisement.

(G) Write an ad for your dream job. Include the job title, skills, preferences, pay, and any other necessary information.

Have each student write his or her own ad, even if working with a partner. Make sure students use abbreviations. You may want to specify a minimum number of abbreviations they should use.

Activity Bank

Lesson 3, Worksheet 1: Job Ad Abbreviations

Lesson 3, Worksheet 2: Classified Job Search

E Read the descriptions and decide which job or jobs from page 107 each person should apply for. Write the job titles.

1. Lance recently moved here and needs to find a job. At his old job, he answered the phone, typed letters, and filed paperwork. He would like a job doing the same thing. What jobs should he apply for?

   receptionist, administrative assistant

2. Kyung was recently laid off from his janitorial job at the local school district. He had been working there for ten years and took care of all the maintenance and repairs for the school. What job should he apply for?

   custodian

3. Kim has two kids and wants to work while they are in school. She doesn't have any clerical skills, but she is cheerful and friendly. What job should she apply for?

   photographer

4. Rita manages a bakery but wants to find a job closer to home. She is smart and willing to work hard. She really likes to work with people and would like to find a job in the same line of work. What job should she apply for?

   manager

F Answer the following questions about yourself. (Answers will vary.)

1. Which job advertised on page 107 would you be best at? Why?

2. Which job would you most like to have? Why?

3. Which job would you like the least? Why?

G Write an ad for your dream job. Include the job title, skills, preferences, pay, and any other necessary information. (Answers will vary.)

Employment history

GOAL ➤ Fill out a job application

A Look at the ways people apply for jobs. How did you get your last job? What's the best way to get a job? Discuss your answers with a partner.

➤ personal connection (you know someone at the company)

➤ go to an employment agency

➤ reply to a classified ad

➤ see a *Help Wanted* sign and fill out an application

➤ introduce yourself to the manager and fill out an application

➤ send a resume to a company

B Not every business advertises available positions. If you want to work somewhere, you should go in and ask for an application. Read the conversation below.

Ramona: Excuse me. May I speak to the manager, please?
Employee: She's not here right now. Can I help you?
Ramona: Are you hiring now?
Employee: As a matter of fact, we are.
Ramona: What positions are you hiring for?
Employee: We need a <u>manicurist</u> and a <u>receptionist</u>.
Ramona: Great. Can I have an application, please?
Employee: Here you go. You can drop it off any time.
Ramona: Thanks a lot.
Employee: Sure. Good luck.

C Practice the conversation above. Fill in your own job titles.

D On a job application, you have to fill out certain information. Match the type of information to its description.

_c_ 1. Personal Information   a. people that can be called who know you

_b_ 2. Employment History   b. previous jobs you had

_e_ 3. Availability   c. name, address, special skills

_d_ 4. Education   d. schools you attended

_a_ 5. References   e. when you are free to work

AT-A-GLANCE PREP

Objective: Fill out a job application
Academic Strategy: Focused listening
Vocabulary: *connection, job application, resume, position, employment agency, hiring, manager, correction fluid, wrinkle*

RESOURCES

Activity Bank: Lesson 4, Worksheets 1–3
Reading and Writing Challenge: Unit 6

Grammar Challenge 3: Unit 6, Challenge 4
Audio: CD 1, Track 13

■ 1.5 hour classes ■ 2.5 hour classes ■ 3⁺ hour classes

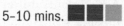
AGENDA
Discuss ways to apply for a job.
Ask for an application.
Read a job application.
Listen to rules for filling out an application.
Fill out a job application.

Warm-up and Review   10–15 mins. ■■■

Have students take out their job advertisements that they wrote in Lesson 3. Ask volunteers to write their ads on the board. Quiz students on what the abbreviations mean. Then poll the class to see which ad offered the most desirable.

Introduction   5–10 mins. ■■■

Discuss with students what they need to do once they find an opening for a good job. Explain that to get most jobs they will have to fill out a job application. Ask them how they would go about getting an application. Write some of their ideas on the board. State the objective: *Today we will be learning how to fill out a job application.*

Presentation 1   15–20 mins. ■■■

(A) Look at the ways people apply for jobs. How did you get your last job? What's the best way to get a job? Discuss your answers with a partner.

As a class, go over the ways people apply for jobs. Then have students discuss their answers with a partner. After about ten minutes, call on volunteer pairs to report what they discussed.

(B) Not every business advertises available positions. If you want to work somewhere, you should go in and ask for an application. Read the conversation below.

Have students read the conversation silently and then go over it as a class. Ask volunteers to role-play the conversation.

Practice 1   5–10 mins. ■■■

(C) Practice the conversation above. Fill in your own job titles.

Have students work with a partner to practice the conversation a few times, switching roles each time.

Evaluation 1   5–10 mins. ■■■

Observe students as they practice.

Presentation 2   5–10 mins. ■■■

First, ask students what information items go on an application. Make a list on the board and add items students didn't mention. Ask them to take out a sheet of paper and copy the list. Have them put a check mark next to every item they know. Have them underline the items they have to find out about at home. Have them circle the information that is not applicable to them or that they have no way of finding out.

(D) On a job application, you have to fill out certain information. Match the type of information to its description.

Do this activity as a class.

STANDARDS CORRELATIONS

CASAS: 4.1.2 (See CASAS Competency List on pages 169–175.)
SCANS: **Information** Acquire and evaluate information, organize and maintain information, interpret and communicate information
Interpersonal Participate as a member of a team, teach others, exercise leadership, negotiate to arrive at a decision, work with cultural diversity
Systems Understand systems, monitor and correct performance, improve and design systems
Basic Skills Reading, writing, arithmetic, listening, speaking
Thinking Skills Creative thinking, decision making, problem solving, seeing things in the mind's eye
Personal Qualities Responsibility, sociability, self-management
EFF: **Communication** Reading with understanding, convey ideas in writing, speak so others can understand, listen actively
Decision Making Solve problems and make decisions
Interpersonal Cooperate with others
Lifelong Learning Reflect and evaluate, use information and communications technology (optional)

Practice 2   15-20 mins.

E Look at Ramona's job application. Discuss the sections with your classmates and teacher.

Have students work with a partner to find the information on Ramona's application. Have them refer to Exercise D.

Evaluation 2   15-20 mins. ■■□

Help students with vocabulary as needed.

Presentation 3   5-10 mins. ■■■

To prepare for focused listening, have students look at the set of incomplete rules in Exercise F. Ask students if they can figure out what the missing words might be.

Practice 3   5-10 mins. ■

F Read the rules for filling out an application below. What words could go in the blanks? Now, listen and fill in the missing words.

Play the recording with students' books closed. Tell students just to listen. Then have students open their books and see if they can fill in any missing information in the rules that they remember. Play the recording again, pausing for students to complete the rules.

 Listening Script   *CD 1, Track 13*

The listening script matches the list of rules in Exercise F.

Evaluation 3   3-5 mins. ■

After students share their answers with a partner, go over them as a class. Talk about the rules and their importance.

GOAL ➤ **Fill out a job application**

E Look at Ramona's job application. Discuss the sections with your classmates and teacher.

JOB APPLICATION

Position Applied for: **Manicurist**   Interviewed by _____

PERSONAL INFORMATION

Name **Jimenez**   **Ramona**   Phone   **(714) 555-9765**
            last   first   mi

Last Five Year Employment History (Please list most recent positions first)

Employer (company, address)	Position	Dates from	Dates to	Reason for Leaving
Jardin Nails 8976 Flower Lane Garden Grove, CA 92842	manicurist	1/05	3/07	salon closed

AVAILABILLITY Write an "x" if available		Sun	Mon	Tue	Wed	Thu	Fri	Sat
	Morning	X	X	X	X		X	X
	Afternoon	X	X	X	X		X	X
	Evening							

EDUCATION	School and Address	Course of Study	Number of Years Completed	Degree or Diploma
Elementary School	Escuela do los Arboles Mexico	Basic skills	8 years	certificate of completion
High School	Garden Grove High School 11271 Stanford Ave., Garden Grove, CA 92840	general education	2 years	none

REFERENCES	Name	Position	Company	Telephone
	Kim Nguyen	Manager	Jardin Nails	(714) 555-3635

CD 1
TR 13

F Read the rules for filling out an application below. What words could go in the blanks? Now, listen and fill in the missing words.

Rules for Filling Out an Application

1. Use a dark _____**pen**_____, blue or _____**black**_____ ink.

2. Don't ____**cross out**____ any mistakes. Use correction fluid to _____**correct**_____ any mistakes.

3. Answer every ____**question**____. If the question doesn't apply to you, write _____**NA**_____ (Not Applicable).

4. Tell the _____**truth**_____! Never _____**lie**_____ on your job application.

5. Don't _____**bend**_____ or wrinkle the application.

6. Keep the application _____**clean**_____ no food or coffee stains!

7. Write as _____**neatly**_____ as possible. _____**Type**_____ it if you can.

8. If you don't ____**understand**____ the question, ask someone before you answer it.

 Fill out the job application with your own information. (Answers will vary.)

JOB APPLICATION

Date _____

Position Applied for: _____   Interviewed by _____

PERSONAL INFORMATION

Name _____   Phone ( ) _____
        last   first   mi

Present Address _____

City _____   State _____   Zip _____

Special Skills _____

Type WPM _____   Languages _____

Computer Skills _____

Last Five Years Employment History (Please list most recent positions first)

Employer (company, address)	Position	Dates		Reason for Leaving
		from	to	

AVAILABILITY

		Sun	Mon	Tue	Wed	Thu	Fri	Sat
Write an "x" if available	Morning							
	Afternoon							
	Evening							

EDUCATION

	School and Address	Course of Study	Number of Years Completed	Degree or Diploma
Elementary School				
High School				
College(s)				
Other				

REFERENCES

Name	Position	Company	Telephone

I certify that the above information is true to the best of my knowledge. I authorize previous employers to provide any information they feel appropriate.

Signature _____

Refer students to *Stand Out 3 Grammar Challenge*, Unit 6, Challenge 4 for an introduction and practice with *used to*.

Application   10–20 mins. ▪▪▪

G Fill out the job application with your own information.

Have students fill out the application as fully as they can. Make sure they follow the rules in Exercise F for filling out an application.

Activity Bank

Lesson 4, Worksheet 1: Job Application Requirements

Lesson 4, Worksheet 2: Application Data

Lesson 4, Worksheet 3: Job Application

Objective: Interview for a job
Grammar: *Would rather*
Academic Strategy: Reading for understanding
Vocabulary: *personality, character traits, self-confidence, enthusiasm, warmth, sensitivity*

RESOURCES

Activity Bank: Lesson 5, Worksheets 1–3
Reading and Writing Challenge: Unit 6

Grammar Challenge 3: Unit 6, Challenge 5
Audio: CD 1, Track 14

■ 1.5 hour classes ■ 2.5 hour classes ■ 3⁺ hour classes

AGENDA

Discuss job interview experiences.
Listen and read about interviewing.
Discuss desirable character traits.
Indentify appropriate interview clothing.
Use would rather to discuss preferences.
Answer interview questions.

Warm-up and Review 5–10 mins.

Have students turn to the applications in Lesson 4. In pairs, have them review the rules on page 111 and see if the partner followed them.

Go over the steps of the application process that you have discussed so far in this unit: decide what job you want; find an opening for that type of job in a newspaper or by using the suggestions on page 110, Exercise A; get an application; fill out the application; and turn in the application. Ask students if they know the next step.

Introduction 5–10 mins.

 Have you ever had a job interview? What happened? Tell your partner.

Have pairs talk for a few minutes. Ask volunteers to share with the class. State the objective: *Today we will learn how to interview for a job.*

Presentation 1 5–10 mins.

Ask students what they think interviewers want in a candidate. Have them brainstorm in groups or as a class. Write their ideas on the board.

Practice 1 10–15 mins.

Have students read the passage. Ask them not to use their dictionaries. Give students as much time as they need to understand the gist.

 During a job interview, an employer will try to find out about an applicant's character and personality. Read and listen to find out what interviewers look for during an interview.

Play the recording.

> 🎧 **Listening Script** *CD 1, Track 14*
> The listening script matches the reading on page 113.

 Discuss the following questions with a partner.

Evaluation 1 10–15 mins.

Discuss the questions in Exercise C as a class. Answer any questions students have about the reading. Ask students for examples of how they could show each trait in an interview. You might make a chart on the board with traits and examples.

STANDARDS CORRELATIONS

CASAS: 4.1.5, 4.1.7 (See CASAS Competency List on pages 169–175.)
SCANS: **Information** Acquire and evaluate information, organize and maintain information, interpret and communicate information
Interpersonal Participate as a member of a team, teach others, negotiate to arrive at a decision, work with cultural diversity
Systems Monitor and correct performance
Basic Skills Reading, writing, listening, speaking

Thinking Skills Creative thinking, decision making
Personal Qualities Responsibility, sociability, self-management
EFF: **Communication** Reading with understanding, convey ideas in writing, speak so others can understand, listen actively
Decision Making Solve problems and make decisions
Interpersonal Cooperate with others
Lifelong Learning Take responsibility for learning, reflect and evaluate

Why do you want to work here?

GOAL ➤ Interview for a job

  A Have you ever had a job interview? What happened? Tell your partner.

 B During a job interview, an employer will try to find out about an applicant's character and personality. Read and listen to find out what interviewers look for during an interview.

CD 1
TR 14

Your job interview is the most important part of the application process. This is when the employer gets to meet you and learn more about you. Employers are interested in your skills and experience, but they also look for personality and character traits.

Do you stand tall and smile confidently? Employers will notice your self-confidence. Managers want to hire employees who have confidence in themselves and will have confidence in the job they are doing.

Do you like to work hard and do a good job? Another important thing an interviewer looks for is enthusiasm about work. People who are enthusiastic about a job make great employees. They are happy with the work and usually stay with the company for a while.

Are you friendly and easy to talk to? Do you pay attention to how other people are feeling? Warmth and sensitivity are also very important traits. A person with these characteristics will make a good coworker, someone who can work well with others.

Do you have some or all of these traits? Can you show that you have these traits in an interview? If the answer is yes, you will have a good chance of getting the job.

C Discuss the following questions with a partner.

1. In your opinion, which is the most important trait: self-confidence, enthusiasm, or a friendly personality? (Answers will vary.)

   Smile and stand tall.

2. According to the reading, how can you use body language to show you are self-confident? Can you think of any other ways you can show confidence through body language?

   (Answers will vary.)

3. How can you show an employer that you are enthusiastic about the job and the company?
   You can act interested in the company.

4. According to the article, why do employers like to hire warm, sensitive people?

   They like to hire them because they make good coworkers who work well with others.

5. Do you think there are other character traits that employers like? What are they?
   (Answers will vary.)

D Imagine you are interviewing someone for a job as an administrative assistant in a busy doctor's office. List six character traits you would look for. Use ideas from the box or your own. (Answers will vary.)

honest	confident	funny	friendly	sensitive	thoughtful	enthusiastic
arrogant	motivated	warm	helpful	careful	intelligent	sneaky

1. _____   3. _____   5. _____

2. _____   4. _____   6. _____

E With your classmates, discuss what kind of clothing and accessories are appropriate or not appropriate for a job interview. Fill in the chart. Use the words from the box and add some of your own ideas. (Answers may vary.)

Men	Appropriate	Not appropriate
	long-sleeved shirt	T-shirt
	tie	earrings handbag
	pants	tattoos long hair
	suit	makeup jeans
	belt	sneakers nail polish
	cuff links	shorts jewelry
	briefcase	dress
	jacket	

Women	Appropriate	Not appropriate
	earrings handbag	tattoos
	makeup briefcase	sneakers
	pants jacket	tie
	suit long hair	shorts
	belt nail polish	T-shirt
	cuff links jewelry	jeans
	dress	

Word box:
earrings
tattoos
makeup
sneakers
tie
pants
suit
belt
shorts
cuff links
dress
handbag
briefcase
jacket
t-shirt
long hair
jeans
nail polish
jewelry

Evaluation 1 *(continued)*

D Imagine you are interviewing someone for a job as an administrative assistant in a busy doctor's office. List six character traits you would look for. Use ideas from the box or your own.

Discuss each of the words in the box with students and, as a class, decide what character traits this employee should have.

Presentation 2   10–15 mins. ■■■

Ask a few students to stand up, choosing students who are wearing a variety of styles. Ask the class about whether they would be dressed appropriately for a job interview.

Teaching Tip

Cooperative learning technique (Sit Down and Share)

You could do this exercise as an alternative to the presentation above.

1. Ask the whole class to stand up.
2. Ask students who are wearing jeans to sit down.
3. Ask students who are wearing sneakers to sit down.
4. Repeat the steps above, substituting things that are inappropriate to wear to an interview (baseball hats, tank tops, shorts, etc.). Everyone left standing should be wearing an outfit appropriate for an interview.
5. Ask the class why they think this group of people is left standing.
6. Discuss what these people are wearing and why these outfits are appropriate for a job interview.

Practice 2   15–20 mins. ■■

E With your classmates, discuss what kind of clothing and accessories are appropriate or not appropriate for a job interview. Fill in the chart. Use the words from the box and add some of your own ideas.

Evaluation 2   10–20 mins. ■■

Go over students' responses as a class.

Presentation 3   5-10 mins. ■■■

Ask students the following questions and take a class poll: *Would you rather work alone or with people? Would you rather work outside or inside? Would you rather work full time or part time?*

F Study the chart with your classmates and teacher.

Practice 3   10-15 mins. ■

G Which work situation do you prefer? Talk to your partner about your preferences.

Model the conversation with a few volunteers before you have students work in pairs.

H Write two sentences about your ideal work situation.

Activity Bank

Lesson 5, Worksheet 2: Expressing Likes and Preferences

Evaluation 3   10-15 mins. ■

Observe students as they discuss work situations in Exercise G. Ask volunteers to write their sentences from Exercise H on the board. Evaluate them as a class.

Refer students to *Stand Out 3 Grammar Challenge*, Unit 6, Challenge 5 for more practice with *would rather*.

Application   10-20 mins. ■■■

I Imagine you are preparing for a job interview. Choose a job from the ads on page 107 or one of your own. Work with a partner and answer the questions below.

Have students write down their answers to the questions. Then have them practice asking and answering the questions with a partner. If you have time, you may want to conduct mock interviews with students.

Activity Bank

Lesson 5, Worksheet 1: Interview Skills Reading
Lesson 5, Worksheet 3: The Interview

Refer students to *Stand Out 3 Grammar Challenge*, Unit 6, Extension Challenges 1–2 for more practice with present perfect continuous and adverbs of manner.

Instructor's Notes

GOAL ➤ **Interview for a job**

F Study the chart with your classmates and teacher.

Would rather					
Subject	*would rather*	**Base form**	*than*	**Base form**	**Example sentence**
I, you, she, he, it, we, they	would ('d) rather	work alone	than	work with people	I would rather work alone than work with people.
Note: You can omit the second verb if it is the same as the first verb. Example: I would rather work nights than (work) days.					

G Which work situation do you prefer? Talk to your partner about your preferences.

(Answers will vary.)

EXAMPLE: *Student A:* Would you rather work inside or outside?
Student B: I'd rather work inside because I hate the cold.

1. work alone / on a team
2. work days / nights
3. get paid hourly / weekly
4. have your own business / work for someone else
5. retire at 65 / work until you are 70
6. have a male boss / a female boss

H Write two sentences about your ideal work situation. (Answers will vary.)

EXAMPLE: <u>I'd rather work on a team than alone because I like talking to people.</u>

1. _____

2. _____

I Imagine you are preparing for a job interview. Choose a job from the ads on page 107 or one of your own. Work with a partner and answer the questions below.

(Answers will vary.)

1. What are your skills? _____

2. Why do you think you would be good at this job? _____

3. How would you describe your personality? _____

4. What did you like and dislike about your last job? _____

5. Would you rather work full time or part time? _____

6. What salary do you expect? _____

Review

A Read each skill below and write a job title on the line. (Lesson 1)

1. cleans teeth   dental hygienist

2. types, files, and does general office work   administrative assistant

3. takes a patient's temperature and blood pressure   nurse

4. fixes pipes   plumber

5. cleans office buildings   custodian

6. operates machinery   machine operator

7. takes care of children   nanny

8. maintains yards   landscaper

B List six job skills you have. (Lesson 2)   (Answers will vary.)

1. _____

2. _____

3. _____

4. _____

5. _____

6. _____

C Complete these sentences using a gerund or an infinitive form of the verb in parentheses. (Lesson 2)

1. I like ___working/to work___ on a team. (work)

2. I am good at ___talking___ to customers. (talk)

3. They hate ___answering/to answer___ the phone. (answer)

4. I decided ___to study___ computers next semester. (study)

5. He is interested in ___repairing___ cars. (repair)

6. We finished ___writing___ our reports yesterday. (write)

Objectives: All unit objectives
Grammar: All unit grammar
Academic Strategy: Reviewing
Vocabulary: All unit vocabulary

AGENDA

Discuss unit objectives.
Complete the review.
Do My Dictionary.
Evaluate and reflect on progress.

RESOURCES

Activity Bank Worksheets: Unit 6, Lessons 1–5
Reading and Writing Challenge: Unit 6

Grammar Challenge 3: Unit 6, Challenges 1–5

■ 1.5 hour classes   ■ 2.5 hour classes   ■ 3⁺ hour classes

Stand Out 3 Assessment CD-ROM with Exam*View*®

Warm-up and Review   5-10 mins.

In groups, have students list questions they might be asked at a job interview.

Introduction   5-10 mins. ■■■

Ask students as a class to try to recall (in general) all the goals of this unit without looking at their books. Then remind them which goals they omitted, if any. (Unit goals: identify job titles and skills, identify job skills and preferences, interpret job advertisements, fill out a job application, and interview for a job) Write all the goals from Unit 6 on the board. Show students the first page of the unit and mention the five objectives. State the objective: *Today we will be reviewing everything you have learned in this unit.*

Presentation 1   10-15 mins.

This presentation will cover the first three pages of the review. Quickly go to the first page of each lesson and discuss the objective. Ask questions to remind students of what they learned.

Note: Since there is little presentation in the review, you can assign the review exercises for homework and go over them in class the following day.

Practice 1   20-25 mins.

Note: There are two ways to do the review: (1) Go through each exercise one at a time and, as students complete each one, go over the answers. (2) Briefly go through the instructions of each exercise, allow students to complete all of the exercises at once, and then go over the answers.

Ⓐ **Read each skill below and write a job title on the line. (Lesson 1)**

Ⓑ **List six job skills you have. (Lesson 2)**

Ⓒ **Complete these sentences using a gerund or an infinitive form of the verb in parentheses. (Lesson 2)**

Evaluation 1   20-25 mins.

Go around the classroom and check on students' progress. Help individuals when needed. If you see consistent errors among several students, interrupt the class and give a mini lesson or review to help students feel comfortable with the concept.

STANDARDS CORRELATIONS

CASAS: 7.2.1 (See CASAS Competency List on pages 169-175.)
SCANS: Resources Allocate time
Information Acquire and evaluate information
Interpersonal Participate as a member of a team, teach others, negotiate to arrive at a decision, work with cultural diversity
Systems monitor and correct performance
Basic Skills Reading, writing, arithmetic, listening, speaking
Thinking Skills Creative thinking, decision making, problem solving, seeing things in the mind's eye

Personal Qualities Responsibility, sociability, self-management
EFF: Communication Convey ideas in writing, speak so others can understand, listen actively
Decision Making Solve problems and make decisions
Interpersonal Guide others, cooperate with others
Lifelong Learning Take responsibility for learning, reflect and evaluate, learn through research

Practice 1 *(continued)*   25–30 mins. ■■■

(**D**) Read the job ads. (Lesson 3)

(**E**) Write the correct job title(s) on the line: *administrative assistant*, *cashier*, or *custodian*.

(**F**) Fill out the partial job application. (Lesson 4)

Evaluation 1 *(continued)*   25–30 mins. ■■■

Go around the classroom and check on students' progress. Help individuals when needed. If you see consistent errors among several students, interrupt the class and give a mini lesson or review to help students feel comfortable with the concept.

Teaching Tip

Recycling/Review

The review exercises and the project that follows are part of the recycling/review process. Students at this level often need to be reintroduced to concepts to solidify what they have learned. Many concepts are forgotten while learning other new concepts. This is because students learn but are not necessarily ready to acquire language concepts.

Therefore, it becomes very important to review and to show students how to review on their own. It is also important to recycle the new concepts in different contexts.

Read the job ads. (Lesson 3)

1. Administrative Assistant,
weekdays: 10 A.M.- 6 P.M. Requires HS diploma
and 1 year experience. **Excellent phone &**
organizational skills along with a pleasant
attitude a must! Please apply in person to:
7790 Maribel Avenue, Los Angeles, CA 90066.

2. Fast-growing supermarket chain
is looking for personable, motivated
cashiers. Must be good with numbers.
Excellent salary and benefits.
Fax resume to: 626-555-8879

3. Reliable **custodian** for local school
district. Min 1 yr exp. **cleaning, plumbing,**
carpentry, painting, repair. Will provide
supplies and tools. $12-14/hr + benefits.
Call 818-555-6879.

E Write the correct job title(s) on the line: *administrative assistant*, *cashier*, or *custodian*.

1. For which job do you have to be good with numbers?   *cashier*

2. Which jobs require experience?   *administrative assistant, custodian*

3. Which job requires a high school diploma?   *administrative assistant*

4. Which job requires a resume?   *cashier*

5. Which jobs offer benefits?   *cashier, custodian*

6. Personality is NOT important for which job?   *custodian*

F Fill out the partial job application. (Lesson 4)   (Answers will vary.)

JOB APPLICATION

Position Applied for: _____   Date _____
Interviewed by _____

PERSONAL INFORMATION

Name _____   Phone ( ) _____
　　　　last　　　　　first　　　　　mi

Special Skills _____

Last Five Years Employment History (Please list most recent positions first)

Employer (company, address)	Position	Dates from	to	Reason for Leaving

AVAILABILITY

Write an "x" if available		Sun	Mon	Tue	Wed	Thu	Fri	Sat
	Morning							
	Afternoon							
	Evening							

EDUCATION

	School and Address	Course of Study	Number of Years Completed	Degree or Diploma
Elementary School				
High School				

REFERENCES

Name	Position	Company	Telephone

Review

G What would you rather do? Think about the things you don't like about your current job. Write four sentences using *would rather* to express your preferences. (Lesson 5)

(Answers will vary.)

1. _____
2. _____
3. _____
4. _____

H What kind of personality should people have for these jobs? Write two adjectives for each job. Share your answers with a partner. (Lesson 5)   (Answers may vary.)

1. home health-care aide: **responsible, caring** _____

2. manager in a clothing store: bright, motivated _____

3. receptionist in a dentist's office: pleasant, friendly _____

4. nanny: caring, responsible _____

5. custodian in a school: clean, dependable _____

6. teacher: patient, enthusiastic _____

I Write six interview questions for one of the following jobs. Interview a partner. (Lesson 5)

(Answers will vary.)

landscaper	receptionist	furniture store manager	computer technician
bookkeeper	waiter	assembler in a factory	home health-care aide

EXAMPLE: receptionist Can you type? _____

1. _____
2. _____
3. _____
4. _____
5. _____
6. _____

Practice 1 *(continued)*   25–30 mins. ■■■

G What would you rather do? Think about the things you don't like about your current job. Write four sentences using *would rather* to express your preferences. (Lesson 5)

H What kind of personality should people have for these jobs? Write two adjectives for each job. Share your answers with a partner. (Lesson 5)

I Write six interview questions for one of the following jobs. Interview a partner. (Lesson 5)

Evaluation 1 *(continued)*   25–30 mins. ■■■

Go around the classroom and check on students' progress. Help individuals when needed. If you see consistent errors among several students, interrupt the class and give a mini lesson or review to help students feel comfortable with the concept.

Presentation 2
My Dictionary

5-10 mins. ■■■

Ask students to brainstorm new vocabulary items they learned in this unit. Have them do this without looking in their books. Using some of the words that students came up with as examples, explain word stress. Show students how to find the stress in their dictionaries.

Practice 2
15-20 mins. ■■

(Shorter classes can do these exercises for homework.)

Look up the following words in the dictionary. Write them with the correct syllable stress.

Evaluation 2
15-20 mins. ■■

Walk around the classroom and help students.

Presentation 3
5-10 mins. ■■■

Learner Log

In this unit, you learned many things about getting hired. How comfortable do you feel doing each of the skills listed below? Rate your comfort level on a scale of 1 to 4.

Go over the instructions with students and make sure they understand what to do. You may want to read the skills out loud with the class and answer any questions they may have.

Teaching Tip

Learner Logs

Learner logs function to help students in many different ways.

1. They serve as part of the review process.
2. They help students to gain confidence and document what they have learned. Consequently, students see that they are making progress and want to move forward in learning.
3. They provide students with a tool that they can use over and over to check and recheck their understanding. In this way, students become independent learners.

Practice 3
5-10 mins. ■

Have students complete the Learner Log.

Evaluation 3
5-10 mins. ■

Walk around the classroom and help students.

Application
10-15 mins. ■■■

Go over the two reflection questions with students and have them complete the answers by themselves.

Assessment
■■■

TB ⊙

Use the Stand Out 3 Assessment CD-ROM with Exam*View*® to create a post-test for Unit 6.

Instructor's Notes

_____
_____
_____
_____
_____
_____
_____
_____
_____
_____
_____
_____
_____
_____
_____
_____
_____
_____
_____
_____
_____
_____

My Dictionary

Word Stress

Your dictionary will tell you where to put the stress in each word. Dictionaries use different symbols to show stress. What symbol does your dictionary use?

EXAMPLE: 'ap-ple (The stress is on the first syllable.)

Look up the following words in the dictionary. Write them with the correct syllable stress.

1. applicant 'ap-pli-cant   5. computer com-'put-er

2. previous 'pre-vi-ous   6. equipment e-'quip-ment

3. bookkeeper 'book-keep-er   7. environment en-'vi-ron-ment

4. technician tech-'ni-cian   8. require re-'quire

Now practice saying the words, using the correct stress.

Learner Log

In this unit, you learned many things about getting hired. How comfortable do you feel doing each of the skills listed below? Rate your comfort level on a scale of 1 to 4.

1 = Need more practice   **2** = OK   **3** = Good   **4** = Great!

Life Skill	Comfort Level	Page
I can identify job titles and skills.	1 2 3 4	101
I can describe my job skills.	1 2 3 4	104
I can interpret job advertisements.	1 2 3 4	107
I can fill out a job application.	1 2 3 4	110
I know what is appropriate to wear to an interview.	1 2 3 4	113
I am familiar with interview questions.	1 2 3 4	114

If you circled 1 or 2, write down the page number where you can review this skill.

Reflection

1. What was the most useful skill you learned in this unit?_____

_____

2. How will this help you in life? _____

Team Project

Create a job application portfolio.

With your team, you will plan the contents and layout for a job application portfolio. Each student will create his or her own job application portfolio.

What does a job application portfolio include?

➤ a job application information sheet
➤ a list of rules for filling out a job application
➤ a list of skills
➤ sample interview questions and answers
➤ certificates

➤ awards
➤ transcripts
➤ performance reviews
➤ letters of recommendation

1. Form a team with four or five students. Choose a position for each member of your team.

POSITION	JOB DESCRIPTION	STUDENT NAME
Student 1: Leader	See that everyone speaks English and participates.	
Student 2: Secretary	Write list for job application portfolio.	
Student 3: Designer	Design order of job application portfolio.	
Students 4/5: Member(s)	Help secretary and designer with their work.	

2. Make a list of all the information you want to include in your portfolio. Look at the list above for help. Decide how many pages you will need.

3. With your team, decide the best order for your portfolio.

4. Collect and create items to put in your individual portfolio. Put your portfolio together.

5. Share your portfolio with at least two other students.

6. Set up an interview with your teacher and share your portfolio with him or her.

Create a job application portfolio.

Each student will create a portfolio of items that will prepare him or her to apply and interview for a job.

The team project is the final application for the unit. It gives students a chance to show that they have mastered all of the Unit 6 objectives.

Note: Shorter classes can extend this project over two class meetings.

Stage 1   5 mins.

Form teams with four or five students. Choose a position for each member of your team.

Tell students that they will work both collectively and individually on this project. Have them decide who will lead each step as described on the student page. Provide well-defined directions on the board for how teams should proceed. Explain that all the students do every step as a team. Teams shouldn't go to the next stage until the previous one is complete.

Stage 2   10–15 mins.

Make a list of all the information you want to include in your portfolio. Look at the list above for help. Decide how many pages you will need.

Ask each team to report to the class on what they have decided should go into individual portfolios.

Stage 3   5–10 mins.

With your team, decide the best order for your portfolio.

Stage 4   20–30 mins.

Collect and create items to put into your individual portfolio. Put your portfolio together.

Students may have to collect items or information from home to add to their portfolios. Tell them they can bring them in on the next day of class.

Stage 5   10 mins.

Share your portfolio with at least two other students.

Stage 6   5 mins. (per student)

Set up an interview with your teacher and share your portfolio with him or her.

Objective: Compare employee behavior and attitudes
Grammar: Possessive adjectives and possessive pronouns
Academic Strategy: Focused listening
Vocabulary: *behavior, ideal, coworker, reserved, courteous, strict, easygoing, ambitious, demanding, opinionated, patient*

AGENDA

Listen and identify behaviors.
Discuss employee attitudes.
Use possessive adjectives
*   and pronouns.*
Describe an ideal manager.
Compare your jobs.

RESOURCES

Activity Bank: Lesson 1, Worksheets 1–2
Reading and Writing Challenge: Unit 7

Grammar Challenge 3: Unit 7, Challenge 1
Audio: CD 1, Track 15

Stand Out 3 Assessment CD-ROM with Exam*View*®

 1.5 hour classes ■ 2.5 hour classes ■ 3· hour classes

 Preassessment *(optional)* ■■■

Use the Stand Out 3 Assessment CD-ROM with Exam*View*® to create a pretest for Unit 7.

Warm-up and Review   5–10 mins. ■■■

Have students give examples of good and bad behavior at school. Write their ideas on the board.

Introduction   5–10 mins. ■■■

Asks students for ideas of good and bad behavior at work. State the objective: *Today we will talk about employee behavior and attitudes.*

Presentation 1   5 mins. ■■■

Have students open their books and discuss what is happening in each picture. Tell students they will be listening to each of these employees talk about their jobs.

Practice 1   10–15 mins. ■■■

 Listen to two employees talk about their jobs. What does Leticia do? What does So do?

 With a partner, write examples of the two employees' behavior in the chart below.

 **Listening Script**   *CD 1, Track 15*

Leticia: *Hi. I'm Leticia. I work for New Wave Graphics as an administrative assistant. I really like my job. I come to work on time every day and I never leave early. I try to keep my work space very clean and*

I never eat at my desk. When my manager asks me to do something, I get it done as soon as I can. I obey all the company policies, especially the safety rules. I try to be friendly to everyone I work with, even when I'm having a bad day. I am constantly learning new computer skills, so I can be ready to move up the ladder when a position becomes available. New Wave Graphics is a great company to work for and I hope to stay here a long time.

So: *Hey, I'm So. I stock shelves at Johnson's Market. I'm supposed to come in at twelve and leave at eight, but I figure as long as I get my work done, it doesn't matter what time I get there. I've got long hair and my manager always tells me to keep it back, but he's never around, so I usually leave it down. It's my hair. I should be able to wear it how I want, shouldn't I? The best part about this job is the food. I stock the shelves with all the dry goods, such as cereal, crackers, and pasta. And there's always some extra stuff that doesn't fit on the shelves, so I usually take a few things home with me. I figure they should be paying me more for all the work I do, so I take a few things home to make up for it. I don't really like the guys I work with. They try too hard to impress the manager, so that they can get raises. I try to stay away from them and just get my work done as fast as I can. It's an OK job. I'll find something better soon.*

Evaluation 1   5 mins.

 In your opinion, who is the better employee? Why? Can you think of other examples of good and bad employee behavior?

Go over these questions as a class.

Note: Standards Correlations are on the next page.

GOALS

➤ **Compare employee behavior and attitudes**

➤ **Interpret a pay stub**

➤ **Interpret benefit information**

➤ **Identify safe workplace behavior**

➤ **Communicate at work**

LESSON **1**

Attitudes at work

GOAL ➤ Compare employee behavior and attitudes

CD 1
TR 15

A Listen to two employees talk about their jobs. What does Leticia do? What does So do?

Leticia is an administrative assistant. So stocks shelves at a supermarket.

B With a partner, write examples of the two employees' behavior in the chart below.

Leticia	So
comes to work on time never leaves work early keeps work space clean doesn't eat at her desk does tasks when asked obeys company policies is friendly learns new skills	doesn't always come in on time leaves his hair down takes food home from work (steals) isn't friendly to coworkers

C In your opinion, who is the better employee? Why? Can you think of other examples of good and bad employee behavior?

Answers may vary. Leticia is the better employee because she follows the rules, is friendly to coworkers, and works hard

LESSON 1

GOAL ➤ **Compare employee behavior and attitudes**

D Read the conversation below. Look at the words in *italics*. Which are possessive adjectives and which are possessive pronouns?

possessive adjectives: my, her, your
possessive pronouns: mine, yours

Ellen: *My* boss is quite demanding and she always wants *her* reports on time.
Leticia: Yes, *your* manager is more demanding than *mine*.
Ellen: Yeah, but *yours* is less friendly.

E Study the chart. Which possessive pronouns have an *s* at the end? Which possessive adjectives and possessive pronouns are the same?

Possessive Adjectives and Possessive Pronouns		
Possessive adjectives	**Rule**	**Example sentence**
my, your, his, her, our, their	*Possessive adjectives* show possession of an object and come before the noun.	This is *her* office.
Possessive pronouns	**Rule**	**Example sentence**
mine, yours, his, hers, ours, theirs	*Possessive pronouns* show possession of an object and act as a noun.	This office is *hers*.

F Underline the possessive adjective in each sentence. Circle the possessive pronoun.

EXAMPLE: <u>My</u> sister's manager is generous, but <u>my</u> manager is more generous than (hers)

1. <u>Their</u> job is boring, but <u>our</u> job is more boring than (theirs.)

2. <u>My</u> husband gets a good salary. <u>His</u> salary is better than (mine.)

3. <u>My</u> brother says <u>his</u> coworkers are friendly, but <u>my</u> coworkers are friendlier than (his.)

4. I like <u>her</u> manager, but (mine) is much more easygoing.

5. <u>His</u> office is clean, but (ours) is bigger.

Presentation 2   10-20 mins. ■■■

Ask volunteers if they are good or bad employees. Encourage them to tell you why. Ask them to respond with a statement such as this: *I am a good employee because I always finish my work on time.* Then ask the other students why the volunteers are good or bad employees, based on their own statements. This gives the other students an opportunity to restate what they heard and change the verb form to third person. For example: *Nora is a good employee because she always finishes her work on time.*

Write down any pronouns or possessive adjectives students use. Put them into two lists on the board. You will add more adjectives and pronouns to the lists in Exercise E.

D Read the conversation below. Look at the words in *italics*. Which are possessive adjectives and which are possessive pronouns?

E Study the chart. Which possessive pronouns have an *s* at the end? Which possessive adjective and possessive pronouns are the same?

Go over the chart and give more examples.

Practice 2   10-15 mins. ■■

F Underline the possessive adjective in each sentence. Circle the possessive pronoun.

After students do this activity alone, have them form pairs. Have one partner keep his or her book open. That partner will read a sentence from Exercise F to the other, repeating the underlined and circled words after reading the sentence. The partner must identify the correct form of each repeated word (italicized in the example below):

A: *My* sister's manager is generous, but *my* manager is more generous than *hers*. *My!*

B: Possessive adjective.

A: Yes. OK, *hers!*
B: Object pronoun?
A: No, try again.
B: Possessive pronoun.
A: Good.

Instructor's Notes

STANDARDS CORRELATIONS

CASAS: 4.1.9, 4.4.1 (See CASAS Competency List on pages 169-175.)
SCANS: **Information** Acquire and evaluate information, organize and maintain information, interpret and communicate information
Interpersonal Participate as a member of a team, teach others, negotiate to arrive at a decision, work with cultural diversity
Systems Monitor and correct performance
Basic Skills Reading, writing, listening, speaking
Thinking Skills Creative thinking, decision making, problem solving, seeing things in the mind's eye

Personal Qualities Responsibility, sociability, self-management
EFF: **Communication** Read with understanding, convey ideas in writing, speak so others can understand, listen actively
Decision Making Solve problems and make decisions
Interpersonal Advocate and influence, cooperate with others
Lifelong Learning Reflect and evaluate, use information and communications technology (optional)

Practice 2 (continued)

G Circle the correct word in each sentence below.

Evaluation 2 5 mins. ■■

Observe students as they work. When they have finished, go over the answers to Exercises F and G as a class.

Presentation 3 5–10 mins. ■■■

H Leticia and Ellen are comparing the people they work with.

Have students look at the picture of Leticia and Ellen. Read the conversation with the class.

Practice 3 15–20 mins. ■

I What is an ideal manager like? What are ideal coworkers like? Use the adjectives from the box and have a conversation with your partner.

Go over the vocabulary with students.

📖 Refer students to *Stand Out 3 Grammar Challenge*, Unit 7, Challenge 1 for more practice with possessive pronouns and adjectives.

Evaluation 3 5–10 mins. ■

Ask volunteer pairs to perform their conversations for the class.

Application 10–20 mins. ■■■

J Form groups of three or four students. Compare your jobs. Then, write four sentences about your group using possessive pronouns.

Have students complete the activity and choose a group representative to read the sentences to the class.

Activity Bank

Lesson 1, Worksheet 1: Employee Behavior
Lesson 1, Worksheet 2: Possessive Pronouns
                          and Adjectives

 LESSON 1

GOAL ➤ **Compare employee behavior and attitudes**

 G Circle the correct word in each sentence below.

EXAMPLE: She keeps (her / hers) work space very clean.

1. She never eats at (her / hers) desk, but they always eat at (they / theirs).

2. That office is (you / yours).

3. (Theirs / Their) company has more employees than his.

4. That's (your / yours) book. Where is (my / mine) book?

5. We will give you (our / ours) proposal so you can compare it with (your / yours).

 H Leticia and Ellen are comparing the people they work with.

Leticia: I think an ideal manager should be demanding.
Ellen: I agree. A manager shouldn't be too easygoing.

 I What is an ideal manager like? What are ideal coworkers like? Use the adjectives from the box and have a conversation with your partner. (Answers will vary.)

friendly	courteous	funny	serious	demanding	respectful
strict	quiet	interesting	ambitious	hardworking	patient
relaxed	intelligent	easygoing	lazy	opinionated	reserved

 J Form groups of three or four students. Compare your jobs. Then, write four sentences about your group using possessive pronouns. (Answers will vary.)

EXAMPLE: Anita has a friendly manager, but Jun's manager is friendlier than hers.

1._____

2._____

3._____

4._____

It's pay day!

GOAL ➤ Interpret a pay stub

A Discuss the following vocabulary with your classmates and teacher.

year-to-date	marital status	rate of pay
earnings	Medicare	social security
federal	net pay	state disability
gross pay	payroll ending date	tax deductions
401K	pre-tax deductions	

B Look at Leticia's pay stub. Find the vocabulary words from the box above.

Employee Name: Leticia Rosales
Check number: 0768
SS number: 000-23-4567

Marital Status: single
Payroll Begin/End Dates:
5/14/08-5/27/08

HOURS AND EARNINGS

Description	Rate of Pay	Hours/Units	Earnings
Hourly/ Day/Monthly	14.75	80	1,180.00

TAX DEDUCTIONS

Tax Description	Current Amount	Calendar Year-to-Date
Federal	102.78	205.56
State	19.72	39.44
Social Security	10.68	21.36
Medicare	14.29	18.58
State Disability		

PRE-TAX DEDUCTIONS

Description	Amount
401K	50.00
Current Total	50.00
Year-to-Date Total	100.00

	Gross Pay	Pre-Tax Deductions	Pre-Tax Retirement	Tax Deductions	Net Pay
Current	1,180.00	50.00		147.47	982.53

Objective: Interpret a pay stub

Vocabulary: *calendar, year-to-date, check number, current amount, current total earnings, federal, gross pay, marital status, Medicare, net pay, payroll ending date, pre-tax deductions, pre-tax retirement, rate of pay, Social Security (SS) number, state disability, tax deductions, year-to-date total, 401K*

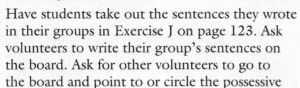

AGENDA
Discuss pay stub vocabulary.
Read and interpret a pay stub.

RESOURCES

Activity Bank: Lesson 2, Worksheet 1
Reading and Writing Challenge: Unit 7

Grammar Challenge 3: Unit 7, Challenge 2

■ 1.5 hour classes   ■ 2.5 hour classes   ■ 3⁺ hour classes

Warm-up and Review   5–10 mins. ■■■

Have students take out the sentences they wrote in their groups in Exercise J on page 123. Ask volunteers to write their group's sentences on the board. Ask for other volunteers to go to the board and point to or circle the possessive pronouns and possessive adjectives.

Introduction   5–10 mins. ■■■

Ask students what a *pay stub* is. Ask them what sort of information can be found on a pay stub. Make a list of their ideas on the board. State the objective: *Today we will be learning how to interpret a pay stub.*

Presentation 1   10–15 mins. ■■■

 Discuss the following vocabulary with your classmates and teacher.

 Look at Leticia's pay stub. Find the vocabulary words from the box above.

Give students a few minutes to look over Leticia's pay stub. Call out a few terms found on the stub and ask students to point to them in their books. Walk around the classroom and make sure they are pointing to the correct items. Go through the pay stub step by step, explaining each part. Make sure you cover all of the vocabulary in the box in Exercise A. You may need to explain how the amounts are calculated in some cases.

STANDARDS CORRELATIONS

CASAS: 4.2.1, 4.4.3 (See CASAS Competency List on pages 169–175.)
SCANS: Information Acquire and evaluate information, organize and maintain information, interpret and communicate information
Interpersonal Participate as a member of a team, teach others, exercise leadership, negotiate to arrive at a decision, work with cultural diversity
Systems Understand systems, monitor and correct performance
Basic Skills Reading, writing, arithmetic, listening, speaking

Thinking Skills Creative thinking, decision making, problem solving, seeing things in the mind's eye
Personal Qualities Responsibility, sociability, self-management
EFF: Communication Read with understanding, speak so others can understand, listen actively
Decision Making Use math to solve problems and communicate
Interpersonal Guide others, cooperate with others

Practice 1   5-10 mins. ■■■

C Where can you find this information on the pay stub? Write the number of each section of Leticia's pay stub.

Evaluation 1   5 mins. ■■■

Observe the students as they work on Exercise C. Go over the answers when students have finished.

Presentation 2   5 mins. ■■■

Tell students they will be asking and answering questions about a pay stub. Demonstrate with one or two volunteers to make sure that students understand the activity.

Practice 2   10-15 mins. ■■

D Work with a partner to answer the questions about Leticia's pay stub. Student A looks at the pay stub. Student B asks the questions and writes the answers. Then, switch roles.

Evaluation 2   5-10 mins. ■■

Observe students as they practice the conversations in Exercise D.

E Discuss these questions with a partner.

Students may also form groups to discuss these questions.

LESSON **2**   **GOAL** ➤ Interpret a pay stub

 Where can you find this information on the pay stub? Write the number of each section of Leticia's pay stub.

Pay stub information	Section
1. weeks the paycheck covers	1
2. total amount she takes home	4
3. information about retirement savings	3
4. information about taxes	2
5. hourly wage	1

D Work with a partner to answer the questions about Leticia's pay stub. Student A looks at the pay stub. Student B asks the questions and writes the answers. Then, switch roles.

EXAMPLE: *Student A*: Is she married?
           Student B: No.

1. Did she pay into social security this pay period? _____Yes_____

   If so, how much? _____$10.68_____

2. Does she pay Medicare? _____Yes_____

3. Does she pay state disability insurance? _____No_____

4. How much federal tax has she paid this year? _____$205.56_____

5. How much money did she make this pay period before taxes? _____$1,180.00_____

6. How much state tax did she pay this pay period? _____$19.72_____

7. What does she get paid per hour? _____$14.75_____

8. What is her social security number? _____000-23-4567_____

 Discuss these questions with a partner. (Answers will vary.)

1. Would you rather get paid every week, twice a month, or once a month? Why?

2. Would you rather get paid a salary or get paid hourly? Why?

F Skim So's pay stub and answer the questions below.

Employee Name: So Tran			Tax Deductions		
Check Number: 0498			**Tax Deductions**	**Current Amount**	**Calendar Year-to-Date**
S.S. Number: 000-56-8976					
Marital Status: Married			Federal	27.16	488.88
Payroll Begin/End Dates:			State	5.29	95.22
9/01/08–9/15/08			Social Security	6.68	126.92
			Medicare	9.29	167.22
Hours and Earnings			State Disability		
Description: Hourly/Day/Monthly			Pre-Tax Deductions		
Rate of Pay: 9.25			**Description**	**Amount**	
Hours/Units: 80			401K	25.00	
Earnings: 740.00			Current Total	25.00	
			Year-to-Date Total	475.00	

	Gross Pay	Pre-Tax Deductions	Pre-Tax Retirement	Tax Deductions	Net Pay
Current	740.00	25.00		48.42	666.28

1. Did So pay into social security this pay period? ___Yes___ If so, how much? ___$6.68___

2. Does he pay Medicare? ___Yes___

3. Does he pay state disability insurance? ___No___

4. How many hours did he work during this pay period? ___80___

5. How much federal tax has he paid this year? ___$488.88___

6. Does so contribute to a retirement account? ___Yes___ If so, how much? ___$25___

7. How much money did he make this pay period after taxes? ___$666.28___

8. How much money did he make this pay period before taxes? ___$740___

9. How much state tax did he pay this month? ___$5.29___

10. Is he married? ___Yes___

11. What does he get paid per hour? ___$9.25___

12. What is his social security number? ___000-56-8976___

Presentation 3   5-10 mins. ■■■

Write *year-to-date* on the board and ask students what this term means. Come up with a definition as a class and write it on the board. Tell students they will formulate definitions in the same way but within their groups.

Practice 3   15-20 mins. ■

In groups, have students write definitions for the vocabulary words in Exercise A on page 124. After they have agreed on a definition as a group, have one group member write down the definition.

Evaluation 3   10-15 mins. ■

Ask each group to read its definitions out loud. Then have the class vote on the best ones. Write the winning definitions on the board.

Application   10-20 mins. ■■■

(F) **Skim So's pay stub and answer the questions below.**

Have students work individually to answer these questions. When they have finished, they may compare their answers with a partner.

Activity Bank
Lesson 2, Worksheet 1: Pay Stub Practice

Refer students to *Stand Out 3 Grammar Challenge*, Unit 7, Challenge 2 for practice with *how much* and *how many*.

AT-A-GLANCE PREP

Objective: Interpret benefit information
Academic Strategies: Focused listening, reading for understanding
Vocabulary: *bonus, health insurance, dental insurance, disability insurance, family leave, maternity leave, medical leave, overtime, personal days, sick days, vacation days*

RESOURCES

Activity Bank: Lesson 3, Worksheet 1
Reading and Writing Challenge: Unit 7

Grammar Challenge 3: Unit 7, Challenge 3
Audio: CD 1, Track 16

 1.5 hour classes   2.5 hour classes   3⁺ hour classes

AGENDA

Identify employee benefits.
Listen to a career counselor.
Read a newsletter.
Choose the best company.
Create a company benefits package.

Warm-up and Review 5 mins.

Ask students if they looked at a pay stub at home.

Introduction 5-10 mins.

Write *benefits* on the board. Ask students what it means in the workplace. State the objective: *Today we will interpret benefit information.*

Presentation 1 10-15 mins.

A Read the list of benefits. Put a check mark (✓) next to the ones given at your present or last job. Add another benefit that you know.

Go through each benefit with the students.

Practice 1 15-20 mins.

B Benefits are extra things that a company offers its employees in addition to a salary. Listen to the career counselor talk about the benefits that three companies offer. Fill in the chart.

Go over the chart with students. Play the recording as many times as it takes for students to fill in the correct information.

🎧 **Listening Script**   *CD 1, Track 16*

Counselor: *Hello, future employees. My name is Kevin Daly and today's workshop is on company benefits. Can someone tell me what benefits are?*
Participant: *That's when the company pays for you to go to the doctor.*
Counselor: *Yes, that's true, but companies offer more than just health benefits. To give you an example of*

---

the different types of benefits that companies offer their employees, I'm going to talk about three different companies.

The first company is Set-It-Up Technology. This company helps small businesses set up computers in their offices. Their employees work six days a week, but they are paid a good salary. All employees are given full medical and dental insurance. In addition, employees are given twelve sick days and two weeks vacation a year. But the best benefit this company offers is its 401K retirement account. The company will match every dollar an employee contributes to the account.

The second company I'd like to talk about is Machine Works, an assembly plant that makes sewing machines. This company offers its full-time employees health benefits. There is no dental insurance. Machine Works gives their employees one week of sick leave and one week of vacation. This company pays a generous amount of overtime but there is no 401K offered by Machine Works.

The final company I'm going to talk about is Lino's Ristorante. This is a big chain restaurant so their benefits are pretty good. Employees receive health insurance but no dental benefits. Full-time employees receive eight sick days a year. All employees are given one week of paid vacation time every year. Lino's offers a 401K plan and they will contribute fifty cents for every dollar that you contribute.

So, these are some examples of benefits that different companies offer. Are there any questions?

Evaluation 1 5 mins.

Have students fill in the chart on the board.

C Which company would you rather work for? Why? Discuss your answer with a partner.

Note: Standards Correlations are on the next page.

What are the benefits?

GOAL ➤ Interpret benefit information

Vocabulary · Grammar · Life Skills · Academic · Pronunciation

A Read the list of benefits. Put a check mark (✓) next to the ones given at your present or last job. Add another benefit that you know. *(Answers will vary.)*

☐ 401K

☐ bonus

☐ dental insurance

☐ disability insurance

☐ family leave

☐ health insurance

☐ daycare

☐ maternity leave

☐ medical leave

☐ overtime

☐ paid personal days

☐ paid sick days

☐ paid vacation days

☐ _____

CD 1
TR 16

B Benefits are extra things that a company offers its employees in addition to a salary. Listen to the career counselor talk about the benefits that three companies offer. Fill in the chart.

Company	Health/Dental insurance	Sick days	Vacation days	401K
Set-It-Up Technology	full medical and dental insurance	12 days	2 weeks	yes—$1 for every dollar you contribute
Machine Works	health insurance, no dental	1 week	1 week	no 401K
Lino's Ristorante	health insurance, no dental	8 days	1 week	yes—50¢ for every dollar you contribute

C Which company would you rather work for? Why? Discuss your answer with a partner.
(Answers will vary.)

D Read about the benefits offered by some local companies in a small town in Utah.

Employment Monthly
Your Source for Employment Information in Well Springs, Utah

First Marketing offers medical benefits, including dental insurance, disability insurance, family leave, medical leave, and maternity leave to all full-time employees. You'll get paid for up to six sick or personal days you need to take. In addition to the great health benefits, you'll have the opportunity to contribute to a 401K as well as receive bonuses based on productivity at the end of the year. Most employees work full-time and receive time and a half for any overtime they work.

Quick Clean is a large chain of cleaners and there are employment opportunities at local areas in your community. All full-time employees receive health insurance. You can pay extra for dental insurance, but Quick Clean offers medical and maternity leave. All employees receive a certain number of sick days as well as vacation days, based on how long they have been with the company. Quick Clean doesn't offer any bonuses or 401K plans, but they encourage their employees to meet with their financial planner to help plan for retirement.

Ernie's Electrical offers medical, dental, maternity, disability, family, and medical leave to all full- and part-time employees. They give all of their employees three weeks a year to do with as they please—they can be used as sick days, personal days, or vacation days. No employees work overtime at Ernie's Electrical, which helps cut down on costs, but everyone receives a holiday bonus.

E Read about each person. Decide which company would be best for him or her.

1. Alicia is a young, hardworking student who can only work part time. She needs benefits because she lives by herself and has no family in Utah.

   Ernie's Electrical

2. Lars needs full benefits and likes to work overtime to make as much money as possible. He already has a 401K from another company that he would like to transfer to his new company.

   First Marketing

3. The most important thing for Su is maternity benefits. She and her husband are ready to start their family, but she still needs to work. She doesn't need dental insurance because her husband's company covers her.

   First Marketing / Quick Clean / Ernie's Electrical

Presentation 2

10–15 mins.

 Read about the benefits offered by some local companies in a small town in Utah.

Ask three volunteers to each read a paragraph out loud. Go over the reading as a class, answering any questions students might have.

Practice 2

5–10 mins.

E Read about each person. Decide which company would be best for him or her.

Have students complete this exercise alone and then compare their answers with a partner or in a group.

Evaluation 2

5 mins.

Go over the answers as a class.

STANDARDS CORRELATIONS

CASAS: 4.2.1 (See CASAS Competency List on pages 169–175.)
SCANS: **Resources** Allocate human resources
Information Acquire and evaluate information, organize and maintain information, interpret and communicate information
Interpersonal Participate as a member of a team, teach others, exercise leadership, negotiate to arrive at a decision, work with cultural diversity
Systems Monitor and correct performance, improve and design systems
Basic Skills Reading, writing, listening, speaking

Thinking Skills Creative thinking, decision making, problem solving, seeing things in the mind's eye
Personal Qualities Responsibility, sociability, self-management
EFF: **Communication** Read with understanding, listen actively
Decision Making Solve problems and make decisions, plan
Interpersonal Resolve conflict and negotiate, advocate and influence, cooperate with others
Lifelong Learning Reflect and evaluate, use information and communications technology (optional)

Presentation 3　　　　5 mins. ■ ■ ■

Go over the directions and the example in Exercise F.

Practice 3　　　　5-10 mins. ■

F Complete the statements with a word or phrase from Exercise A on page 127.

Evaluation 3　　　　5 mins. ■

Go over the answers as a class.

Application　　　　15-25 mins. ■ ■ ■

Tell student groups to pretend they are starting a new company and that they must decide what benefits they will offer their employees. (Remind students that two weeks of vacation is standard in the United States for most jobs. Vacation benefits and student expectations regarding amount of vacation is a good topic for a cross-cultural discussion.)

Have each group first decide what kind of company they wish to form. (For example, do they produce goods or offer a service? What do they produce or what do they offer?)

G With a group, imagine that you are starting a company. Decide what benefits you will offer. Answer the questions below.

Groups by now will have settled on which benefits to offer so they will be prepared for the questions. When groups have finished answering, ask each of them to report to the class.

Activity Bank

Lesson 3, Worksheet 1: Benefits

Refer students to *Stand Out 3 Grammar Challenge*, Unit 7, Challenge 3 for practice with *prefer . . . to*.

(F) **Complete the statements with a word or phrase from Exercise A on page 127.**

1. ___Disability insurance___ is for those who get injured at work.

2. At times, employees need to take time to care for a sick family member. This is

   called _____family leave_____.

3. Most companies are required to offer their employees _____benefits_____
   to take care of them and their families when they are sick.

4. Some companies offer a retirement plan called a _____401K_____.

5. When a company shares its profits with the employees, each employee gets a

   _____bonus_____.

6. When a woman has a new baby, she is allowed to take _____maternity leave_____.

7. When you take a day off to do something for yourself, it is called a

   _____personal day_____.

8. Some companies pay _____overtime_____ when you work more than forty
   hours a week, or on weekends and holidays.

(G) **With a group, imagine that you are starting a company. Decide what benefits
you will offer. Answer the questions below.** (Answers will vary.)

1. How many sick days will each employee receive? _____

2. How many personal days will you give each employee? _____

3. How many vacation days will each employee get? _____

4. Will you offer overtime pay? If yes, how much will you pay employees for

   overtime work? _____

5. What other benefits will you offer your employees? List them below.

   _____

   _____

Workplace safety

GOAL ➤ **Identify safe workplace behavior**

A Look at the pictures below. What type of job does each person have? (Answers will vary.)
Who needs to consider health issues? Who needs to consider safety issues?

Minh

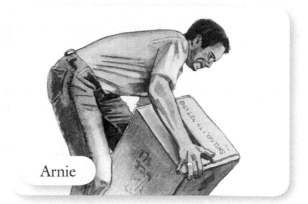

Arnie

Wassim

Robin

B Write the name of the person who should wear the safety items below.

1. a back support belt _____Arnie_____

2. safety goggles _____Wassim_____

3. earplugs _____Robin_____

4. a hairnet _____Minh_____

C Ask your partner if he or she wears safety items at work.

Objective: Identify safe workplace behavior
Grammar: Modals *could* and *might*
Vocabulary: *safety items, back support belt, earplugs, gloves, hard hat, hairnet, safety goggles, seat belt*

AGENDA
Match jobs and safety equipment.
Use could and might for possibility.
Identify safety hazards.
Write classroom safety rules.

RESOURCES

Activity Bank: Lesson 4, Worksheet 1
Reading and Writing Challenge: Unit 7

Grammar Challenge 3: Unit 7, Challenge 4

■ 1.5 hour classes   ■ 2.5 hour classes   ▨ 3+ hour classes

Warm-up and Review   10–15 mins.

Have students take out a sheet of paper and list the benefits that they currently have at their jobs. Then ask them to make a list of benefits they would like to have but don't. Have them share their lists with a small group.

Introduction   5–10 mins.

Write *workplace safety* on the board and ask students what the concept means to them. Ask them to help you think of unsafe workplace scenarios. Write them on the board. Write *safety equipment* on the board and ask students to come up with examples of protective equipment they use or have seen used at work. Make a list on the board. State the objective: *Today we will identify safe workplace behavior.*

Presentation 1   10–15 mins.

Ⓐ **Look at the pictures below. What type of job does each person have? Who needs to consider health issues? Who needs to consider safety issues?**

As a class, discuss each of the employees, including the health and safety issues each may face at work.

Practice 1   5 mins.

Ⓑ **Write the name of the person who should wear the safety items below.**

Evaluation 1   10–15 mins.

Review the answers as a class. Briefly discuss other types of safety gear people might wear at work and then have students form pairs in preparation of Exercise C.

Ⓒ **Ask your partner if he or she wears safety items at work.**

Have each pair make a list of the safety items they wear or use at work. When pairs have finished, ask one person from each pair to write their safety items on the board.

STANDARDS CORRELATIONS

CASAS: 4.3.3, 4.3.4, 4.5.1 (See CASAS Competency List on pages 169–175.)
SCANS: **Information** Acquire and evaluate information, organize and maintain information, interpret and communicates information
Interpersonal Participate as a member of a team, teach others, exercise leadership, negotiate to arrive at a decision, work with cultural diversity
Systems Monitor and correct performance
Basic Skills Reading, writing, listening, speaking

Thinking Skills Creative thinking, decision making, problem solving, seeing things in the mind's eye
Personal Qualities Responsibility, sociability, self-management
EFF: **Communication** Read with understanding, convey ideas in writing, speak so others can understand
Decision Making Solve problems and make decisions
Interpersonal Cooperate with others
Lifelong Learning Take responsibility for learning, reflect and evaluate

Presentation 2 10–15 mins.

D Read the conversation between Arnie and his manager, Fred. Do you think Fred is right?

Ask students to read the conversation in pairs. Encourage animated expression and intonation. Then discuss the situation as a class. Ask students if they agree with Fred.

E Underline the words *might* and *could* in the conversation above. Circle the verb that comes after each modal. Then, study the chart below.

Have students underline these words before explaining what they mean. Then use the situations in the conversation to define *might* and *could* and ask students to come up with more situations to help define these words. Now ask students about grammatical structure. Help them see that modals are followed by the base form of the verb.

Practice 2 5–10 mins.

F We also use *might* and *could* in conditional sentences with *if* when we are talking about possibilities. Complete the sentences.

Evaluation 2 5–10 mins.

Call on individuals to complete the sentences. There may be more than one possible answer. To check that students have used the correct grammatical structure, you may ask them to write their sentences on the board.

Activity Bank

Lesson 4, Worksheet 1: *Could* and *Might*

D **Read the conversation between Arnie and his manager, Fred. Do you think Fred is right?**

Fred: Arnie, why aren't you wearing a back support belt?
Arnie: Oh, I don't need one.
Fred: If you don't wear a belt, you <u>might</u> get hurt.
Arnie: I don't think so. I'm really careful.
Fred: I know, but you <u>could</u> fall. Or you <u>might</u> lift something that is too heavy.
Arnie: You're right. If I get hurt, I <u>might</u> miss work. I <u>could</u> lose a lot of money if I can't work.
Fred: Exactly. Let me get you a belt.

E **Underline the words *might* and *could* in the conversation above. Circle the verb that comes after each modal. Then, study the chart below.**

Modals: *Could* and *Might*			
Subject	**Modal**	**Verb**	**Example sentence**
I, you, he, she,	could	fall	You could fall.
it, we, they	might	miss	I might miss work.
We use the modals *could* and *might* to say that there is a chance that something will happen in the future.			

F **We also use *might* and *could* in conditional sentences with *if* when we are talking about possibilities. Complete the sentences.** (Answers may vary.)

EXAMPLE: If Arnie doesn't wear a back support belt, <u>he could get hurt.</u>

1. If Minh forgets to tie her hair back, <u>she could get her hair caught in a mixer</u>.

2. José <u>could hurt his head</u> if he doesn't wear a hard hat.

3. Wassim <u>could get sparks in his eyes</u> if he doesn't wear safety goggles.

4. Robin <u>could damage his hearing</u> if he doesn't wear earplugs.

5. If Lilly doesn't buckle her seat belt, she <u>could get hurt in an accident</u>.

G **Look at the safety hazards below. What's wrong in each picture?**

1.

3.

2.

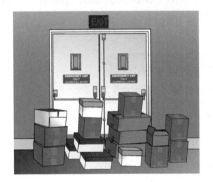

4.

H **Write sentences about what** *could* **and** *might* **happen in the situations above.**
(Answers may vary.)

1. The electric socket could give someone a shock or start a fire.

   _____

2. The trash could catch fire.

   _____

3. People might not be able to use the door in an emergency.

   _____

4. Someone might slip in the cooking oil.

   _____

I **Work with a small group to make a list of safety rules for your classroom.**

Presentation 3

10-15 mins.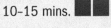

G Look at the safety hazards below. What's wrong in each picture?

Go through each picture with the class, eliciting vocabulary from students to describe each picture. Write the vocabulary they give you on the board and add any relevant words they don't know.

Practice 3

0-15 mins. ■

H Write sentences about what *could* and *might* happen in the situations above.

Ask students to work on the sentences in groups.

Evaluation 3

10-15 mins. ■

Put four columns on the board, one for each situation shown in Exercise G. Ask one person from each group to come to the board and write their group's sentences.

 Refer students to *Stand Out 3 Grammar Challenge*, Unit 7, Challenge 4 for more practice with *could* and *might*.

Application

10-20 mins. ■■

I Work with a small group to make a list of safety rules for your classroom.

When students have finished, have them present their rules to the class. Then as a class, come up with a list of the ten best safety rules for the classroom.

Objective: Communicate at work
Grammar: Polite requests
Pronunciation: Rising intonation for polite requests, tone of voice for agreeing and refusing
Academic Strategy: Focused listening
Vocabulary: *criticism, request, compliment*

AGENDA

Understand compliments and criticism.
Respond to compliments and criticism.
Make polite requests.
Agree and refuse politely.
Use rising intonation.

RESOURCES

Activity Bank: Lesson 5, Worksheets 1–2
Reading and Writing Challenge: Unit 7

Grammar Challenge 3: Unit 7, Challenge 5
Audio: CD 1, Tracks 17–18

■ 1.5 hour classes ■ 2.5 hour classes ■ 3⁺ hour classes

Warm-up and Review   5-10 mins. ■■■

Describe some unsafe workplace situations and ask students what *could* or *might* happen.

Introduction   5-10 mins. ■■■

Write *workplace communication* on the board. Ask students when they communicate with coworkers and why. State the objective: *Today we will be learning how to communicate at work.*

Presentation 1   10-15 mins. ■■■

 **Look at the picture. Is the manager criticizing or complimenting her employee? What do you think they are saying?**

Have students look at the picture and guess what is happening. Write *compliment* and *criticize* on the board. Ask students to tell you the difference.

Practice 1   10-15 mins. ■■■

 Identify the different types of communication. Write *compliment* or *criticism* next to each sentence below.

Have students complete this exercise alone.

Evaluation 1   5-10 mins. ■■■

Let students check their answers with a partner before the class goes over them.

Presentation 2   5-10 mins. ■■■

Tell students they will hear conversations between two employees and decide if the second employee is responding to a compliment or a criticism. First, have them read each sentence and guess what the speaker is responding to.

Practice 2   15-20 mins. ■■■

 Are these people responding to a criticism or a compliment? Write *compliment* or *criticism* next to each sentence below. Then, listen and check your answers.

Have students write their answers before listening. When they listen to check their answers, tell them listen to the tone of the speakers' voices.

> 🎧 **Listening Script**   CD 1, Track 17
>
> The responses to the statements below match the sentences in Exercise C.
>
> 1. *That was an excellent presentation!*
> 2. *You need to work a little faster.*
> 3. *You are a talented salesperson.*
> 4. *You shouldn't wear that shirt to work.*
> 5. *You are one of our best workers.*
> 6. *Please don't take such long breaks.*

 Use the sentences and responses in Exercises B and C to make conversations with a partner.

Students should talk with a partner, then switch partners and talk again until you tell them to stop.

Evaluation 2   15-20 mins. ■■

Observe students as they work.

Note: Standards Correlations are on the next page.

Good job!

GOAL ➤ **Communicate at work**

A Look at the picture. Is the manager criticizing or complimenting her employee? What do you think they are saying?

> *criticize:* to say something negative
>
> *compliment:* to say something nice

B Identify the different types of communication. Write *compliment* or *criticism* next to each sentence below.

1. Good job! _____ compliment
2. You need to work a little faster. _____ criticism
3. You shouldn't wear that shirt to work. _____ criticism
4. That was an excellent presentation. _____ compliment
5. You are really friendly to the customers. _____ compliment
6. Please don't take such long breaks. _____ criticism
7. You are one of our best workers. _____ compliment

CD 1
TR 17

C Are these people responding to criticism or a compliment? Write *compliment* or *criticism* next to each sentence below. Then, listen and check your answers.

1. Thanks. I'm glad to hear it. _____ compliment
2. I'm sorry. I'll try to do better next time. _____ criticism
3. Thanks. _____ compliment
4. I'm sorry. I won't wear it again. _____ criticism
5. Thank you. I appreciate your telling me that. _____ compliment
6. OK. It won't happen again. _____ criticism

D Use the sentences and responses in Exercises B and C to make conversations with a partner.

EXAMPLE: *Student A:* Good job!
             Student B: Thank you. I appreciate your telling me that.

LESSON **GOAL** ➤ **Communicate at work**

E Compare the two conversations. Then, study the charts.

Conversation 1

Employee: Excuse me. Would you mind looking over this report for me before I send it out?
Manager: Yes, of course. That's no problem.

Conversation 2

Susan: Could you give me a hand with this box?
Coworker: Sure, I'll be right over.

Polite Requests	
Would you mind helping me?	Polite and formal
Could you help me, *please*?	Polite and friendly
Can you give me a hand?	Polite and informal
Come here!	Very informal and impolite
When we speak to friends or colleagues, it is polite to be less formal. When we speak to a boss or a manager, it is polite to be more formal.	

Agree	Refuse
Sure.	No. I'm really sorry.
That's fine.	I'm sorry but I can't.
Of course.	I'd like to but I can't because . . .
No problem.	
Certainly.	

Pronunciation

Rising Intonation for Polite Requests

➤ Would you mind helping me?

➤ Can you give me a hand?

Tone of Voice for Agreeing and Refusing

➤ When you *agree* to something, your voice should sound *happy* and *upbeat*.

➤ When you *refuse* something, you should sound *apologetic*.

Presentation 3   5-10 mins. ■■■□

E Compare the two conversations. Then, study the charts.

Introduce polite requests by going over the conversations with the class. Talk about formal and informal situations and how to make polite requests.

Pronunciation

Rising intonation for polite requests and tone of voice for agreeing and refusing

Go over the examples in the pronunciation box and talk about agreeing and refusing. Have students repeat after you as you model each example. Then model and have the students repeat each example from the two charts above.

STANDARDS CORRELATIONS

CASAS: 4.4.1, 4.6.1 (See CASAS Competency List on pages 169-175.)
SCANS: Information Acquire and evaluate information, organize and maintain information, interpret and communicate information
Interpersonal Participate as a member of a team, teach others, exercise leadership, negotiate to arrive at a decision, work with cultural diversity
Systems Understand systems, monitor and correct performance
Basic Skills Reading, writing, listening, speaking
Thinking Skills Creative thinking, decision making, problem solving, seeing things in the mind's eye

Personal Qualities Responsibility, sociability, self-management
EFF: Communication Read with understanding, convey ideas in writing, speak so others can understand
Decision Making Solve problems and make decisions
Interpersonal Cooperate with others
Lifelong Learning Take responsibility for learning, reflect and evaluate

Instructor's Notes

Practice 3   10-15 mins. ◼

F Listen to these people talking to their bosses, coworkers, and employees. Are they being impolite or polite? Check the correct answer.

See how many students can get all the answers right the first time. Then play the recording again to make sure all the students hear the difference between being polite and being impolite.

 Listening Script   CD 1, Track 18

1. *Bob, could you come to my office for a minute?*
2. *Give me that hammer.*
3. *Hey, we need more coffee.*
4. *Would you mail this package?*

 Refer students to *Stand Out 3 Grammar Challenge,* Unit 7, Challenge 5 for more practice with polite requests.

Evaluation 3   5-10 mins. ◼

Go over the answers as a class. Have students practice the requests with a partner.

Application   10-20 mins. ◼◼◼

G Complete the conversations below with a partner. Then, practice your conversations and present them to the class.

H Work with a partner. Practice making and responding to polite requests, and complimenting and criticizing.

Activity Bank

Lesson 5, Worksheet 1: Conversation Completion
Lesson 5, Worksheet 2: Communicating at Work

 Refer students to *Stand Out 3 Grammar Challenge,* Unit 7, Extension Challenges 1–2 for practice with reported speech and three-word phrasal verbs.

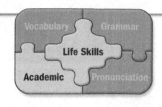

LESSON 5

GOAL ➤ **Communicate at work**

CD 1
TR 18

(F) **Listen to these people talking to their bosses, coworkers, and employees. Are they being impolite or polite? Check the correct answer.**

1. ___ impolite   _✓_ polite   3. _✓_ impolite   ___ polite

2. _✓_ impolite   ___ polite   4. ___ impolite   _✓_ polite

(G) **Complete the conversations below with a partner. Then, practice your conversations and present them to the class.** (Answers will vary.)

Conversation 1

A: That was an excellent project you turned in.

B: _____

A: I'm going to share it with all the other employees.

B: _____

Conversation 2

A: Please don't be late to work anymore.

B: _____

A: It's really affecting your work.

B: _____

Conversation 3

A: _____

B: Sure, I'd be happy to.

A: _____

(H) **Work with a partner. Practice making and responding to polite requests, and complimenting and criticizing.**

1. Your manager gave you a good employee review.
2. Ask your coworker to give you a ride home.
3. Your coworker is always late.
4. Ask your boss to help you check some accounts.

Review

A Work with a partner. Imagine that you need to hire several new employees for your business. Use the vocabulary from the box to talk about the qualities you are looking for. (Lesson 1)

EXAMPLE: *Student A*: I think an ideal employee is serious.
   Student B: I agree. Good employees shouldn't be lazy.

friendly	courteous	funny	serious	demanding	respectful
strict	quiet	interesting	ambitious	hardworking	patient
relaxed	intelligent	easygoing	lazy	opinionated	reserved

B Circle the correct word in each sentence. (Lesson 1)

1. Have you seen (my / mine) new pen?

2. (They / Their) cafeteria has delicious food but (our / ours) is awful.

3. Can I use (your / yours) stapler? I can't find (my / mine.)

4. (Our / Ours) salary is low but we get a lot of tips.

5. (My / Mine) benefits are really good but (her / hers) are better.

C Match the description to the benefit. (Lesson 3)

Benefit	Description
_d_ 1. 401K	a. for work injuries
_f_ 2. bonus	b. a day off to do something for yourself
_a_ 3. disability insurance	c. time off to have a baby
_g_ 4. family medical leave	d. retirement savings
_c_ 5. maternity leave	e. a day off if you are sick
_b_ 6. personal day	f. when a company shares its profits
_e_ 7. sick day	g. time off to care for a sick family member

AT-A-GLANCE PREP

Objectives: All unit objectives
Grammar: All unit grammar
Academic Strategy: Reviewing
Vocabulary: All unit vocabulary

AGENDA

Discuss unit objectives.
Complete the review.
Do My Dictionary.
Evaluate and reflect on progress.

RESOURCES

Activity Bank Worksheets: Unit 7, Lessons 1–5
Reading and Writing Challenge: Unit 7

Grammar Challenge 3: Unit 7, Challenges 1–5

■ 1.5 hour classes   ■ 2.5 hour classes   ■ 3⁺ hour classes

Stand Out 3 Assessment CD-ROM with Exam *View*®

Warm-up and Review   5-10 mins.

Have student turn to page 135 and do Exercise
G again with a different partner. Ask volunteers
to practice their conversations for the class.

Introduction   5-10 mins.

Ask students as a class to try to recall (in general) all
the goals of this unit without looking at their books.
Then remind them which goals they omitted, if
any. (Unit goals: compare employee behavior and
attitudes, interpret a pay stub, interpret benefit
information, identify safe workplace behavior, and
communicate at work) Write all the Unit 7 goals on
the board. Show students the first page of the unit
and mention the five objectives. State the objectives
for the review: *Today we will be reviewing everything
you have learned in this unit.*

Presentation 1   10-15 mins. ■■■

This presentation will cover the first three pages
of the review. Quickly go to the first page of
each lesson. Discuss the objective of each. Ask
simple questions to remind students of what they
have learned.

Note: Since there is little presentation in the
review, you can assign Exercises B–E for homework
and go over them in class the following day.

Practice 1   20-25 mins.

Note: There are two ways to do the review:
(1) Go through each exercise one at a time and,
as students complete each one, go over the
answers. (2) Briefly go through the instructions
of each exercise, allow students to complete all
of the exercises at once, and then go over
the answers.

Ⓐ Work with a partner. Imagine that you need
to hire several new employees for your business.
Use the vocabulary from the box to talk about the
qualities you are looking for. (Lesson 1)

Ⓑ Circle the correct word in each sentence.
(Lesson 1)

Ⓒ Match the description to the benefit.
(Lesson 3)

Evaluation 1   20-25 mins.

Go around the classroom and check on students'
progress. Help individuals when needed. If you
see consistent errors among several students,
interrupt the class and give a mini lesson or
review to help students feel comfortable with
the concept.

STANDARDS CORRELATIONS

CASAS: 7.2.1 (See CASAS Competency List on pages 169–175.)
SCANS: **Resources** Allocate time
Information Acquire and evaluate information
Interpersonal Participate as a member of a team, teach others, negotiate
to arrive at a decision, work with cultural diversity
Systems Monitor and correct performance
Basic Skills Reading, writing, arithmetic, listening, speaking
Thinking Skills Creative thinking, decision making, problem solving,
seeing things in the mind's eye

Personal Qualities Responsibility, sociability, self-management
EFF: **Communication** Convey ideas in writing, read with understanding,
speak so others can understand, listen actively
Decision Making Solve problems and make decisions
Interpersonal Guide others, cooperate with others
Lifelong Learning Take responsibility for learning, reflect and evaluate,
learn through research

Practice 1 *(continued)*   25–30 mins. ■■■□

D Skim Ali's pay stub and answer the questions below. (Lesson 2)

Evaluation 1 *(continued)*   25–30 mins. ■■■□

Go around the classroom and check on students' progress. Help individuals when needed. If you see consistent errors among several students, interrupt the class and give a mini lesson or review to help students feel comfortable with the concept.

Teaching Tip

Recycling/Review

The review exercises and the project that follows are part of the recycling/review process. Students at this level often need to be reintroduced to concepts to solidify what they have learned. Many concepts are learned and forgotten while learning other new concepts. This is because students learn but are not necessarily ready to acquire language concepts.

Therefore, it becomes very important to review and to show students how to review on their own. It is also important to recycle the new concepts in different contexts.

Instructor's Notes

Skim Ali's pay stub and answer the questions below. (Lesson 2)

Employee Name: Ali Ramsey Check Number: 89765 S.S. Number: 000-89-2524	Marital Status: Single Payroll Begin/End Dates 8/01/07–8/15/07

HOURS AND EARNINGS

Description	Rate of Pay	Hours/Units	Earnings
Hourly/Day/Monthly	11.75	56	658.00

TAX DEDUCTIONS

Tax Description	Current Amount	Calendar Year-to-Date
Federal	17.65	141.20
State	6.75	54.00
Social Security	5.23	41.84
Medicare	3.26	26.08
State Disability	4.25	34.00

PRE-TAX DEDUCTIONS

Description	Amount
401K	1005.00
Current Total	100.00
Year-to-Date Total	800.00

	Gross Pay	Pre-Tax Deductions	Pre-Tax Retirement	Tax Deductions	Net Pay
Current	658.00	100.00		37.14	520.86

1. Did Ali pay into social security this pay period? _____Yes_____

   If so, how much? _____$5.23_____

2. Does Ali pay Medicare? _____Yes_____

3. Does he pay state disability insurance? _____Yes_____

4. How many hours did he work during this two-week pay period? _____56_____

5. How much federal tax has Ali paid this year? _____$141.20_____

6. Does he contribute any money to a retirement account? _____Yes_____

   If so, how much? _____$100_____

7. How much money did he make this pay period after taxes? _____$520.86_____

8. How much money did he make this pay period before taxes? _____$658_____

9. How much state tax did he pay this pay period? _____$6.75_____

10. What does he get paid per hour? _____$11.75_____

E Complete the following sentences about work situations. Use a conditional with *might* or *could*. **(Lesson 4)** (Answers will vary.)

1. If you don't mop the wet floor, _____.

2. If the truck driver drives too fast, _____.

3. If those construction workers don't wear earplugs, _____.

4. If the gardener doesn't wear gloves, _____.

5. If your manager sees you leaving early, _____.

6. If I quit my job, _____.

F Work with a partner. Practice responding to compliments and criticism using the sentences below. **(Lesson 5)**

EXAMPLE: *Student A:* You look very professional today.
Student B: Thanks. It's nice of you to say so.

1. Your report was excellent!

2. I noticed you were late again today.

3. Can you be a little neater with your work?

4. You finished that project so quickly!

G Work with a partner. Practice making and responding to polite requests using the situations below. **(Lesson 5)**

1. Ask your coworker to let you use her computer.

2. Ask your employee to send a fax.

3. Ask your coworker to help you lift a heavy box.

4. Ask your manager to give someone a message.

Practice 1 *(continued)*   25–30 mins. ■■■□

(E) Complete the following sentences about work situations. Use a conditional with *might* or *could*. (Lesson 4)

(F) Work with a partner. Practice responding to compliments and criticism using the sentences below. (Lesson 5)

(G) Work with a partner. Practice making and responding to polite requests using the situations below. (Lesson 5)

Evaluation 1 *(continued)*   25–30 mins. ■■■□

Go around the classroom and check on students' progress. Help individuals when needed. If you see consistent errors among several students, interrupt the class and give a mini lesson or review to help students feel comfortable with the concept.

Presentation 2
5-10 mins.

My Dictionary

Ask students to brainstorm new vocabulary items they learned in this unit. Have them do this without looking in their books. Then choose one of the words they came up with that has other word forms, such as *compliment*. Ask them if they can come up with another word that is very close to this one but not exactly the same—*complimentary*. Explain how these words are related but are different parts of speech. Consequently, they are used differently in sentences. Go over as many examples as you need to until students understand.

Practice 2
15-20 mins. ■■

(Shorter classes can do these exercises for homework.)

Use your dictionary to look up different word forms of vocabulary in this unit. Use the new word form in a sentence.

Evaluation 2
15-20 mins. ■■

Walk around the room and help students.

Presentation 3
5-10 mins. ■■■

Learner Log

In this unit, you learned many things about being on the job. How comfortable do you feel doing each of the skills listed below? Rate your comfort level on a scale of 1 to 4.

Go over the instructions with students and make sure they understand what to do. You may want to read the skills out loud with the class to make sure they understand them.

Practice 3
5-10 mins. ■

Have students complete the Learner Log.

Evaluation 3
5-10 mins. ■

Walk around the classroom and help students as necessary.

Application
5-10 mins. ■■■

Go over the two reflection questions with students and have them complete the answers by themselves.

Assessment
■■■

Use the Stand Out 3 Assessment CD-ROM with Exam*View*® to create a post-test for Unit 7.

Learner Logs

Learner logs function to help students in many different ways:

1. They serve as part of the review process.
2. They help students to gain confidence and document what they have learned. Consequently, students see that they are making progress and want to move forward in learning.
3. They provide students with a tool that they can use over and over to check and recheck their understanding. In this way, students become independent learners.

Instructor's Notes

_____
_____
_____
_____
_____
_____
_____
_____
_____
_____
_____
_____
_____
_____
_____
_____
_____
_____
_____

My Dictionary

Word Form: Parts of Speech

Use your dictionary to look up different word forms of vocabulary in this unit.
Use the new word form in a sentence. (Sentences will vary.)

EXAMPLE: nouns: employee, employer   verb: __to employ__

Our company wants to employ people with good computer skills.

1. noun: promotion   verb: _____ to promote _____

_____

2. verb: to retire   noun: _____ retirement, retiree _____

_____

3. verb: to commute   noun (person): _____ commuter _____

_____

4. noun: accomplishment   verb: _____ to accomplish _____

_____

Learner Log

In this unit, you learned many things about being on the job. How comfortable do you feel doing each of the skills listed below? Rate your comfort level on a scale of 1 to 4.

1 = Need more practice   **2** = OK   **3** = Good   **4** = Great!

Life Skill	Comfort Level				Page
I can compare employee behavior and attitudes.	1	2	3	4	121
I can interpret a pay stub.	1	2	3	4	124
I understand benefits.	1	2	3	4	127
I can discuss workplace safety.	1	2	3	4	130
I can respond to compliments and criticism.	1	2	3	4	133
I can make and respond to polite requests.	1	2	3	4	134

If you circled 1 or 2, write down the page number where you can review this skill.

Reflection

1. What was the most useful skill you learned in this unit? _____

_____

2. How will this help you in life? _____

Team Project

Employee Handbook Table of Contents
- Pay Stub Information **3**
- Benefits **7**
- Workplace Safety **19**
- Workplace Communications **23**

Create an employee handbook.

With your team, you will create one section of an employee handbook. With your class, you will create a complete employee handbook.

1. Form a team with four or five students.
   Choose a position for each member of your team.

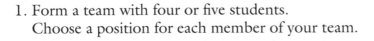

POSITION	JOB DESCRIPTION	STUDENT NAME
Student 1: Leader	See that everyone speaks English and participates.	
Student 2: Secretary	Write information for the handbook.	
Student 3: Designer	Design brochure layout and add artwork.	
Students 4/5: Member(s)	Help secretary and designer with their work.	

2. With your class, decide what will be in your employee handbook. (Look at the table of contents in the illustration above for ideas.) Decide what part of the handbook each team will create. (Lessons 1–5)

3. Create the text for your section of the employee handbook. (Lessons 1–5)

4. Create artwork for your section of the employee handbook.

5. As a class, create a table of contents and a cover. Put your handbook together.

6. Display your handbook so that other classes can see it.

Create an employee handbook.

The class will create an employee handbook based on information they learned in this unit. Each team will create one section for the handbook and then all the sections will be put together to create one handbook.

The team project is the final application for the unit. It gives students a chance to show that they have mastered all of the Unit 7 objectives.

Note: Shorter classes can extend this project over two class meetings.

Stage 1   5 mins.

Form a team with four or five students. Choose a position for each member of your team.

Have students decide who will lead each step as described on the student page. Provide well-defined directions on the board for how teams should proceed. Explain that all the students do every step as a team. Teams shouldn't go to the next stage until the previous one is complete.

Stage 2   5-10 mins.

With your class, decide what will be in your employee handbook. (Look at the table of contents in the illustration above for ideas.) Decide what part of the handbook each team will create. (Lessons 1–5)

You may lead this step and write students' ideas on the board or ask a volunteer to come up and lead this step. Encourage the class to brainstorm many different ideas and then choose the best ones, basing the number of ideas on how many teams there are. Each team should only work on one section.

Stage 3   20-25 mins.

Create the text for your section of the employee handbook. (Lessons 1–5)

Have each team work individually on their assigned section.

Stage 4   15-20 mins.

Create artwork for your section of the employee handbook.

Stage 5   5-10 mins.

As a class, create a table of contents and a cover. Put your handbook together.

Choose a few students to work on this together and ask for one of the teams to be in charge of putting the book together.

Stage 6

Display your handbook.

STANDARDS CORRELATIONS

CASAS: 4.8.1, 4.8.5, 4.8.6 (See CASAS Competency List on pages 169–175.)
SCANS: Resources Allocate time
Information Acquire and evaluate information, organize and maintain information, interpret and communicate information, use computers to process information
Systems Understand systems, improve and design systems
Technology Select technology, apply technology to exercise
Basic Skills Writing
Thinking Skills Creative thinking, decision making, problem solving, seeing things in the mind's eye, reasoning

Personal Qualities Responsibility, self-esteem, self-management, integrity/honesty
EFF: Communication Convey ideas in writing, speak so others can understand
Decision Making Solve problems and make decisions, plan
Interpersonal Guide others, resolve conflict and negotiate, advocate and influence, cooperate with others
Lifelong Learning Take responsibility for learning, reflect and evaluate, use information and communication technologies (optional)

Objective: Identify U.S. geographical locations
Academic Strategy: Focused listening
Vocabulary: names of states, *port, colony, capital, producer*

AGENDA
Study a map of the U.S.
Identify U.S. cities.
Identify states from their abbreviations.
Talk about U.S. tourist attractions.
Listen to and discuss lecture about important cities.

RESOURCES

Activity Bank: Lesson 1, Worksheet 1
Reading and Writing Challenge: Unit 8

Grammar Challenge 3: Unit 8, Challenge 1
Audio: CD 1, Track 19

 1.5 hour classes 2.5 hour classes 3⁺ hour classes

Stand Out 3 Assessment CD-ROM with *ExamView*®

TB Preassessment *(optional)*

Use the Stand Out 3 Assessment CD-ROM with *ExamView*® to create a pretest for Unit 8.

Warm-up and Review   10-15 mins.

Ask students how many states make up the United States. Then give them about ten minutes to write down the names of as many states as they can.

Introduction   5-10 mins.

Have students share their lists with their classmates and add states they missed to their own lists. After one volunteer has written his or her list on the board, ask others to supplement the list until all fifty states are named. You may need to add some to complete the list. State the objective: *Today we will be identifying U.S. geographical locations.*

Presentation 1   10-15 mins.

As you display a large map of the United States (a paper map or a transparency), have students look at the map in their books. Point to different states on the map you are using and ask students to name them. (If you don't have a large map and are relying instead on the one in the students' books, provide students with the approximate location of the states you want them to name.) As you present them, write the state names on the board so students become familiar with the correct spelling.

Practice 1   10-15 mins.

 Look at the map of the United States. How many states are there? Find your state and circle it. Put an *X* on the states you have visited. Write the names of the cities in the spaces provided.

Evaluation 1   5 mins.

Go over the answers as a class.

STANDARDS CORRELATIONS

CASAS: 5.2.1, 5.2.4 (See CASAS Competency List on pages 169–175.)
SCANS: Information Acquire and evaluate information, organize and maintain information, interpret and communicate information
Interpersonal Participate as a member of a team, teach others, exercise leadership, negotiate to arrive at a decision, work with cultural diversity
Systems Understand systems, monitor and correct performance
Basic Skills Reading, writing, listening, speaking
Thinking Skills Creative thinking, decision making, problem solving, seeing things in the mind's eye

Personal Qualities Responsibility, sociability, self-management
EFF: Communication Read with understanding, convey ideas in writing, speak so others can understand, listen actively, observe critically
Decision Making Solve problems and make decisions, plan
Interpersonal Guide others, advocate and influence, cooperate with others
Lifelong Learning Reflect and evaluate, learn through research, use information and communications technology (optional)

Citizens and Community

GOALS

➤ **Identify U.S. geographical locations**

➤ **Compare and contrast ideas**

➤ **Interpret the system of U.S. government**

➤ **Express opinions about community issues**

➤ **Write a speech**

The United States

GOAL ➤ **Identify U.S. geographical locations**

A Look at the map of the United States. How many states are there? Find your state and circle it. Put an *X* on the states you have visited. Write the names of the cities in the spaces provided.

| Philadelphia | Los Angeles | Jamestown | New York | San Francisco | Houston |

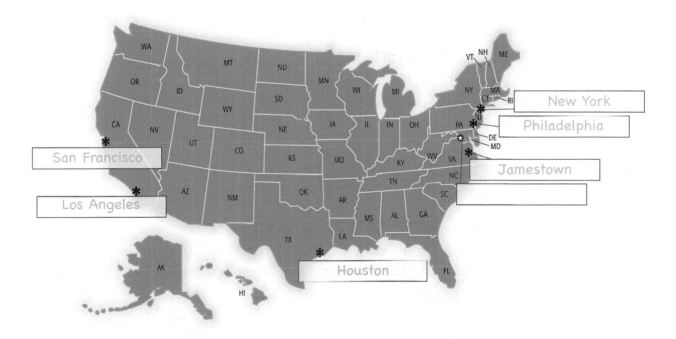

GOAL ➤ **Identify U.S. geographical locations**

B Read the state abbreviations and write the full state name. Ask a classmate or your teacher if you need help.

AL	Alabama	MT	Montana
AK	Alaska	NE	Nebraska
AZ	Arizona	NV	Nevada
AR	Arkansas	NH	New Hampshire
CA	California	NM	New Mexico
CO	Colorado	NJ	New Jersey
CT	Connecticut	NY	New York
DE	Delaware	NC	North Carolina
FL	Florida	ND	North Dakota
GA	Georgia	OH	Ohio
HI	Hawaii	OK	Oklahoma
ID	Idaho	OR	Oregon
IL	Illinois	PA	Pennsylvania
IN	Indiana	RI	Rhode Island
IA	Iowa	SC	South Carolina
KS	Kansas	SD	South Dakota
KY	Kentucky	TN	Tennessee
LA	Louisiana	TX	Texas
ME	Maine	UT	Utah
MD	Maryland	VT	Vermont
MA	Massachusetts	VA	Virginia
MI	Michigan	WA	Washington
MN	Minnesota	WV	West Virginia
MS	Mississippi	WI	Wisconsin
MO	Missouri	WY	Wyoming

Note: Washington, DC, is not a state.

C Ask your partner about the states he or she has visited. Who has visited the most states?

Presentation 2   5-10 mins. ■■■

Look at Exercise B with the class and ask students what the two letter codes before the state names are called (abbreviations). Ask them what the abbreviation is for your state. Go over the ones that have already been completed.

Practice 2   10-15 mins. ■■

B Read the state abbreviations and write the full state name. Ask a classmate or your teacher if you need help.

Have students work in pairs or small groups to complete the entire exercise.

Evaluation 2   10-15 mins. ■■

Go over the state names and the abbreviations (postal codes) with the class.

C Ask your partner about the states he or she has visited. Who has visited the most states?

Activity Bank

Lesson 1, Worksheet 1: The United States

Refer students to *Stand Out 3 Grammar Challenge*, Unit 8, Challenge 1 for practice with contrasting statements with *but* and *however*.

Instructor's Notes

Presentation 3   5-10 mins. ■■■

Have students turn back to the map on page 141 and find the cities marked with an asterisk. Ask them if they have heard of these cities before and, if so, what they know about each one.

D Look at the pictures of popular tourist attractions in the United States. What are they? Where are they located?

Practice 3   15-20 mins. ■

Prepare students for the focused listening activity in Exercise E by previewing its vocabulary.

E Listen to the lecture on notable cities in the United States. Match the city on the right with the information on the left. Review the vocabulary with your teacher before you start.

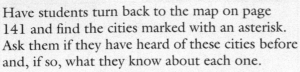

Listening Script   CD 1, Track 19

Now that we've talked about various states in the United States, I'd like to tell you about a few important cities. I'll start with one that really isn't called a city, but it's definitely very important—Washington, DC. DC stands for District of Columbia, which is what it is, a district. This is where the federal government is located: the White House, the Capitol building, and the Supreme Court.

Historically, two of the most important cities are Jamestown and Philadelphia. When the settlers first came from England in the 1600s, they came to Jamestown, Virginia, and named this first colony after King James of England. Many years later, the representatives of the thirteen colonies declared themselves an independent nation and wrote the Declaration of Independence in Philadelphia, which was the same place the Constitution was written.

Also on the East Coast, New York City was established. This is where European immigrants first came. They came to an island off the coast of New York called Ellis Island. Also off the coast of New York is Liberty Island. Liberty Island is the home of the Statue of Liberty, which was given to the United States by France in 1886.

Other famous cities include San Francisco, Los Angeles, and Houston. San Francisco, where the famous Golden Gate Bridge is located, was one of the first established cities in California because it was a port for ships coming in from the Pacific Ocean. Los Angeles became the film capital of the world in the mid 1900s and has grown ever since. And finally Houston, Texas, put itself on the map by being one of the largest oil producers in the United States.

And who could forget Mickey Mouse, Donald Duck, and the whole Disney gang? Yes, Disneyland is in California, but Disney World is located in Orlando, Florida.

These are some of the most notable cities in the United States. Can you think of some other notable cities?

Evaluation 3   5-10 mins. ■

Go over the answers as a class. More information is given about each city in the recording than is listed in the matching activity. Ask students if they can recall any information they heard but weren't asked about.

F What else do you know about the cities listed above? Discuss your ideas with your classmates and teacher.

Ask students to work in groups and write down information about the cities that they either heard in the recording or knew beforehand. Play the recording several more times.

Application   10-20 mins. ■■■

G What are some other cities in the United States? What are they known for? Include your own city or the city nearest you.

Write the following questions on the board: *What city and state do you live in? Why is your city important? Why is your state important?*

Have student groups write a paragraph about a city and its state. Groups should choose a city which at least one of its members has visited or lived in. Make sure all members participate in writing and editing the paragraph.

GOAL ➤ **Identify U.S. geographical locations**

Vocabulary · Grammar · Life Skills · Academic · Pronunciation

D Look at the pictures of popular tourist attractions in the United States. What are they? Where are they located?

Golden Gate Bridge
San Francisco, California

Statue of Liberty
New York, New York

Liberty Bell
Philadelphia, Pennsylvania

CD 1
TR 19

E Listen to the lecture on notable cities in the United States. Match the city on the right with the information on the left. Review the vocabulary with your teacher before you start.

Information

1. __g__ where the federal government is located
2. __d__ home of the Statue of Liberty
3. __f__ a major port for the Pacific Ocean
4. __b__ an English colony named after an English king
5. __e__ where the Declaration of Independence was written
6. __c__ the film capital of the world
7. __a__ a major oil producer
8. __h__ where Disney World is located

City

a. Houston, TX
b. Jamestown, VA
c. Los Angeles, CA
d. New York, NY
e. Philadelphia, PA
f. San Francisco, CA
g. Washington, DC
h. Orlando, FL

F What else do you know about the cities listed above? Discuss your ideas with your classmates and teacher.

G What are some other cities in the United States? What are they known for? Include your own city or the city nearest you. (Answers will vary.)

_____

_____

Which party?

GOAL ➤ Compare and contrast ideas

A The mayor is the top person in city government in most cities in the United States. Do you know who the mayor of your city is? (Answers will vary.)

B Imagine that you are getting ready to vote for a new mayor of your city. Two candidates gave speeches about what is important to them. Read about their different points of view.

Kim Vo wants to . . .	Dawson Brooks wants to . . .
➤ build more parks.	➤ drill for oil on empty land.
➤ lower class size in elementary schools.	➤ increase number of teachers per classroom.
➤ lower the tuition at city colleges for immigrant students.	➤ raise the tuition at city colleges for immigrant students.
➤ spend tax dollars on wider sidewalks in neighborhoods.	➤ spend tax dollars to improve library facilities.
➤ increase the number of police officers who patrol the streets.	➤ spend money to retrain current police officers.
➤ offer job training programs for homeless people.	➤ offer incentives for individuals to start their own businesses.

C With a partner, compare the two candidates using *but* and *however*.

EXAMPLE: Kim Vo wants to build more parks, but Dawson Brooks wants to drill for oil on empty land.

Dawson Brooks wants to drill for oil on empty land; however, Kim Vo wants to build more parks.

D Write two sentences comparing Kim Vo and Dawson Brooks using *but* or *however*.
(Answers will vary.)

1. _____

_____

2. _____

_____

E Which candidate would you vote for? Why? Write a paragraph on a separate piece of paper.
(Answers will vary.)

Objective: Compare and contrast ideas

Grammar: Comparing and contrasting ideas using *but, however, both . . . and, neither . . . nor*

Academic Strategy: Active reading

Vocabulary: *tuition, drill for oil, incentives, bilingual education*

RESOURCES

Activity Bank: Lesson 2, Worksheets 1–2

Reading and Writing Challenge: Unit 8

Grammar Challenge 3: Unit 8, Challenge 2

AGENDA

Discuss the mayor.

Compare two mayoral candidates.

Express opinions.

Compare and contrast ideas and opinions.

■ 1.5 hour classes　■ 2.5 hour classes　■ 3⁺ hour classes

Warm-up and Review　5–10 mins. ■■■

Have groups take out the paragraphs they wrote in Lesson 1. Ask one member of each group to read the paragraph out loud. Make a list on the board of the types of information each paragraph includes. State the objective: *Today we will be learning how to compare and contrast ideas.*

Introduction　5–10 mins. ■■■

 A The mayor is the top person in city government in most cities in the United States. Do you know who the mayor of your city is?

Presentation 1　10–15 mins. ■■■

B Imagine that you are getting ready to vote for a new mayor of your city. Two candidates gave speeches about what is important to them. Read about their different points of view.

Let students silently read the information. When they have finished, check their comprehension by asking questions about each candidate's opinion. For example: *What does Kim Vo want to do for homeless people?*

Practice 1　10–15 mins. ■■■

Explain that *but* and *however* are used when we want to contrast two ideas. Give them examples, such as: *I like pizza, but I don't like lasagna.* The two ideas should be somewhat related: Give an example sentence that contrasts two ideas that are not related, such as: *I like movies, but I hate onions.*

C With a partner, compare the two candidates using *but* and *however*.

Ask students to do this exercise orally.

D Write two sentences comparing Kim Vo and Dawson Brooks using *but* or *however*.

Ask students to write sentences similar to the ones they produced in Exercise C.

Evaluation 1　5 mins. ■■■

Ask volunteers to share their sentences comparing the candidates.

 E Which candidate would you vote for? Why? Write a paragraph on a separate piece of paper.

STANDARDS CORRELATIONS

CASAS: 5.1.4, 5.1.6 (See CASAS Competency List on pages 169–175.)

SCANS: **Information** Acquire and evaluate information, organize and maintain information, interpret and communicate information

Interpersonal Participate as a member of a team, teach others, exercise leadership, negotiate to arrive at a decision, work with cultural diversity

Systems Monitor and correct performance, improve and design systems

Basic Skills Reading, writing, listening, speaking

Thinking Skills Creative thinking, decision making, problem solving, seeing things in the mind's eye

Personal Qualities Responsibility, sociability, self-management

EFF: **Communication** Convey ideas in writing, speak so others can understand, listen actively

Decision Making Solve problems and make decisions

Interpersonal Cooperate with others

Lifelong Learning Reflect and evaluate, learn through research, use information and communications technology (optional)

Presentation 2   5-10 mins. ■■■

Write the word *opinion* on the board and ask students what it means. Ask one student how he or she feels about homework. Most likely, the reply will either be *I like homework* or *I don't like homework.* Write the reply on the board. Ask another student. Keep asking until you get an answer opposite to the one you got from the first student. You then have the opportunity to make the following statement: *(Chun Ling) likes homework, but (Flavio) doesn't.* Tell students that they will be asking their classmates for their opinions and writing them down in Exercise F.

Practice 2   10-15 mins. ■■

(F) Ask students what their feelings are about the topics below. Ask two students about each topic and fill in the chart. Ask: *How do you feel about . . . . ?* Think of your own topic for the last question.

Read the directions out loud and write the following question starter on the board: *How do you feel about _____?* Then go over the example and the topics before students start the activity.

Note: Shorter classes can do this activity at home with family or friends by asking what their opinions are about the topics.

Evaluation 2   5 mins. ■■

Observe students as they work. Ask volunteers to share the information they gathered.

Presentation 3   5-10 mins. ■■■

(G) Study the chart with your classmates and teacher.

F Ask students what their feelings are about the topics below. Ask two students about each topic and fill in the chart. Ask: *How do you feel about . . . ?* Think of your own topic for the last question. (Answers will vary.)

Name	Topic	Agree	Disagree
Enrico	increasing the number of students in our class	✓	
Liz			✓

Name	Topic	Agree	Disagree
	building more schools in our community		

Name	Topic	Agree	Disagree
	providing bilingual education for children		

Name	Topic	Agree	Disagree

G Study the chart with your classmates and teacher.

Comparing and Contrasting Ideas		
If two people share the same opinion, use *both . . . and* or *neither . . . nor.*		
Both	Enrico **and** Liz	want to increase the number of students in our class.
Neither	Suzanna **nor** Ali	wants to increase the number of students in our class.
If two people don't share the same opinion, use *but* or *however.*		
Enrico agrees with bilingual education,		**but** Liz doesn't.
Ali doesn't agree with bilingual education;		**however,** Suzanna does.
Punctuation Note: Use a semicolon (;) before and a comma (,) after *however.*		

H **Complete each sentence with *both, and, neither, nor, but,* or *however.***

1. Neither Alicia _____nor_____ Hoa wants the city to build a school instead of a park.

2. _____Both_____ Kim and Su want to increase the number of hours that our class meets.

3. Jeeva thinks ESL students should be in class with native English speakers;

   _____however_____, Adam thinks they should have their own class.

4. Bruno believes all children should study a second language, _____but_____ Liza thinks children should only learn their native language.

5. _____Neither_____ Lim nor Jeremy wants more homework.

6. Both Elizabeth _____and_____ Parker want to do more writing in class.

I **Look back at the information you collected on your classmates in Exercise F. Write sentences comparing their ideas.** (Answers will vary.)

1. _____

   _____

   _____

2. _____

   _____

   _____

3. _____

   _____

   _____

4. _____

   _____

   _____

Practice 3
5-10 mins. ■

(H) Complete each sentence with *both, and, neither, nor, but,* or *however.*

Evaluation 3
5 mins. ■

Call on volunteers to read the completed sentences out loud.

Application
10-20 mins. ■■■

(I) Look back at the information you collected on your classmates in Exercise F. Write sentences comparing their ideas.

Activity Bank 💿

Lesson 2, Worksheet 1: Compare and Contrast Ideas

Lesson 2, Worksheet 2: The Mayor's Speech

📖 Refer students to *Stand Out 3 Grammar Challenge*, Unit 8, Challenge 2 for more practice with *both* and *neither.*

Objective: Interpret the system of U.S. government

Academic Strategies: Active reading, focused listening, paragraph writing

Vocabulary: *executive, judicial, legislative, president, vice-president, cabinet, city officials, Congress, House of Representatives, Senate, Supreme Court*

RESOURCES

Activity Bank: Lesson 3, Worksheet 1
Reading and Writing Challenge: Unit 8

Grammar Challenge 3: Unit 8, Challenge 3
Audio: CD 1, Track 20

■ 1.5 hour classes   ■ 2.5 hour classes   ■ 3⁺ hour classes

AGENDA

Understand the three branches of the U.S. Government.
Identify city officials and their job duties.
Write an opinion paragraph.

Warm-up and Review   5 mins.

Have students form groups and discuss a few of the following topics: capital punishment, minimum wage increase, higher taxes, funding for public schools, and so on. List a few topics on the board and have groups elicit and discuss among themselves the opinions of their members. After about ten minutes, ask someone from each group to report on its discussions, using *and, but,* and *however.* For example: *Cecilia believes in higher wages for jobs, but Jen doesn't.* Give each group a chance to report. State the objective: *Today we will be interpreting the system of U.S. government.*

Note: This lesson only has two practices since Practice 1 will take a considerable amount of time.

Introduction   5-10 mins.

A Look at the diagram of the three branches that make up the U.S. government. What do you know about them?

Write *U.S. government* on the board and ask students what they know about its three branches. Briefly explain each branch.

Presentation 1   15-20 mins. ■■■

Before students begin Exercise B, remind them that when they read to get information, it is not important to understand every word. Suggest that they read the questions after each section of Exercise B *before* reading the section itself. That way, they will know in advance what information to look for. Go through the first few questions with them.

Practice 1   20-25 mins. ■■■

B Read about the U.S. government. Then, answer the questions after each section.

Allow students time to read and answer the questions on pages 147–148 on their own.

STANDARDS CORRELATIONS

CASAS: 5.1.4, 5.2.1(See CASAS Competency List on pages 169–175.)
SCANS: Information Acquire and evaluate information, organize and maintain information, interpret and communicate information
Interpersonal Participate as a member of a team, teach others, exercise leadership, negotiate to arrive at a decision, work with cultural diversity
Systems Understand systems, monitor and correct performance, improve and design systems
Basic Skills Reading, writing, listening, speaking

Thinking Skills Creative thinking, decision making, problem solving, seeing things in the mind's eye
Personal Qualities Responsibility, sociability, self-management
EFF: Communication Read with understanding, convey ideas in writing, listen actively
Decision Making Solve problems and make decisions, plan
Lifelong Learning Take responsibility for learning, reflect and evaluate, learn through research, use information and communications technology (optional)

U.S. government

GOAL ➤ Interpret the system of U.S. government

A Look at the diagram of the three branches that make up the U.S. government. What do you know about them?

Legislative

Executive

Judicial

B Read about the U.S. government. Then, answer the questions after each section.

The U.S. Government

The U.S. government has three branches—the executive branch, the legislative branch, and the judicial branch. The government was set up this way so no one person would have too much power. With three branches, each branch balances out the others.

The Executive Branch

In the executive branch are the president, the vice president, and the cabinet. The president is the leader of the country and of the executive branch. He can sign new laws, prepare the budget, and command the military. The vice president helps the president and is the leader of the Senate. Both the president and the vice president serve for four years and can be reelected only once. The president's cabinet is a group of experts who advise the president. The president chooses his cabinet members. They include the Secretary of State, the Secretary of Defense, and the Secretary of Education.

1. What does the president do? <u>signs new laws, prepares the budget, commands the military</u>

2. What does the vice president do? <u>helps the president, is the leader of the Senate</u>

3. How long do the president and vice president serve? <u>four years</u>

4. What does the cabinet do? <u>advises the president</u>

5. Are cabinet members elected? <u>No, the president chooses his cabinet members.</u>

The Legislative Branch

The legislative branch, also known as Congress, makes the laws for the United States. Congress has the power to declare war, collect taxes, borrow money, control immigration, set up a judicial and postal system, and the most important power, to make laws.

This branch has the greatest connection to the people of the United States because this branch represents citizens. Congress has two parts—the House of Representatives and the Senate. The House of Representatives has 435 state representatives. Each state gets a certain number of representatives based on its population. Each representative serves for two years and can be reelected. The Senate has 100 senators, two from each of the 50 states. Senators serve for six years and can also be reelected.

1. What is another name for the legislative branch? _____ Congress _____

2. What does this branch do? _____ makes laws _____

3. What are the two parts of this branch called? _____ House of Representatives, Senate _____

4. How many representatives are in the House? _____ 435 _____

5. What determines the number of representatives each state gets? _____ population _____

6. How long do representatives serve? _____ 2 years _____

7. How many senators does each state have? _____ 2 _____

8. How long do senators serve? _____ 6 years _____

The Judicial Branch

The third branch of the U.S. government is the judicial branch, which includes the Supreme Court and the federal courts. The job of the courts is to interpret the laws made by the legislative branch. The Supreme Court is the highest court in the United States, and has nine judges called justices. The justices listen to cases and make judgments based on the Constitution and the laws of the United States. The president and Congress choose the justices of the Supreme Court.

1. What is the role of the judicial branch? interpret the laws

2. What is the highest court in the United States? the Supreme Court

3. How does a person become a judge on the Supreme Court? The president and Congress choose the judges on the Supreme Court.

Active reading

The purpose of active reading is to help students engage their reading comprehension skills so they can tackle any reading with confidence. Explain that they may not understand the passage on the first reading. Help them realize that to understand a reading, they may need to read it more than once—perhaps as many as three or four times.

Pre-reading: Teach students that anticipating the content of a reading and recalling information they may already know about the topic will help make the reading easier to comprehend. Help students predict what they will be reading about by first looking at the title, pictures, highlighted or key vocabulary, and questions that may follow the reading.

First reading: Focus students' attention on main ideas by asking them to find the topic sentence in each paragraph, or have them summarize the main point of each paragraph.

Second reading: Show students how to scan the reading quickly to find details that support the main ideas or that answer the post-reading questions.

Guessing from context: Encourage students to guess the meaning of new words from context by analyzing the words surrounding the new vocabulary items. They should try not to let unknown words slow down their reading and should use a dictionary only after they are familiar with the context.

Critical thinking: Encourage students to express a personal opinion about the reading and to compare the ideas cross-culturally. Students might want to write comments and thoughts in their journals as they read.

Evaluation 1   15–20 mins.

If some students finish before others, have them work with a partner to compare answers. When all of the students have finished, go through each question with them, asking them to point out where they found the answers in the text. Supplement the reading with your own knowledge about the three branches of the government.

For longer classes, have students draw and label the three branches of government in small groups. If time, do a jigsaw activity in which a group of students becomes expert on one of the branches and reviews important points in the material with other students.

Instructor's Notes

_____

_____

_____

_____

_____

_____

_____

_____

_____

_____

_____

_____

_____

_____

Presentation 2   5-10 mins.

Discuss each of the titles of officials in Exercise C with students. Ask students if they know what each city official does.

Practice 2   10-15 mins.

C Most cities have government officials who are elected to help run the city. Listen to the following people talk about their jobs and fill in the chart with their duties.

 Listening Script   *CD 1, Track 20*

1. *Hi, my name is Jim, and I'm the tax assessor. I help set tax rates by deciding the value of property. Some people don't like me because they think I cause higher taxes, but I'm just doing my job.*

2. *Hello there, I'm Su Young. I'm the city clerk. As city clerk, I keep track of records of property, local businesses, and registered voters. I also issue birth certificates and marriage licenses. So, if you're going to get married or have a baby, come see me!*

3. *I'm Christopher Erikson, a city council member. I help to represent this community. All the council members meet with the mayor to discuss and solve community problems. It's really important to help make our community a better place to live.*

4. *Hi, my name is Sheryl, and I'm the superintendent of schools. I oversee the city schools and I help them do their job to provide a good education to our children. It's a very important job!*

5. *My name is Matt Peterson, and I'm the mayor of this town. I'm the head of the city government and I work with all the city council members to keep our community strong and happy.*

Activity Bank

Lesson 3, Worksheet 1: The Three Branches of Government

 Refer students to *Stand Out 3 Grammar Challenge*, Unit 8, Challenge 3 for more practice with active and passive voice.

Evaluation 2   5 mins.

Go over the answers.

Application   15-25 mins.

D Discuss the positions in the chart above with a group. Which position would you most like to have? Why? Which one would you least like to have? Why? Write a paragraph below.

To help students with their paragraphs, write the following question on the board: *If you could have any position in city government, which one would you want and why?*

Instructor's Notes

GOAL ➤ Interpret the system of U.S. government

CD 1
TR 20

Most cities have government officials who are elected to help run the city. Listen to the following people talk about their jobs and fill in the chart with their duties.

Official	Duties
Tax Assessor	1. helps county set tax rates 2. decides on the value of property
City Clerk	1. keeps track of records of property, local businesses, and registered voters 2. issues birth certificates and marriage licenses
City Council Member	1. helps represent the community meets with the mayor to discuss and solve community 2. problems
Superintendent of Schools	1. oversees the city schools 2. helps the schools provide a good education to the children
Mayor	1. is the head of the city government 2. works with the city council members

D Discuss the positions in the chart above with a group. Which position would you most like to have? Why? Which one would you least like to have? Why? **Write a paragraph below.** (Answers will vary.)

_____

_____

_____

_____

_____

_____

_____

_____

_____

_____

Community concerns

GOAL ➤ **Express opinions about community issues**

A Cherie lives in a small town in California, but it's not as nice as it used to be. Read about the problems in Cherie's community.

Hi, my name is Cherie. I live in a small community called Rosshaven in California. I moved here about ten years ago with my family because we wanted to live in a nice, safe community, but many things have happened in the past ten years.

First of all, the neighborhood schools are overcrowded. Because our school system is so good, many families from outside neighborhoods send their kids to our schools. There are over 35 students in each classroom.

Another problem is that there are many homeless people on our streets. It sometimes makes me nervous to have my kids walking home by themselves. I wish they could take a bus, but that's another problem. We don't have any public transportation here. When Rosshaven was first built, many wealthy people moved here. They all had cars, so there was no need for public transportation, but now things have changed. I think it's time for me to go to a city council meeting to see what I can do for our community.

B Cherie talks about three different problems in the reading above. List them below.

1. The neighborhood schools are overcrowded.

2. There are many homeless people on the streets.

3. There is no public transportation.

Objective: Express opinions about community issues
Grammar: Modal *should*
Academic Strategy: Active reading
Vocabulary: *overcrowded, homeless, wealthy, curfew, fine, tickets, resident*

RESOURCES

Activity Bank: Lesson 4, Worksheet 1
Reading and Writing Challenge: Unit 8

Grammar Challenge 3: Unit 8, Challenge 4

■ 1.5 hour classes   ■ 2.5 hour classes   ■ 3+ hour classes

AGENDA

Read about community issues.
Discuss solutions to community problems.
Give suggestions.

Warm-up and Review   10-15 mins. ■■■

Begin by asking students questions about the different branches of government. You might play a game where students in teams have to guess which branch is responsible for which activities.

Introduction   5-10 mins. ■■■

Write *community problems* on the board and ask students to help you identify such problems. Write every response on the board. State the objective: *Today we will be expressing opinions about community issues.*

Presentation 1   10-15 mins. ■■■

 Cherie lives in a small town in California. It's not as nice as it used to be. Read about the problems in Cherie's community.

Have students look at the picture of Cherie and her family before they begin reading. Ask them to imagine what kind of community problems Cherie might face. Then have students silently read the paragraph about Cherie. After they finish, ask them some basic comprehension questions: *Where do Cherie and her family live? Does she have children?* Then read the paragraph out loud to the students.

 Cherie talks about three different problems in the reading above. List them below.

Have students list the problems on their own before discussing them as a class.

STANDARDS CORRELATIONS

CASAS: 5.5.7, 5.5.8 (See CASAS Competency List on pages 169-175.)
SCANS: **Resources** Allocate time, allocate money, allocate materials and facility resources, allocate human resources
Information Acquire and evaluate information, organize and maintain information, interpret and communicate information
Interpersonal Participate as a member of a team, teach others, exercise leadership, negotiate to arrive at a decision, work with cultural diversity
Systems Understand systems, monitor and correct performance, improve and design systems
Basic Skills Reading, writing, listening, speaking

Thinking Skills Creative thinking, decision making, problem solving, seeing things in the mind's eye
Personal Qualities Responsibility, sociability, self-management
EFF: **Communication** Read with understanding, speak so others can understand, listen actively, observe critically
Decision Making Solve problems and make decisions, plan
Interpersonal Guide others, resolve conflict and negotiate, advocate and influence, cooperate with others
Lifelong Learning Take responsibility for learning, reflect and evaluate

Practice 1   10–15 mins.

C With a group, discuss possible solutions to each problem in Cherie's community. Write your ideas below. Report your answers to the class.

Tell each group to try to come up with at least two solutions to each problem. Make sure each group has a member taking notes.

Evaluation 1   10–15 mins.

Write the three problems on the board. Have each group report their solutions to the class and write what they say on the board. After each group has presented their ideas, read each solution out loud. Have the class vote on which solution they think best solves each problem.

Presentation 2   2 mins.

Go over the instructions for Exercise D.

Practice 2   10–15 mins.

D Rosshaven is a nice place to live, but like every community, it has some problems. Match each problem with a possible solution. Then, compare answers with a partner and say if you agree or disagree with each solution.

Evaluation 2   5–10 mins.

Circulate around the classroom and observe students as they work. Offer help with vocabulary as needed.

Presentation 3   5–10 mins.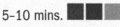

E We use *should* to give a strong suggestion. Study the chart below with your teacher.

Have students practice stating different community problems and solutions with their partners. Write the following example exchange on the board.

Student A: *We have a traffic problem. Our streets are too busy.*

Student B: *I think the city council should see that more traffic police are posted at busy intersections.*

Practice 3   10–15 mins. ◼

F With your group, use *should* to talk about the solutions you wrote in Exercise C.

Evaluation 3   10–15 mins. ◼

Observe students as they work in groups.

Instructor's Notes

_____

_____

_____

_____

_____

_____

_____

_____

_____

_____

_____

_____

_____

_____

_____

_____

_____

_____

_____

_____

_____

_____

C With a group, discuss possible solutions to each problem in Cherie's community. Write your ideas below. Report your answers to the class. (Solutions will vary.)

Problem	Possible solutions
overcrowded schools	1. 2.
many homeless people	1. 2.
no public transportation	1. 2.

D Rosshaven is a nice place to live, but like every community, it has some problems. Match each problem with a possible solution. Then, compare answers with a partner and say if you agree or disagree with each solution.

Problem

___c___ 1. Visitors park in resident parking spaces.

___b___ 2. People don't clean up after their animals.

___a___ 3. Teenagers are out late at night getting into trouble.

___d___ 4. The parks are not well kept up.

Solution
The city council should . . .

a. set a curfew for teenagers.

b. fine people who don't clean up after their pets.

c. give tickets to visitors who park in resident spaces.

d. raise taxes to help with recreation improvements.

E We use *should* to give a strong suggestion. Study the chart below with your teacher.

Should			
Subject	**Modal**	**Base verb**	
The city council	*should*	set	a curfew for teenagers.
People	*should*	clean up	after their pets.

F With your group, use *should* to talk about the solutions you wrote in Exercise C.

GOAL ➤ Express opinions about community issues

G With a group, form a city council. Decide how you will solve the following problems and present your ideas to the class. The class will vote on which group would be the best city council. (Answers will vary.)

1. There are no sidewalks on the busy streets in our town, and it is very dangerous. Many people get hurt because they walk too close to the cars. There is no space on the street to build sidewalks. What should we do to solve this problem?

_____

_____

_____

_____

_____

2. The housing prices are going up in our community. It's difficult to find affordable rent and almost impossible to buy a house. Many people are moving away from the community to find cheaper housing. The community wants to maintain diversity, but only the very wealthy can afford to stay. What should we do about the housing costs?

_____

_____

_____

_____

_____

3. The town's river was very dirty, but groups of citizens did a lot to clean it up. We want to increase taxes so we can build a new park along the river, but the growing town needs a new supermarket and more office space, too. Is there a way to make everyone happy?

_____

_____

_____

_____

_____

Refer students to *Stand Out 3 Grammar Challenge*, **Unit 8, Challenge 4 for more practice with** *should*.

Application   20–25 mins. ■■■

G With a group, form a city council. Decide how you will solve the following problems and present your ideas to the class. The class will vote on which group would be the best city council.

Tell each group that at least one of its members will have to come to the board and present its solutions.

Note: If you are short on time, give each group only one problem to solve.

AT-A-GLANCE PREP

Objective: Write a speech
Grammar: Contrary-to-fact conditional statements
Academic Strategies: Active reading, speech writing
Vocabulary: *penalty, retirement, wage, casinos*

AGENDA

Read a paragraph.
Express your opinions.
Write conditional sentences.
Write a paragraph.

RESOURCES

Activity Bank: Lesson 5, Worksheets 1–2
Reading and Writing Challenge: Unit 8

Grammar Challenge 3: Unit 8, Challenge 5

■ 1.5 hour classes   ■ 2.5 hour classes   ■ 3+ hour classes

Warm-up and Review   5-10 mins.

Ask students what kinds of problems they had to deal with in the previous lesson. Then ask about the solutions they came up with.

Introduction   5-10 mins.

Ask students: *What would you do if you were president?* Allow a few students to respond and write their answers on the board. Take one answer and write a conditional statement on the board. For example: *If Luis were president, he would raise the minimum wage.* State the objective: *Today we will learn how to write a speech.*

Presentation 1   10-15 mins.

(A) Rosario's teacher asked her to write a paragraph about what she would do if she became president of the United States. Read what she wrote below.

Read Rosario's speech out loud. Answer any questions students might have.

(B) Study these expressions with your classmates and teacher. Underline the ones Rosario used in her paragraph above.

Help students understand how to use each expression by giving them examples that include each phrase and asking them to give you examples in return.

Practice 1   10-15 mins.

(C) Write your opinion about the topics. Use the expressions from the box.

Evaluation 1   5-10 mins.

Ask for volunteers to read their sentences to the class.

If I were president

GOAL ➤ Write a speech

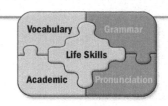

A Rosario's teacher asked her to write a paragraph about what she would do if she became president of the United States. Read what she wrote below.

> If I won the presidential election, I would be the first
> female president. If I were president, nobody would be poor
> or homeless. Personally, I think if people had more money, they
> wouldn't commit crimes. In my opinion, we shouldn't spend so much
> money on the military. If scientists didn't have to build weapons,
> they would have more time to study other things. Maybe they
> would find a cure for cancer. I think that I'd be a great president!

B Study these expressions with your classmates and teacher. Underline the ones Rosario used in her paragraph above.

> **Expressing an Opinion**
>
> In my opinion, …   I believe that …
>
> As I see it, …   I think that …
>
> Personally, I think …   I feel that …

C Write your opinion about the topics. Use the expressions from the box.

(Answers will vary.)

EXAMPLE: the environment

    <u>I believe that the president of the United States should be</u>

    <u>more concerned about the environment.</u>

1. homeless people _____

2. homework _____

3. public transportation in my city _____

4. learning English _____

LESSON **5** GOAL ➤ Write a speech

D Study the chart with your classmates and teacher.

Contrary-to–Fact Conditional Statements						
If	**Subject**	**Past tense verb**	**Subject**	*Would*	**Base verb**	**Example sentence**
If	I, you, she, he, we, they	had / didn't have	I	would wouldn't	buy	If I had more money, I would buy a new house.
If	I, you, she, he, we, they	were was / were't (wasn't)	I	would wouldn't	spend	If I were (was) president, I would spend more money on education.

Contrary-to-fact (or unreal) conditional statements are sentences that are not true and that the speaker thinks will probably never be true.
Note: In written English, we use *were* instead of *was* in contrary-to-fact conditionals, but in spoken English we often use *was*.

E Complete the sentences below with the correct form of the verbs in parentheses.

1. I ___would give___ (give) money to the homeless if ___I were___ (be) president.

2. If people ___had___ (have) more money, they ___would be___ (be) happier.

3. If the president ___spent___ (spend) more on health, scientists ___would discover___ (discover) a cure for cancer.

4. If our classes ___were___ (be) larger, the teacher ___would not have___ (not have) much time for each student.

5. Maria ___would go___ (go) to medical school if she ___were___ (be) younger.

6. We ___would walk___ (walk) more if we ___drove___ (drive) less.

F Look at the list of city officials on page 149. On a piece of paper, write a conditional statement for each official. Then, share your statements with a partner.

(Answers will vary.)

EXAMPLE: ___If I were the sheriff, I would hire more police officers.___

Presentation 2   5-10 mins. ■■■

Write some of the students' ideas from Exercise C on the board, using conditional statements. For example: *If I were the president, I would be more concerned about homeless people.*

(D) Study the chart with your classmates and teacher.

Present the chart to the class.

Practice 2   15-20 mins. ■■

(E) Complete the sentences below with the correct form of the verbs in parentheses.

Have students complete this activity individually. Have them compare answers with a partner when they finish.

(F) Look at the list of city officials on page 149. On a piece of paper, write a conditional statement for each official. Then, share your statements with a partner.

📖 Refer students to *Stand Out Grammar Challenge*, Unit 8, Challenge 5 for more practice with conditional statements.

Evaluation 2   10-20 mins. ■■

Go over the answers as a class. Ask a volunteer to write each of the positions listed on page 149 on the board at the top of separate columns. Now ask different students to read one of their conditional statements out loud. Have the volunteer note in the corresponding column the actions students say they would take if they held one of the positions. Have a class discussion about which actions are realistic and which are not.

Presentation 3   5–10 mins.

(G) **What would you do if you were president? Talk about the things you would like to change.**

Ask two volunteers to perform the conversation. Then ask a few different students both the leading question in the conversation—*What would you do . . . ?*—and the follow-up question—*How . . . ?* Point out that the follow-up question is meant to get more information.

Practice 3   10–15 mins. ▪

(H) **Think about the following topics. What would you do if you were president? Write your ideas.**

Give students time to work alone to write their ideas. Then have them discuss their ideas in small groups.

Evaluation 3   10–15 mins. ▪

Observe students as they work.

Application   10–20 mins. ▪▪▪

(I) **Using the ideas you wrote above, write a paragraph about what you would do if you were president. Use Rosario's paragraph on page 153 as an example. Then, share your paragraph with the class. Who would the class elect to be president?**

When students have finished their paragraphs, ask them to share their paragraphs with their groups. Ask each group to vote on which of their members would make the best candidate for president. Then ask each group's candidate to read his or her paragraph out loud to the class. When they finish, have the class vote on who should be president.

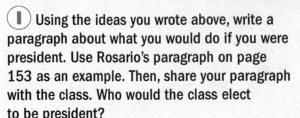

> **Activity Bank**
>
> Lesson 5, Worksheet 1: What Do You Think?
> Lesson 5, Worksheet 2: Conditional Statements

📖 Refer students to *Stand Out 3 Grammar Challenge*, Unit 8, Extension Challenges 1–2 for more practice with the passive voice and reported speech.

GOAL ➤ Write a speech

 G What would you do if you were president? Talk about the things you would like to change.

EXAMPLE: *Student A:* What would you do if you were president?
Student B: Let's see. I think we need to improve our schools.
Student A: How would you do that?
Student B: I would pay teachers more. I would spend money on things like computers.

H Think about the following topics. What would you do if you were president? Write your ideas. (Answers will vary.)

Topic	My ideas
eliminating the death penalty	
raising the retirement age to 70	
raising the cost of gasoline so people would drive less	
smoking in public places	
raising the minimum wage	
building casinos to raise money for schools	

I Using the ideas you wrote above, write a paragraph about what you would do if you were president. Use Rosario's paragraph on page 153 as an example. Then, share your paragraph with the class. Who would the class elect to be president? (Answers will vary.)

_____

_____

_____

_____

_____

_____

Review

 Write the full name of each state next to its abbreviation. See how many you can remember before you look back at page 142. (Lesson 1)

1. NY ___New York___
2. CA ___California___
3. WA ___Washington___
4. FL ___Florida___
5. TX ___Texas___

6. ME ___Maine___
7. IL ___Illinois___
8. NV ___Nevada___
9. HI ___Hawaii___
10. NJ ___New Jersey___

B Read the chart below. Write sentences using *both . . . and, neither . . . nor, but,* and *however.* (Lesson 2) (Answers will vary.)

EXAMPLE: ___Both Sophia and Jamal want to increase class size.___

Name	Topic	Agree	Disagree
Sophia	increasing the number of students in our class	✓	
Jamal		✓	
Sophia	building more parks in the community		✓
Jamal		✓	
Sophia	hiring more police officers	✓	
Jamal			✓
Sophia	building more freeways		✓
Jamal			✓

1. ___Jamal wants to build more parks in the community, but Sophia doesn't. (or)___
   ___Jamal wants to build more parks in the community; however, Sophia doesn't.___

2. ___Sophia wants to hire more police officers; however, Jamal doesn't. (or)___
   ___Sophia wants to hire more police officers, but Jamal doesn't.___

3. ___Neither Sophia nor Jamal wants to build more freeways.___

AGENDA

Discuss unit objectives.
Complete the review.
Do My Dictionary.
Evaluate and reflect on progress.

Objective: All unit objectives
Grammar: All unit grammar
Academic Strategy: Reviewing
Vocabulary: All unit vocabulary

RESOURCES

Activity Bank: Lessons 1–5
Reading and Writing Challenge: Unit 8

Grammar Challenge: Unit 8, Challenges 1–5

■ 1.5 hour classes ■ 2.5 hour classes ■ 3⁺ hour classes

Stand Out 3 Assessment CD-ROM with *ExamView®*

Warm-up and Review   5–10 mins.

In groups, have students come up with a list of as many states as they can think of. See which group comes up with the most.

Introduction   5–10 mins.

Ask students as a class to try to recall (in general) all the goals of this unit without looking at their books. Then remind them which goals they omitted, if any. (Unit goals: identify U.S. geographical locations, compare and contrast ideas, interpret the system of the U.S. government, express opinions about community issues, write a speech) Write all the goals from Unit 8 on the board. Show students the first page of the unit and mention the five objectives. State the objective for the review: *Today we will be reviewing everything you have learned in this unit.*

Presentation 1   10–15 mins.

This presentation will cover the first three pages of the review. Quickly go to the first page of each lesson. Discuss the objective of each. Ask simple questions to remind students of what they have learned.

Note: Since there is little presentation in the review, you can assign the review exercises for homework and go over them in class the following day.

Practice 1   20–25 mins.

Note: There are two ways to do the review:
(1) Go through each exercise one at a time and, as students complete each one, go over the answers.
(2) Briefly go through the instructions of each exercise, allow students to complete all of the exercises at once, and then go over the answers.

(A) Write the full name of each state next to its abbreviation. See how many you can remember before you look back at page 142. (Lesson 1)

(B) Read the chart below. Write sentences using *both . . . and, neither . . . nor, but,* and *however.* (Lesson 2)

Evaluation 1   20–25 mins.

Go around the classroom and check on students' progress. Help individuals when needed. If you see consistent errors among several students, interrupt the class and give a mini lesson or review to help students feel comfortable with the concept.

STANDARDS CORRELATIONS

CASAS: 7.2.1 (See CASAS Competency List on pages 169–175.)
SCANS: **Resources** Allocates time
Information Acquire and evaluate information
Interpersonal Participate as a member of a team, teach others, negotiate to arrive at a decision, work with cultural diversity
Systems Monitor and correct performance
Basic Skills Reading, writing, arithmetic, listening, speaking
Thinking Skills Creative thinking, decision making, problem solving, seeing things in the mind's eye

Personal Qualities Responsibility, sociability, self-management
EFF: **Communication** Convey ideas in writing, read with understanding, speak so others can understand, listen actively
Decision Making Solve problems and make decisions
Interpersonal Guide others, cooperate with others
Lifelong Learning Take responsibility for learning, reflect and evaluate, learn through research

Lesson Planner: Unit 8, Review   **156a**

Practice 1 *(continued)*　　25-30 mins. ■ ■ ■

C Check (✓) the correct branch of government after each statement. (Lesson 3)

D Look at the community problems below. Write a solution for each problem using *should*. (Lesson 4)

Evaluation 1 *(continued)*　　25-30 mins. ■ ■ ■

Go around the classroom and check on students' progress. Help individuals when needed. If you see consistent errors among several students, interrupt the class and give a mini lesson or review to help students feel comfortable with the concept.

Teaching Tip

Recycling/Review

The review process and the project that follows are part of the recycling/review process. Students at this level often need to be reintroduced to concepts to solidify what they have learned. Many concepts are learned and forgotten while learning other new concepts. This is because students learn but are not necessarily ready to acquire language concepts.

Therefore, it becomes very important to review and to show students how to review on their own. It is also important to recycle the new concepts in different contexts.

Instructor's Notes

C Check (✓) the correct branch of government after each statement. (Lesson 3)

	Legislative	Executive	Judicial
1. listens to cases and makes judgments			✓
2. interprets the laws			✓
3. signs new laws		✓	
4. includes the president's cabinet		✓	
5. includes the House of Representatives	✓		
6. makes laws	✓		
7. can control immigration	✓		
8. commands the military		✓	
9. includes the Congress	✓		
10. chooses the justices of the Supreme Court	✓	✓	

D Look at the community problems below. Write a solution for each problem using *should*. (Lesson 4)   (Answers will vary.)

1. Problem: traffic on the freeways

   Solution: The city should build more carpool lanes.

2. Problem: smoking in parks near playgrounds

   Solution: _____

3. Problem: cars driving too fast in residential areas

   Solution: _____

4. Problem: potholes

   Solution: _____

5. Problem: high crime

   Solution: _____

Review

E Complete these contrary-to-fact conditionals with the correct form of the verbs in parentheses. (Lesson 5)

1. I _____ would work _____ (work) faster if I _____ had _____ (have) a computer.

2. If she _____ lived _____ (live) in Italy, she _____ would eat _____ (eat) pizza every day.

3. If it _____ stopped _____ (stop) raining, we _____ would play _____ (play) outside.

4. If the town _____ bought _____ (buy) more land, we _____ would build _____ (build) schools.

5. I _____ would spend _____ (spend) more on education if I _____ were _____ (be) president.

6. If the president _____ lowered _____ (lower) taxes, he _____ would be _____ (be) popular with Republicans.

7. People _____ would drive _____ (drive) less if gas _____ were _____ (be) more expensive.

8. If we _____ prohibited _____ (prohibit) smoking in public places, everyone

   _____ would be _____ (be) healthier.

F What would you do if you were mayor of your city? Write a paragraph stating your opinions about various local issues. Then, say what you would do if you were mayor. (Lesson 5)

(Answers will vary.)

EXAMPLE: In my opinion, the public transportation system in this town is

very poor. The buses are always late because there is too much

traffic. If I were mayor, I would build a subway system and . . .

_____

_____

_____

_____

_____

Practice 1 (continued) 25–30 mins. ■■■

E Complete these contrary-to-fact conditionals with the correct form of the verbs in parentheses. (Lesson 5)

F What would you do if you were mayor of your city? Write a paragraph stating your opinions about various local issues. Then, say what you would do if you were mayor. (Lesson 5)

Evaluation 1 (continued) 25–30 mins. ■■■

Go around the classroom and check on students' progress. Help individuals when needed. If you see consistent errors among several students, interrupt the class and give a mini lesson or review to help students feel comfortable with the concept.

Presentation 2

5-10 mins.

My Dictionary

Ask students to brainstorm new vocabulary items they learned in this unit. Have them do this without looking in their books.

Practice 2

15-20 mins.

(Shorter classes can do these exercises for homework.)

In this book, you have learned about ways to acquire vocabulary and use a dictionary. Now put everything together and practice writing an entry in a vocabulary book.

Go over the example entry with students and do one on the board together as a class. Then have students choose two or three of the words they brainstormed and write their own entries. Encourage them to start their own vocabulary notebooks.

Evaluation 2

15-20 mins.

Walk around the room and help students.

Presentation 3

5-10 mins.

Learner Log

In this unit, you learned many things about citizens and community. How comfortable do you feel doing each of the skills listed below? Rate your comfort level on a scale of 1 to 4.

Go over the instructions with students and make sure they understand what to do. You may want to do the first one or two with the class to make sure they understand.

Practice 3

5-10 mins.

Have students complete the Learner Log.

Evaluation 3

5-10 mins.

Walk around the classroom and help students as needed.

Application

5-10 mins.

Go over the two reflection questions with students and have them complete the answers by themselves.

TB Assessment

Use the Stand Out 3 Assessment CD-ROM with Exam*View*® to create a post-test for Unit 8.

My Dictionary

In this book, you have learned about ways to acquire vocabulary and use a dictionary. Now put everything together and practice writing an entry in a vocabulary book.

Word: 'legislature.
Part of speech: noun
Definition: a branch of the U.S. government that passes laws
Related word(s): legislation *(n)*, legislate *(v)*
Example sentence: The <u>legislature</u> passed a new law
　　　　　　　　　on gasoline taxes.

Start a vocabulary notebook of your own. Add any new words you have learned inside or outside of class. Start with a word or words from this unit.

Learner Log

In this unit, you learned many things about citizens and community. How comfortable do you feel doing each of the skills listed below? Rate your comfort level on a scale of 1 to 4.

1 = Need more practice　　　　**2** = OK　　　　**3** = Good　　　　**4** = Great!

Life Skill	Comfort Level				Page
I can identify geographical locations in the U.S.	1	2	3	4	141
I can compare and contrast ideas.	1	2	3	4	144
I can talk about the U.S. system of government.	1	2	3	4	147
I can discuss community issues.	1	2	3	4	150
I can express opinions.	1	2	3	4	150
I can write a speech.	1	2	3	4	153

If you circled 1 or 2, write down the page number where you can review this skill.

Reflection

1. What was the most useful skill you learned in this unit? _____

_____

2. How will this help you in life? _____

Team Project

Create a flyer: Run for mayor.

With your team, you will run a mayoral campaign. You will write a list of community problems and your solutions, and create a flyer that will help you gain votes. You will also write a speech that you would give if you were elected mayor.

1. Form a team with four or five students. Choose a position for each member of your team.

POSITION	JOB DESCRIPTION	STUDENT NAME
Student 1: Leader	See that everyone speaks English. See that everyone participates.	
Student 2: Secretary	Write down the community problems, possible solutions, and the speech.	
Student 3: Designer	Create the flyer.	
Students 4/5: Members	Help the secretary and the designer with their work.	

2. Imagine someone on your team is running for mayor of your city. Answer the following questions:

   Why would you want to be mayor?

   Why would you be the best mayor?

3. Come up with a list of community problems and your solutions to those problems. (Lesson 4)

4. Create a flyer including all your information and any appropriate pictures or art.

5. Write a speech that you would give as mayor. (Lesson 5)

6. Present your flyer and speech to the class.

Create a flyer: Run for mayor.

Each team will prepare one of its members to run for mayor by creating a platform and giving a speech to the class.

The team project is the final application for the unit. It gives students a chance to show that they have mastered all of the Unit 8 objectives.

Note: Shorter classes can extend this project over two class meetings.

Stage 1   5 mins.

Form a team with four of five students. Choose a position for each member of your team.

Have students decide who will lead each step as described on the student page. Provide well-defined directions on the board for how teams should proceed. Explain that all the students do every step as a team. Teams shouldn't go to the next stage until the previous one is complete.

Stage 2   15-20 mins.

Imagine someone on your team is running for mayor of your city. Answer the following questions: Why would you want to be mayor? Why would you be the best mayor?

Have students decide who will be the mayoral candidate and why that person would be a good mayor.

Stage 3   10-15 mins.

Come up with a list of community problems and your solutions to those problems. (Lesson 4)

This stage will work best if students think of the community they live in and what some of the real problems are. Help them get started if they are having difficulty by brainstorming a few options on the board. Don't give them too many ideas or they won't be able to think of any of their own.

Stage 4   10-15 mins.

Create a flyer including all your information and any appropriate pictures or art.

Have students include in their flyer some of the key information they discussed in Stages 2 and 3.

Optional Computer Activity: Students may want to use the computer to design their flyers.

Stage 5   5 mins.

Write a speech that you would give as mayor. (Lesson 5)

Give students a time limit for their speeches. (Two to three minutes should be sufficient.)

Stage 6   15-20 mins.

Present your flyer and speech to the class.

Help teams prepare for their presentations. Suggest that each member (besides the candidate who will give the speech) choose a different part of the flyer to present.

Extension: Have the class vote on who would be the best mayor and why.

STANDARDS CORRELATIONS

CASAS: 4.8.1, 4.8.5, 4.8.6 (See CASAS Competency List on pages 169–175.)
SCANS: Resources Allocate time
Information Acquire and evaluate information, organize and maintain information, interpret and communicate information, use computers to process information
Systems Understand systems, improve and design systems
Technology Select technology, apply technology to exercise
Basic Skills Writing
Thinking Skills Creative thinking, decision making, problem solving, seeing things in the mind's eye, reasoning

Personal Qualities Responsibility, self-esteem, self-management, integrity/honesty
EFF: Communication Convey ideas in writing, speak so others can understand
Decision Making Solve problems and make decisions, plan
Interpersonal Guide others, resolve conflict and negotiate, advocate and influence, cooperate with others
Lifelong Learning Take responsibility for learning, reflect and evaluate, use information and communication technologies (optional)

Stand Out 3 Vocabulary List

Pre-Unit
Registration
date of birth P1
first name P1
last name P1
middle initial P1
occupation P1
Education
achieve P9
college P7
community college P7
elementary school P7
formatting P6
goal P1
graduate school P7
high school P7
indent P5
junior high school P7
kindergarten P7
middle school P7
paragraph margins P5
preschool P7
successful P5
technical college P7
title P5
university P7
vocational P7

Unit 1
accomplish 14
adverbs of frequency 2
balance 13
beneficial 11
benefits 14
concentrate 11
conclusion 8
distractions 11
goals 4
go over
harmful 11
improve 11
obstacle 4
occupational 6
personal 6
routine 1
schedule 1
solution 5
study habits 10
support 8
task 14
time slot 14
topic 8

Unit 2
ad 24
adjectives 28
advantages 31
advertisement 24
bank 21
car wash 21
cash 30
CD-ROM drive 27
check 30
comparative and
    superlative 00
comparison shopping 33
consumer 21
CPU 27
credit card 30
cut 24
debit card 30
delivery 24
department store 21
disadvantages 31
discount 24
drugstore 21
dry cleaners 21
expire 24
gas station 21
goods 21
grocery store 21
guarantee 24
hard drive 27
hardware store 21
hotel 21
installation 24
insured 24
irregular adjectives 28
jewelry store 21
laundromat 21
licensed 24
memory 27
monitor 27
must 32
offer 24
percent off 24
pharmacy 21
post office 21
office supply store 21
regular 24
sale 24
sale price 24
save 24
screen 27
sequence transitions 34

services 21
smart consumer 33
speed 27
tailor's 21
warranty 24

Unit 3
addition 50
air conditioning 44
arrange 47
average 50
balcony 41
baseline 47
carpeting 44
carport 41
cancel 47
charming 41
classified ad 41
condition 41
electrician 53
exterminator 53
fix 53
garage 44
graph 51
hookup 43
maintenance 50
mouse/mice 53
options 00
plumber 53
pool 44
preferences 44
properties 43
repairperson 53
repairs 53
roaches 53
security guard 41
salary 50
spa 43
stand for 41
subtraction 50
tennis courts 44
total 50
therms 47
utility 47
yard 44

Unit 4
ATM 64
borrow 65
branch 65
car registration 61
check out 65

check writing 64
circulation 65
class registration 61
commercial 66
deposit 70
direct deposit 64
disabled 66
distance 68
dry cleaning 70
east 67
errands 70
far 68
fee 66
fine 65
iron 70
librarian 65
loan 65
loss 65
main 65
minimum balance 64
north 67
northeast 67
northwest 67
overdue 65
permit 66
public library 65
reference 65
renew 61
renewal 66
replacement 66
run 67
service fee 64
task 61
teller 64
transactions 64
south 67
southeast 67
southwest 67
unlimited 64
valid 66
west 67

Unit 5
% daily value 91
aerobics 93
allergies 82
amount 91
avoid 00
backache 84
balance 93
calories 91
carbohydrate 91

Stand Out 3 Irregular Verb List

The following verbs are used in *Stand Out 3* and have irregular past tense forms.

Base Form	Simple Past	Past Participle	Base Form	Simple Past	Past Participle
be	was, were	been	lend	lent	lent
become	became	become	lose	lost	lost
break	broke	broken	make	made	made
build	built	built	mean	meant	meant
buy	bought	bought	meet	met	met
catch	caught	caught	pay	paid	paid
choose	chose	chosen	put	put	put
come	came	come	read	read	read
do	did	done	ride	rode	ridden
drink	drank	drunk	run	ran	run
drive	drove	driven	say	said	said
eat	ate	eaten	sell	sold	sold
fall	fell	fallen	shake	shook	shaken
feel	felt	felt	show	showed	shown
fly	flew	flown	sit	sat	sat
forget	forgot	forgotten	sleep	slept	slept
find	found	found	speak	spoke	spoken
get	got	gotten	spend	spent	spent
give	gave	given	stand	stood	stood
go	went	gone	take	took	taken
hang	hung	hanged/hung	teach	taught	taught
have	had	had	tell	told	told
hear	heard	heard	think	thought	thought
hold	held	held	throw	threw	thrown
hurt	hurt	hurt	wake	woke	woken
keep	kept	kept	wear	wore	worn
know	knew	known	win	won	won
learn	learned	learned/learnt	write	wrote	written
leave	left	left			

Comparatives

	Adjective	Comparative	Rule	Example sentence
Short adjectives	cheap	cheaper	Add -er to the end of the adjective.	Your computer was *cheaper* than my computer.
Long adjectives	expensive	more expensive	Add *more* before the adjective.	The new computer was *more expensive* than the old one.
Irregular adjectives	good bad	better worse	These adjectives are irregular.	The computer at school is *better* than this one.
Remember to use *than* after a comparative adjective followed by a noun.				

Superlatives

	Adjective	Superlative	Rule	Example sentence
Short adjectives	cheap	the cheapest	Add -est to the end of the adjective.	Your computer is *the cheapest*.
Long adjectives	expensive	the most expensive	Add *most* before the adjective.	He bought *the most* expensive computer in the store.
Irregular adjectives	good bad	best worst	These adjectives are irregular.	The computers at school are *the best*.
Always use *the* before a superlative.				

Must vs. *Have to*

Subject	Modal	Base verb	
We	have to	save	money for vacation.
I	must	pay off	my credit card every month.

Comparatives Using Nouns

Our new apartment has *more bedrooms* than our old one. Our old apartment had *fewer bedrooms* than our new one.	Use *more* or *fewer* to compare count nouns.
Rachel's apartment gets *more light* than Pablo's apartment. Pablo's apartment gets *less light* than Rachel's apartment.	Use *more* or *less* to compare noncount nouns.

Superlatives Using Nouns

Rachel's apartment has *the most bedrooms*. Phuong's apartment has *the fewest bedrooms*.	Use *the most* or *the fewest* for count nouns.
Rachel's apartment has *the most light*. Phuong's apartment has *the least light*.	Use *the most* or *the least* for non-count nouns.

Yes/No Questions and Answers with *Do*

Questions				Short answers
Do	Subject	Base verb	Example question	
do	I, you, we, they	have	Do they have a yard?	Yes, they do. / No, they don't.
does	he, she, it	want	Does she want air-conditioning?	Yes, she does. / No, she doesn't.

Information Questions

Question words	Example questions
How What When	*How* may I help you? *What* is your current address? *When* would you like your service turned off?

Past Continuous

Subject	*be*	Verb + *ing*	Example sentence
I, he, she, it	was	making	I was making breakfast.
you, we, they	were	studying	She was taking a shower.
Use the past continuous to talk about things that started in the past and continued for a period of time.			

Past Continuous Using *While*

Subject	*be*	Verb + *ing*	Example sentence
I, he, she, it	was	making	While I was making dinner, I saw a mouse.
you, we, they	were	studying	The electricity went out while we were studying.
To connect two events that happened in the past, use the past continuous with *while* for the longer event. Use the simple past for the shorter event.			
Note: You can reverse the two clauses, but you need a comma if the *while* clause comes first.			

Information Questions

Location	Where	is the bank?
	How far	is the school from here?
	What	is the address?
Time	When	does the library open?
	What time	does the restaurant close?
	How often	do the buses run?
Cost	How much	does it cost?

Adverbial Clauses with *Before, After* and *When*

EXAMPLE	RULE
After I returned the books, I stopped by the bank to make a deposit.	The action closest to *after* happened first. (First, she returned the books. Second, she went to the bank)
Before I went grocery shopping, I stopped by the cleaners to pick up some skirts.	The action closest to *before* happened second. (First, she went to the cleaners. Second, she went grocery shopping.)
When everyone left the house, I made my list of errands and off I went.	The action closest to *when* is completed and then next act begins. (First, everyone left. Second, she made her list.)
I went home **when** I finished shopping. **When** I finished shopping, I went home.	You can reverse the two clauses and the meaning stays the same. You need a comma if the adverbial clause goes first.

Present Perfect

Subject	*have*	Past participle		Time	Example sentence
I, you we, they	have	been	sick	since Tuesday	I *have been* sick since Tuesday.
she, he, it	has	had	a backache	for two weeks	She *has had* a backache for two weeks.
Use the present perfect for events starting in the past and continuing up to the present.					

Future Conditional Statements

Cause: *If* + present tense	Effect: future tense
If you *are* very stressed,	you *will have* high blood pressure.
If you *don't eat* enough calcium,	you *won't have* strong bones.

We can connect a cause and an effect by using a *future conditional* statement. The *if*-clause (or the *cause*) is in the present tense and the *effect* is in the future tense.

Effect: future tense	Cause: *if* + present tense
You *will have* high blood pressure	*if* you *are* very stressed.

You can reverse the clauses, but use a comma only when the *if*-clause comes first.

Infinitives and Gerunds
Infinitive = *to* + verb   Gerund = verb + *ing*

Verb	Infinitive or Gerund?	Example sentence	Other verbs that follow the same rule
want	infinitive	He wants *to get* a job.	plan, decide
enjoy	gerund	He enjoys *fixing* bicycles.	finish, give up
like	both	He likes *to talk*. He likes *talking*.	love, hate

Gerunds and Nouns after Prepositions

Subject	Verb	Adjective	Preposition	Gerund/Noun	Example sentence
I	am	good	at	calculating	I am good at *calculating*.
she	is	good	at	math	She is good at *math*.

A gerund or a noun follows an adjective + a preposition. Some other examples of adjectives + prepositions are *interested in, afraid of, tired of, bad at*, and *worried about*.

Would rather

Subject	*would rather*	Base form	*than*	Base form	Example sentence
I, you, she, he, it, we, they	would ('d) rather	work alone	than	work with people	I would rather work alone than work with people.

Note: You can omit the second verb if it is the same as the first verb.
Example: I would rather work nights than (work) days.

Possessive Adjectives and Possessive Pronouns

Possessive adjectives	Rule	Example sentence
my, your, his, her, our, their	*Possessive adjectives* show possession of an object and come before the noun.	This is *her* office.
Possessive pronouns	**Rule**	**Example sentence**
mine, yours, his, hers, ours, theirs	*Possessive pronouns* show possession of an object and act as a noun.	This office is *hers*.

Modals: *Could* and *Might*

Subject	Modal	Verb	Example sentence
I, you, he, she,	could	fall	You could fall.
it, we, they	might	miss	I might miss work.

We use the modals *could* and *might* to say that there is a chance that something will happen in the future.

Comparing and Contrasting Ideas

If two people share the same opinion, use *both . . . and* or *neither . . . nor*.		
Both	Enrico **and** Liz	want to increase the number of students in our class.
Neither	Suzanna **nor** Ali	wants to increase the number of students in our class.
If two people don't share the same opinion, use *but* or *however*.		
Enrico agrees with bilingual education,	**but** Liz doesn't.	
Ali doesn't agree with bilingual education;	**however,** Suzanna does.	

Punctuation Note: Use a semicolon (;) before and a comma (,) after *however*.

Should

Subject	Modal	Base verb	
The city council	should	set	a curfew for teenagers.
People	should	clean up	after their pets.

Contrary-to–Fact Conditional Statements							
If	**Subject**	**Past tense verb**	**Subject**	*Would*	**Base verb**	**Example sentence**	
If	I, you, she, he, we, they	had / didn't have	I	would / wouldn't	buy	If I had more money, I would buy a new house	
If	I, you, she, he, we, they	were / was / were't (wasn't)	I	would / wouldn't	spend	If I were (was) president, I would spend more money on education.	

Contrary-to-fact (or unreal) conditional statements are sentences that are not true and that the speaker thinks will probably never be true.

Note: In written English, we use *were* instead of *was* in contrary-to-fact conditionals, but in spoken English we often use *was*.

CASAS Competencies

0. Basic Communication

0.1 Communicate in interpersonal interactions
0.1.1 Identify or use appropriate non-verbal behavior in a variety of situations (e.g., handshaking)
0.1.2 Identify or use appropriate language for informational purposes (e.g., to identify, describe, ask for information, state needs, command, agree or disagree, ask permission)
0.1.3 Identify or use appropriate language to influence or persuade (e.g., to caution, request, advise, persuade, negotiate)
0.1.4 Identify or use appropriate language in general social situations (e.g., to greet, introduce, thank, apologize, compliment, express pleasure or regret)
0.1.5 Identify or use appropriate classroom behavior
0.1.6 Clarify or request clarification

0.2 Communicate regarding personal information
0.2.1 Respond appropriately to common personal information questions
0.2.2 Complete a personal information form
0.2.3 Interpret or write a personal note, invitation, or letter
0.2.4 Converse about daily and leisure activities and personal interests

1. Consumer Economics

1.1 Use weights, measures, measurement scales, and money
1.1.1 Interpret recipes
1.1.2 Use the metric system (see also 1.1.4, 6.6.1, 6.6.2, 6.6.3, 6.6.4)
1.1.3 Interpret maps and graphs (see also 1.9.4, 2.2.1, 2.2.5)
1.1.4 Select, compute, or interpret appropriate standard measurement for length, width, perimeter, area, volume, height, or weight (see also 1.1.2, 6.6.1, 6.6.2, 6.6.3, 6.6.4, 6.6.5)
1.1.5 Interpret temperatures (see also 6.6.4)
1.1.6 Count, convert, and use coins and currency, and recognize symbols such as ($) and (.) (see also 6.1.1, 6.1.2, 6.1.3, 6.1.4, 6.1.5)
1.1.7 Identify product containers and interpret weight and volume
1.1.8 Compute averages (see also 6.7.5)
1.1.9 Interpret clothing and pattern sizes and use height and weight tables

1.2 Apply principles of comparison-shopping in the selection of goods and services
1.2.1 Interpret advertisements, labels, charts, and price tags in selecting goods and services
1.2.2 Compare price or quality to determine the best buys for goods and services
1.2.3 Compute discounts (see also 6.4.1)
1.2.4 Compute unit pricing
1.2.5 Interpret letters, articles, and information about consumer-related topics

1.3 Understand methods and procedures used to purchase goods and services
1.3.1 Compare different methods used to purchase goods and services
1.3.2 Interpret credit applications and recognize how to use and maintain credit
1.3.3 Identify or use various methods to purchase goods and services, and make returns and exchanges
1.3.4 Use catalogs, order forms, and related information to purchase goods and services
1.3.5 Use coupons to purchase goods and services

1.3.6 Use coin-operated machines

1.3.7 Interpret information or directions to locate merchandise (see also 2.5.4)

1.3.8 Identify common food items

1.3.9 Identify common articles of clothing

1.4 Understand methods and procedures to obtain housing and related services

1.4.1 Identify different kinds of housing, areas of the home, and common household items

1.4.2 Select appropriate housing by interpreting classified ads, signs, and other information

1.4.3 Interpret lease and rental agreements

1.4.4 Interpret information to obtain, maintain, or cancel housing utilities

1.4.5 Interpret information about tenant and landlord rights

1.4.6 Interpret information about housing loans and home-related insurance

1.4.7 Interpret information about home maintenance, and communicate housing problems to a landlord (see also 1.7.4)

1.4.8 Recognize home theft and fire prevention measures

1.5 Apply principles of budgeting in the management of money

1.5.1 Interpret information about personal and family budgets

1.5.2 Plan for major purchases (see also 1.5.1)

1.5.3 Interpret bills (see also 2.1.4)

1.6 Understand consumer protection measures

1.6.1 Interpret food packaging labels (see also 1.2.1, 3.5.1)

1.6.2 Identify consumer protection resources available when confronted with fraudulent practices

1.6.3 Identify procedures the consumer can follow if merchandise or service is unsatisfactory

1.6.4 Check sales receipts

1.7 Understand procedures for the care, maintenance, and use of personal possessions

1.7.1 Interpret product guarantees and warranties

1.7.2 Interpret clothing care labels

1.7.3 Interpret operating instructions, directions, or labels for consumer products (see also 3.4.1)

1.7.4 Interpret maintenance procedures for household appliances and personal possessions

1.7.5 Interpret information to obtain repairs

1.8 Use banking and financial services in the community

1.8.1 Demonstrate the use of savings and checking accounts, including using an ATM

1.8.2 Interpret the procedures and forms associated with banking services, including writing checks

1.8.3 Interpret interest or interest-earning savings plans

1.8.4 Interpret information about the types of loans available through lending institutions

1.8.5 Interpret information on financial agencies and financial planning

1.9 Understand methods and procedures for the purchase and maintenance of an automobile and interpret driving regulations

1.9.1 Interpret highway and traffic signs (see also 2.2.2)

1.9.2 Identify driving regulations and procedures to obtain a driver's license (see also 2.5.7)

1.9.3 Compute mileage and gasoline consumption

1.9.4 Interpret maps related to driving (see also 1.1.3, 2.2.1, 2.2.5)

1.9.5 Interpret information related to the selection and purchase of a car

1.9.6 Interpret information related to automobile maintenance

1.9.7 Recognize what to do in case of automobile emergencies

1.9.8 Interpret information about automobile insurance

2. Community Resources

2.1 Use the telephone and telephone book

2.1.1 Use the telephone directory and related publications to locate information

2.1.2 Identify emergency numbers and place emergency calls (see also 2.5.1)

2.1.3 Interpret information about time zones (see also 2.3.1)

2.1.4 Interpret telephone billings

2.1.5 Interpret telegram rates and procedures

2.1.6 Interpret information about using a pay telephone

2.1.7 Take and interpret telephone messages, leave messages on answering machines, and interpret recorded messages (see also 4.5.4)

2.1.8 Use the telephone to make and receive routine personal and business calls

2.2 Understand how to locate and use different types of transportation and interpret related travel information

2.2.1 Ask for, give, follow, or clarify directions (see also 1.1.3, 1.9.4, 2.2.5)

2.2.2 Recognize and use signs related to transportation (see also 1.9.1)

2.2.3 Identify or use different types of transportation in the community, and interpret traffic information

2.2.4 Interpret transportation schedules and fares

2.2.5 Use maps relating to travel needs (see also 1.1.3, 1.9.4, 2.2.1)

2.3 Understand concepts of time and weather

2.3.1 Interpret clock time (see also 2.1.3, 6.6.6)

2.3.2 Identify the months of the year and the days of the week

2.3.3 Interpret information about weather conditions

2.4 Use postal services

2.4.1 Address letters and envelopes

2.4.2 Interpret postal rates and types of mailing services

2.4.3 Interpret postal service forms and instructions on returned mail

2.4.4 Purchase stamps and other postal items and services

2.4.5 Interpret procedures for tracing a lost letter or parcel

2.4.6 Interpret a postal money order form

2.5 Use community agencies and services

2.5.1 Locate and utilize services of agencies that provide emergency help

2.5.2 Identify how and when to obtain social and governmental services (e.g., low-income housing, Social Security, Medicare), and how to interact with service providers

2.5.3 Locate medical and health facilities in the community (see also 3.1.3)

2.5.4 Read, interpret, and follow directions found on public signs and building directories (see also 1.3.7)

2.5.5 Locate and use educational services in the community, including interpreting and writing school-related communications

2.5.6 Use library services

2.5.7 Interpret permit and license requirements (see also 1.9.2)

2.5.8 (unassigned)

2.5.9 Identify child care services in the community (see also 3.5.7)

2.6 Use leisure time resources and facilities

2.6.1 Interpret information about recreational and entertainment facilities and activities

2.6.2 Locate information in TV, movie, and other recreational listings

2.6.3 Interpret information in order to plan for outings and vacations

2.6.4 Interpret and order from restaurant and fast food menus, and compute related costs

2.7 Understand aspects of society and culture

2.7.1 Interpret information about holidays

2.7.2 Interpret information about ethnic groups, cultural groups, and language groups

2.7.3 Interpret information about social issues (see also 2.7.2)

2.7.4 Interpret information about religion

2.7.5 Interpret literary materials such as poetry and literature

2.7.6 Interpret materials related to the arts, such as fine art, music, drama, and film

3. Health

3.1 Understand how to access and utilize the health care system

3.1.1 Describe symptoms of illness, including identifying parts of the body; interpret doctor's directions

3.1.2 Identify information necessary to make or keep medical and dental appointments

3.1.3 Identify and utilize appropriate health care services and facilities, including interacting with providers (see also 2.5.3)

3.2 Understand medical and dental forms and related information

3.2.1 Fill out medical health history forms

3.2.2 Interpret immunization requirements

3.2.3 Interpret information associated with medical, dental, or life insurance

3.2.4 Ask for clarification about medical bills

3.3 Understand how to select and use medications

3.3.1 Identify and use necessary medications (see also 3.3.2, 3.3.3)

3.3.2 Interpret medicine labels (see also 3.3.1, 3.4.1)

3.3.3 Identify the difference between prescription, over-the-counter, and generic medications (see also 3.3.1)

3.4 Understand basic health and safety procedures

3.4.1 Interpret product label directions and safety warnings (see also 1.7.3, 3.3.2)

3.4.2 Identify safety measures that can prevent accidents and injuries

3.4.3 Interpret procedures for simple first-aid

3.4.4 Interpret information about AIDS and other sexually transmitted diseases (see also 3.1.1)

3.4.5 Recognize problems related to drugs, tobacco, and alcohol and identify where treatment may be obtained

3.5 Understand basic principles of health maintenance

3.5.1 Interpret nutritional and related information listed on food labels (see also 1.6.1)

3.5.2 Select a balanced diet

3.5.3 Interpret food storage information

3.5.4 Identify practices that promote dental health

3.5.5 Identify practices that promote cleanliness and hygiene

3.5.6 Interpret information and identify agencies that assist with family planning (see also 2.5.3, 3.1.3)

3.5.7 Identify child-rearing practices and community resources that assist in developing parenting skills (see also 2.5.9)

3.5.8 Identify practices that promote mental well being

3.5.9 Identify practices that promote physical well being

4. Employment

4.1 Understand basic principles of getting a job

4.1.1 Interpret governmental forms related to seeking work, such as applications for Social Security (see also 2.5.2)

4.1.2 Follow procedures for applying for a job, including interpreting and completing job applications, résumés, and letters of application

4.1.3 Identify and use sources of information about job opportunities such as job descriptions, job ads, and announcements, and about the workforce and job market

4.1.4 Identify and use information about training opportunities (see also 2.5.5)

4.1.5 Identify procedures involved in interviewing for a job, such as arranging for an interview, acting and dressing appropriately, and selecting appropriate questions and responses

4.1.6 Interpret general work-related vocabulary (e.g., experience, swing shift)

4.1.7 Identify appropriate behavior and attitudes for getting a job

4.1.8 Identify common occupations and the skills and education required for them

4.1.9 Identify procedures for career planning, including self-assessment

4.2 Understand wages, benefits, and concepts of employee organizations

4.2.1 Interpret wages, wage deductions, benefits, and timekeeping forms

4.2.2 Interpret information about employee organizations

4.2.3 Interpret employment contract and union agreements

4.2.4 Interpret employee handbooks, personnel policies, and job manuals

4.3 Understand work-related safety standards and procedures

4.3.1 Interpret safety signs found in the workplace (see also 3.4.1)

4.3.2 Interpret work safety manuals and related information

4.3.3 Identify safe work procedures and common safety equipment, including wearing safe work attire

4.3.4 Report unsafe working conditions work-related accidents, injuries, damages

4.4 Understand concepts and materials related to job performance and training

4.4.1 Identify appropriate behavior, attire, attitudes, and social interaction, factors that affect job retention advancement

4.4.2 Identify appropriate skills and education for keeping a job and getting a

4.4.3 Interpret job-related signs, charts, diagrams, forms, and procedures, record information on forms, charts, checklists, etc. (see also 4.2.1, 4.3.4)

4.4.4 Interpret job responsibilities and performance reviews (see also 4.4.2)

4.4.5 Identify job training needs and goals

4.4.6 Interpret work specifications and standards

4.4.7 Demonstrate the ability to apply skills learned in one job situation another

4.4.8 Interpret job-related technical information, such as from service manuals and classes

4.5 Effectively utilize common workplace technology and systems

4.5.1 Identify common tools, equipment, machines, and materials required one's job

4.5.2 Demonstrate simple keyboarding

4.5.3 Demonstrate ability to use a filing or other ordered system (e.g., coded numbered)

4.5.4 Demonstrate use of common business machines (see also 2.1.7, 2.1.8)

4.5.5 Demonstrate basic computer skills use of common software programs, including reading or interpreting computer generated printouts

4.5.6 Demonstrate ability to select, set use tools and machines in order accomplish a task, while operating a technological system

4.5.7 Demonstrate ability to identify resolve problems with machines follow proper maintenance procedures

4.6 Communicate effectively in the workplace

4.6.1 Follow, clarify, give, or provide feedback to instructions; give and respond appropriately to criticism

4.6.2 Interpret and write work-related correspondence, including notes, memos, letters, and e-mail (see also 4.4.3)

4.6.3 Interpret written workplace announcements and notices (see also 4.4.1, 4.4.3)

4.6.4 Report progress on activities, status of assigned tasks, and problems and other situations affecting job completion (see also 4.3.4)

4.6.5 Select and analyze work-related information for a given purpose and communicate it to others orally or in writing

4.7 Effectively manage workplace resources

4.7.1 Interpret or prepare a work-related budget, including projecting costs, keeping detailed records, and tracking status of expenditures and revenue

4.7.2 Identify or demonstrate effective management of material resources, including acquisition, storage, and distribution

4.7.3 Identify or demonstrate effective management of human resources, including assessing skills, making appropriate work assignments, and monitoring performance

4.7.4 Identify, secure, evaluate, process, and/or store information needed to perform tasks or keep records

4.8 Demonstrate effectiveness in working with other people

4.8.1 Demonstrate ability to work cooperatively with others as a member of a team, contributing to team efforts, maximizing the strengths of team members, promoting effective group interaction, and taking personal responsibility for accomplishing goals

4.8.2 Identify ways to learn from others and to help others learn job-related concepts and skills

4.8.3 Demonstrate effective communication skills in working with customers and clients

4.8.4 Demonstrate initiative and resourcefulness in meeting the needs and solving the problems of customers

4.8.5 Demonstrate leadership skills, including effectively communicating ideas or positions, motivating and respecting others, and responsibly challenging existing policies

4.8.6 Demonstrate negotiation skills in resolving differences, including presenting facts and arguments, recognizing differing points of view, offering options, and making compromises

4.8.7 Identify and use effective approaches to working within a multicultural workforce, including respecting cultural diversity, avoiding stereotypes, and recognizing concerns of members of other ethnic and gender groups

4.9 Understand how social, organizational, and technological systems work, and operate effectively within them

4.9.1 Identify the formal organizational structure of one's work environment

4.9.2 Demonstrate how a system's structures relate to its goals

4.9.3 Identify sources of information and assistance, and access resources within a system

4.9.4 Assess the operation of a system or organization and make recommendations for improvement, including development of new systems

5. Government and Law

5.1 Understand voting and the political process

5.1.1 Identify voter qualifications

5.1.2 Interpret a voter registration form

5.1.3 Interpret a ballot

5.1.4 Interpret information about electoral politics and candidates

5.1.5 Interpret information about special interest groups

5.1.6 Communicate one's opinions on a current issue

5.2 Understand historical and geographical information

5.2.1 Interpret information about U.S. history

5.2.2 Identify or interpret U.S. historical documents

5.2.3 Interpret information about world history

5.2.4 Interpret information about U.S. states, cities, geographical features, and points of interest

5.2.5 Interpret information about world geography

5.3 Understand an individual's legal rights and responsibilities and procedures for obtaining legal advice

5.3.1 Interpret common laws and ordinances, and legal forms and documents

5.3.2 Identify individual legal rights and procedures for obtaining legal advice (see also 5.3.1)

5.3.3 Interpret basic court procedures

5.3.4 Interpret laws affecting door-to-door sales (see also 1.6.2)

5.3.5 Interpret information about traffic tickets

5.3.6 Interpret information or identify requirements for establishing residency and/or obtaining citizenship

5.3.7 Identify common infractions and crimes, and legal consequences

5.3.8 Identify procedures for reporting a crime

5.4 Understand information about taxes

5.4.1 Interpret income tax forms

5.4.2 Compute or define sales tax

5.4.3 Interpret tax tables (see also 5.4.1, 5.4.2)

5.4.4 Interpret tax information from articles and publications

5.5 Understand governmental activities

5.5.1 Interpret information about international affairs

5.5.2 Interpret information about legislative activities

5.5.3 Interpret information about judicial activities

5.5.4 Interpret information about executive activities

5.5.5 Interpret information about military activities

5.5.6 Interpret information about law enforcement activities

5.5.7 Interpret information about local policymaking groups

5.5.8 Identify local, state and federal government leaders

5.6 Understand civic responsibilities and activities

5.6.1 Interpret information about neighborhood or community problems and their solutions

5.6.2 Interpret information about civic organizations and public service groups

5.6.3 Interpret civic responsibilities, such as voting, jury duty, taxes

5.7 Understand environmental and science-related issues

5.7.1 Interpret information about environmental issues

5.7.2 Interpret information related to physics, including energy

5.7.3 Interpret information about earth-related sciences

5.7.4 Interpret information about new technologies and scientific issues

5.8 Understand concepts of economics

5.8.1 Interpret economic information and statistics

5.8.2 Interpret information on economic issues and trends

5.8.3 Interpret information on world economic systems

6. Computation

6.0 Demonstrate pre-computation skills

6.0.1 Identify and classify numeric symbols

6.0.2 Count and associate numbers with quantities, including recognizing correct number sequencing

6.0.3 Identify information needed to solve a given problem

6.0.4 Determine appropriate operation to apply to a given problem

6.0.5 Demonstrate use of a calculator

6.1 Compute using whole numbers

6.1.1 Add whole numbers

6.1.2 Subtract whole numbers

6.1.3 Multiply whole numbers

6.1.4 Divide whole numbers

6.1.5 Perform multiple operations using whole numbers

6.2 Compute using decimal fractions

6.2.1 Add decimal fractions

6.2.2 Subtract decimal fractions

6.2.3 Multiply decimal fractions

6.2.4 Divide decimal fractions

6.2.5 Perform multiple operations using decimal fractions

6.2.6 Convert decimal fractions to common fractions or percents

6.3 Compute using fractions

6.3.1   Add common or mixed fractions
6.3.2   Subtract common or mixed fractions
6.3.3   Multiply common or mixed fractions
6.3.4   Divide common or mixed fractions
6.3.5   Perform multiple operations using common or mixed fractions
6.3.6   Convert common or mixed fractions to decimal fractions or percents
6.3.7   Identify or calculate equivalent fractions

6.4 Compute with percents, rate, ratio, and proportion

6.4.1   Apply a percent to determine amount of discount (see also 1.2.3)
6.4.2   Apply a percent in a context not involving money
6.4.3   Calculate percents
6.4.4   Convert percents to common, mixed, or decimal fractions
6.4.5   Use rate to compute increase or decrease
6.4.6   Compute using ratio or proportion (see also 6.4.5)

6.5 Use expressions, equations, and formulas

6.5.1   Recognize and evaluate simple consumer formulas
6.5.2   Recognize and apply simple geometric formulas
6.5.3   Recognize and apply simple algebraic formulas
6.5.4   Recognize and evaluate logical statements

6.6 Demonstrate measurement skills (see also 1.1)

6.6.1   Convert units of U.S. standard measurement and metric system (see also 1.1.2, 1.1.4)
6.6.2   Recognize, use, and measure linear dimensions, geometric shapes, or angles (see also 1.1.2, 1.1.4)
6.6.3   Measure area and volume of geometric shapes (see also 1.1.2, 1.1.4)
6.6.4   Use or interpret measurement instruments, such as rulers, scales, gauges, and dials (see also 1.1.2, 1.1.4, 1.1.5, 4.3.3, 4.4.3)
6.6.5   Interpret diagrams, illustrations, and scale drawings (see also 1.1.4, 4.4.3)
6.6.6   Calculate with units of time
6.6.7   Solve measurement problems in stipulated situations
6.6.8   Interpret mechanical concepts or spatial relationships
6.6.9   Use or interpret switches and controls

6.7 Interpret data from graphs and compute averages

6.7.1   Interpret data given in a line graph (see also 1.1.3)
6.7.2   Interpret data given in a bar graph (see also 1.1.3)
6.7.3   Interpret data given in a picture graph
6.7.4   Interpret data given in a circle graph (see also 1.1.3)
6.7.5   Compute averages, medians, or modes (see also 1.1.8)

6.8 Use statistics and probability

6.8.1   Interpret statistical information used in news reports and articles
6.8.2   Interpret statements of probability

6.9 Use estimation and mental arithmetic

6.9.1   Use computation short cuts
6.9.2   Estimate answers

7. Learning to Learn

7.1 Identify or practice effective organizational and time management skills in accomplishing goals

7.1.1   Identify and prioritize personal, educational, and workplace goals (see also 4.4.5)
7.1.2   Demonstrate an organized approach to achieving goals, including identifying and prioritizing tasks and setting and following an effective schedule
7.1.3   Demonstrate personal responsibility and motivation in accomplishing goals
7.1.4   Establish, maintain, and utilize a physical system of organization, such as notebooks, files, calendars, folders, and checklists (see also 4.5.3)

7.2 Demonstrate ability to use thinking skills

7.2.1   Identify and paraphrase pertinent information
7.2.2   Analyze a situation, statement, or process, identifying component elements and causal and part/whole relationships
7.2.3   Make comparisons, differentiating among, sorting, and classifying items, information, or ideas
7.2.4   Identify or make inferences through inductive and deductive reasoning to hypothesize, predict, conclude, and synthesize; distinguish fact from opinion, and determine what is mandatory and what is discretionary
7.2.5   Evaluate a situation, statement, or process, assembling information and providing evidence, making judgements, examining assumptions, and identifying contradictions
7.2.6   Generate ideas using divergent (brainstorming) and convergent (focus) approaches, and also through creative imagination
7.2.7   Identify factors involved in making decisions, including considering goals, constraints, and consequences, and weighing alternatives

7.3 Demonstrate ability to use problem-solving skills

7.3.1   Identify a problem and its possible causes
7.3.2   Devise and implement a solution to an identified problem
7.3.3   Evaluate the outcome of an implemented solution and suggest modifications to the solution as needed
7.3.4   Utilize problem-solving strategies, such as breaking down the problem into component parts and generating alternative or creative solutions

7.4 Demonstrate study skills

7.4.1   Identify or utilize effective study strategies
7.4.2   Take notes or write a summary or an outline
7.4.3   Identify, utilize, or create devices or processes for remembering information
7.4.4   Identify or utilize appropriate informational resources, including the Internet (see also 4.9.3)
7.4.5   Use reference materials, such as dictionaries and encyclopedias
7.4.6   Use indexes and tables of contents
7.4.7   Identify or utilize test-taking skills

7.4.8 Interpret visual representations, such as symbols, blueprints, flowcharts, and schematics (see also 6.6.5)

7.4.9 Identify personal learning style

7.5 Understand aspects of and approaches to effective personal management

7.5.1 Identify personal values, qualities, interests, abilities, and aptitudes

7.5.2 Identify or use strategies to develop a positive attitude and self-image, and self-esteem

7.5.3 Identify or use strategies to cope with negative feedback

7.5.4 Identify sources of stress, and resources for stress reduction

7.5.5 Identify personal, family, and work responsibilities, and ways to accommodate them and deal with related problems

7.5.6 Identify or use strategies for communicating more successfully

7.5.7 Identify constructive ways of dealing with change, including showing flexibility and adaptability, and updating skills

8. Independent Living

8.1 Perform self-care skills

8.1.1 Recognize and/or demonstrate hygiene and grooming skills (see also 3.5.5)

8.1.2 Recognize and/or demonstrate dressing skills

8.1.3 Recognize and/or demonstrate dining skills and manners

8.1.4 Recognize and/or demonstrate selection and care of clothing and personal property

8.2 Perform home-care skills

8.2.1 Recognize and/or demonstrate meal and snack preparation tasks and activities (see also 1.1.1, 3.5.2)

8.2.2 Recognize and/or demonstrate dishwashing and meal clean-up activities (see also 3.5.5)

8.2.3 Recognize and/or demonstrate housekeeping and house cleaning tasks

8.2.4 Recognize and/or demonstrate laundry skills and related clothing-care skills (see also 1.7.2, 1.7.3)

8.2.5 Recognize and/or demonstrate yard and garden tasks and activities

8.2.6 Recognize and/or demonstrate general household repair and maintenance (see also 1.4.7, 1.7.4)

8.3 Use support services to assist in maintaining independence and achieving community integration

8.3.1 Identify and interact with persons in the home environment who can provide support in achieving goals (e.g., family, friends, caregivers)

8.3.2 Identify and interact with persons in the community who can provide support in achieving goals (e.g., neighbors, contacts from human service agencies and recreation facilities)

Photo Credits

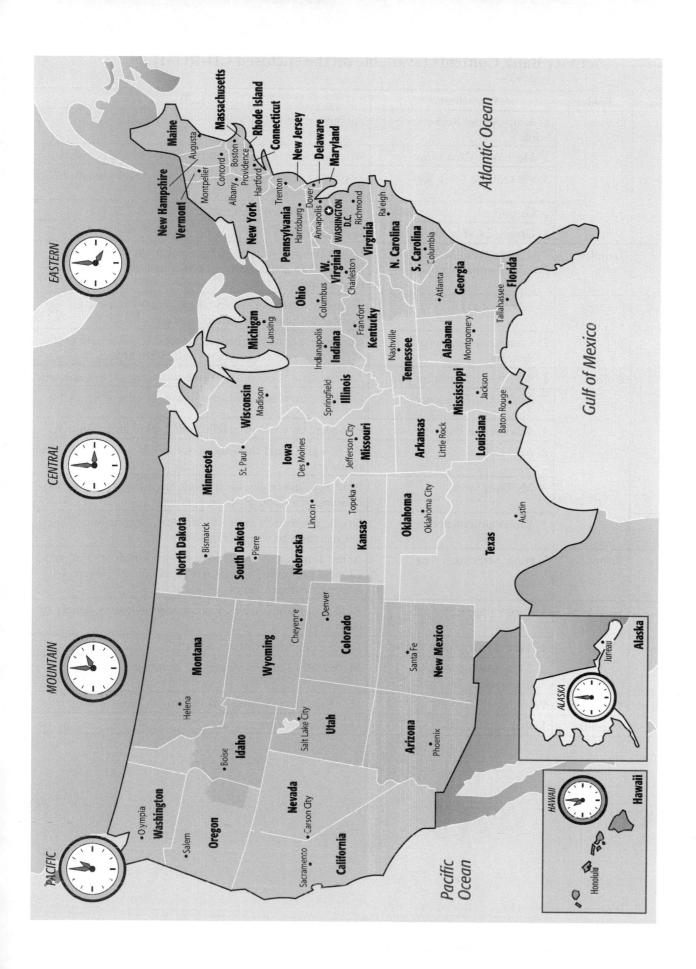

Activity Bank Contents (available on the enclosed CD-ROM)

Unit	Lesson	Folder	Worksheets*	Skill
Pre-Unit	1	Pre-unit	1: Adult School Registration Form	Fill out a registration form.
			2: Meet Your Classmates	Write interview questions and interview four classmates.
			3: Fill Out the Form 🎧	Listen to a meeting between a counselor and student. Fill out a registration form.
			4: Greetings	Write and practice greetings.
			5: Greeting Cards	Greet classmates.
	2	Templates	Paragraph Template.doc Editing_Formatting.doc	In the Templates folder, there are two worksheets for this lesson: a Paragraph Template and a worksheet for Editing (formatting).
	3	Pre-unit	1: Educational History	Complete a chart of classes taken, grades completed. Complete a chart of educational goals.
			2: Compare Educational Systems	Complete a chart comparing the educational system in the U.S. to the system in students' native countries.
Unit 1	1	Unit 1	1: Schedule Information Gap	Ask and answer questions with a partner to fill in a schedule.
			2: Adverbs of Frequency	Complete exercises to practice using adverbs of frequency.
	2		1: *When* in the Future	Complete exercises to practice using *when* in the future.
			2: My Goals	Fill in a goal chart showing personal, educational, and occupational goals.
			3: My Own Store	Read and answer questions about Stephanie's goal. Guess meaning of vocabulary from context.
	3		1: Paragraph Practice	Decide if sentences are topic, support, or conclusion. Then use sentences to write paragraphs.
		Templates	Editing_Sentence Types	In the Templates Folder, there is a worksheet for student to edit and peer-edit for sentences types in their paragraphs: Editing: Sentence Types
	4	Unit 1	1: Parts of Speech	Read about study habits. Practice identifying vocabulary by parts of speech.
	5		1: Time Management Outline	Fill in a time management outline
			2: Time Management Techniques	Make a list of time management techniques.
	Extension	Computer	Worksheets 1.1 – 1.4	Inputting Data, Saving, and Printing in Word and Excel
		Internet	Unit 1 Internet.doc	Using the Internet

Unit	Lesson	Folder	Worksheets*	Skill
Unit 2	1	Unit 2	1: Goods and Services	Read a mall directory to identify where to buy goods and services. Practice asking a partner where to find goods and services.
			2: Store Guessing Game Cards	Guess which store card a student is holding by asking questions about what can be purchased there.
	2	Unit 2	1: Sample Ad Card/ Matching Ad Cards	Ask questions to find students with the matching card. The Sample Ad card can be used as an example to help generate questions.
			2: Ad Practice	Reads ads and fill in a chart with information from the ads.
			3: Radio Ads [2]	Listen to radio ads and fill in a chart with the information.
	3	Unit 2	1: Comparative and Superlative Adjectives	Fill in a chart with the correct comparative and superlative forms.
			2: Comparative Sentence Lists	Decide which purchasing method is best for certain items.
	4	Unit 2	1: Purchasing Methods	Decide the best purchasing method for various items.
			2: *Must* and Have *to*	Answer questions using *must* or *have to*.
	5	Unit 2	1: One Consumer's Story	Read about a purchase. Answer questions and work with vocabulary.
			2: Sequence Writing	Put processes in order. Write about a process.
	Extension	Computer	Worksheet 2.1	Inputting Data, Saving, and Printing *or* Copying and Pasting
		Internet	Computers for Sale	Using the Internet
Unit 3	1	Unit 3	1: Classified Ad Cards	Use cards to compare two properties.
			2: Interpret Classified Ads	Rewrite ads using complete words instead of abbreviations. Compare the two apartments.
			3: Compare Homes	Compare two homes using comparatives and superlative adjectives with nouns.
	2	Unit 3	1: *Yes/No* Questions	Write and answer yes/no questions.
	3	Unit 3	1: Arranging Utilities	Read and listen to conversations about arranging for utilities. Fill in the missing information.
			2: Interpret a Gas Bill	Read a gas bill and answer questions.
	4	Unit 3	1: My Budget	Make a personal budget and graph your expenses.
	5	Unit 3	1: Long Action/Short Action Cards	Use cards to create sentences using past continue with *while*.
			2: Past Continuous with *while*	Write sentences using long and short actions. Complete sentences with the correct verb tense.
	Extension	Unit 3	1. Being a Good Neighbor	Make vocabulary inferences and an outline from a brief reading.
		Computer	Worksheets 3.1 and 3.2	Changing Font Size and Styles *or* Sorting Data
		Internet	Unit 2 Internet.doc	Using the Internet

Unit	Lesson	Folder	Worksheets*	Skill
Unit 4	1	Unit 4	1: Information Questions 🎧	Write, ask and answer information questions.
	2	Unit 4	1: Automated Bank Information	Read and listen to bank account information. Fill in a chart.
			2: The Library	Read and answer questions about internet access at the library. Read a fine schedule and make calculations.
	3	Unit 4	1: Giving Directions	Use imperatives to write, give, and receive directions.
	4	Unit 4	1: Adverbial Time Clauses	Study rules and complete exercises using *after*, *before*, and *when*.
	5	Templates	Editing_Formatting.doc	In the Templates Folder, there is worksheet for student to edit and peer edit for formatting, mechanics, sentence types and transitions in their paragraphs.
	Extension	Unit 4	1. Make a Telephone Directory	Create a class telephone directory of local businesses.
		Computer	Worksheet 4.1	Changing Font Size and Styles, Copy and Paste
		Internet	Unit 3 Internet.doc	Using the Internet
Unit 5	1	Unit 5	1: Parts of the Body	Identify and locate body parts.
			2: Doctors	Identify which doctors treat various illnesses.
	2	Unit 5	1: Present Perfect	Write past participles, *for* or *since*, and present perfect verb forms.
			2: What's the Matter? 🎧	Listen to doctor-patient conversation and fill in missing information.
	3	Unit 5	1: Future Conditional	Complete future conditional statements. Interview classmates about health habits.
			2: Health Cause and Effect Cards	Find the person with the matching cause or effect.
	4	Unit 5	1: Nutrition Label Quiz	Read a nutrition label and answer questions.
	5	Unit 5	1: Fitness Q & A	Answer questions about personal fitness.
			2: Fitness Chart	Complete a chart on weekly exercise.
	Extension	Unit 5	1: Medical History Forms	Fill out a brief medical history form. Fill out medical history form after reading about a patient. Answer questions about a filled out form.
			2: Skin Cancer	Read and answer questions about skin cancer.
		Computer	Worksheets 5.1 – 5.3	Changing Font Styles and Sizes and Using Clipart *or* Designing Bar Graphs
		Internet	Unit 5 Internet.doc	Using the Internet

Unit	Lesson	Folder	Worksheets*	Skill
Unit 6	1	Unit 6	1: Job Titles	Identify personal interests and abilities. Write the correct job title and skills.
	2	Unit 6	1: Infinitives and Gerunds	Write infinitives and gerunds for base verbs. Complete practice exercises. Interview and write about classmates. Write about yourself.
	3	Unit 6	1: Job Ad Abbreviations	Complete abbreviation charts. Rewrite an ad without abbreviations.
			2: Classified Job Search	Find a classified ad in the paper or on the internet and answer questions about it.
	4	Unit 6	1: Job Application Requirements	a checklist of required job application information
			2: Application Data	a sheet for students to fill out and take with them to fill out job applications
			3: Job Application	blank job application for students to fill out
	5	Unit 6	1: Interview Skills Reading	Read and answer questions about what to do after an interview.
			2: Expressing Likes and Preferences	Complete exercises with *would rather*, *prefer*, *like* and *don't like*.
			3: The Interview	Listen to an interview and analyze the candidate.
	Extension	Unit 6	1: Application Letter Practice	Label the parts of an application letter. Answer questions about the letter
		Computer	Worksheets 6.1 and 6.2	Inserting and Manipulating Tables *or* Manipulating Clipart
		Internet	Unit 6 Internet.doc	Using the internet
Unit 7	1	Unit 7	1: Employee Behavior	Complete a chart of good and bad employee behavior.
			2: Possessive Pronouns and Adjectives	Review rules and complete exercises about possessive pronouns and adjectives.
	2	Unit 7	1: Pay Stub Practice	Read a pay stub and answer questions.
	3	Unit 7	1: Benefits	Listen to company representatives talk about benefits and check which benefits each company offers.
	4	Unit 7	1: *Could* and *Might*	Discuss cause and affect of workplace behavior and complete exercises with *could* and *might*.
	5	Unit 7	1: Conversation Completion	Work with a partner to complete and practice workplace conversations.
			2: Communicating at Work	Listen to workplace conversations and guess the topic.
	Extension	Computer	Worksheets 7.1 and 7.2	Designing a Bar Graph
		Internet	Unit 7 Internet.doc	Using the internet

Unit	Lesson	Folder	Worksheets*	Skill
Unit 8	1	Unit 8	1: The United States	Complete a chart about the United States.
	2	Unit 8	1: Compare and Contrast Ideas	Write infinitives and gerunds for base verbs. Complete practice exercises. Interview and write about classmates. Write about yourself.
			2: The Mayor's Speech	Read the platforms of two candidates for mayor. Write sentences comparing their ideas. Listen to a speech.
	3	Unit 8	1: The Three Branches of Government	Read about the three branches of government and complete an outline.
	4	Unit 8	1: Problems in Your Community	Write a paragraph about community problems and ask a partner for solutions.
	5	Unit 8	1: What Do You think?	Ask classmates for their opinions and rewrite their opinions using given expressions.
			2: Conditional Statements	Complete conditional statements. Interview classmates and write sentences about their ideas.
	Extension	Computer	See "Computer Guide"	Creating a Diagram
		Internet	Unit 8 Internet.doc	Using the internet

* Unit worksheets include low, on-level, and high multilevel versions.